KILLING GROUND

At 2 A.M. they were still contesting the scarred, lunar-like surface of Dien Bien Phu. Kubiak was to write:

"I am practically alone on the hilltop in the middle of the battle which continues. I look around me and am scared to see all that is left of our fine battalion.

"Our road of retreat is thick with bodies, with wounded men who moan and even scream at death. And the din from shells and machine guns is still at its height. The battalion radio operator is literally cut in two by a shell. He has just asked for them to fire on our position, for now everything is finished.

"Right to the end, he has done what he could. Not for his country, for he's not French, but for *his* Legion. . . ."

THE DAMNED DIE HARD

Hugh McLeave

BANTAM BOOKS
NEW YORK · TORONTO · LONDON · SYDNEY · AUCKLAND

*This edition contains the complete text
of the original hardcover edition.*
NOT ONE WORD HAS BEEN OMITTED.

THE DAMNED DIE HARD

*A Bantam Falcon Book / published by arrangement with
the author*

PUBLISHING HISTORY

Bantam edition / January 1993

ISBN 0-553-29960-3

Published simultaneously in the United States and Canada

*Bantam Books are published by Bantam Books, a division of Bantam
Doubleday Dell Publishing Group, Inc. Its trademark, consisting of the
words "Bantam Books" and the portrayal of a rooster, is Registered in
U.S. Patent and Trademark Office and in other countries. Marca Reg-
istrada. Bantam Books, 666 Fifth Avenue, New York, New York 10103.*

PRINTED IN THE UNITED STATES OF AMERICA

OPM   0 9 8 7 6 5 4 3 2 1

You legionnaires are soldiers in order to die and I am sending you where you can die.

—General François de Negrier

The only way for us foreigners to repay our debt to France is to die for her.

—Prince Dmitri Amilakvari
(Killed at El Alamein)

Between March 9, 1831, when the Foreign Legion was formed, and October 24, 1962, when it quit Algeria, 902 officers, 3,375 NCOs, and 31,467 legionnaires of more than forty nationalities died for their regiments and the country of their adoption.

To them this book is dedicated.

ACKNOWLEDGMENTS

I am deeply indebted to M. Michel Debré, the French Minister of National Defense, for his permission to use the services of the Foreign Legion and to consult its archives and combat diaries. Without such authorization, this biography of the Legion could never have been contemplated. I am also profoundly grateful to Colonel Letestu, commanding the Foreign Legion, for the help his staff in the Historical Section gave me in answering innumerable queries and in piecing together portraits of the legionnaires whom I chose to represent this unique regiment. I must also thank Colonel Letestu for according me the right to translate the poems and songs of the Legion.

I must express my thanks to the many officers and legionnaires who patiently re-created for me moments as heady as the capture of Narvik or as poignant as the fall of Dien Bien Phu. To name the colonel who witnessed the surrender of Abdel Krim, the eminent soldier who re-enacted the defense of Bir-Hakeim, the brigadier who took me step by step through the Retreat to China, the general who described his role in the Algerian *putsch* would offend their modesty. They would, I know, prefer to stay true to the Legion's sacrosanct tradition of anonymity.

INTRODUCTION

No road's without its stone,
No road's without its pain.
With a world that's off its tack
They need white kepis to walk the track,
They need white kepis to walk the track.

Through the opaque glass roof of the crypt, bluish light filters to play on the faces of the twenty new recruits. In shabby, ill-fitting uniforms they look like the dregs of some conscript unit at the end of a long and hopeless war. Any self-respecting regiment would reject the blond, downy-cheeked German farmer's boy as too young; it would fail the two Spaniards, the Italian, and the Belgian as too old. And what army would bother with the others, knowing most of them as social misfits who have enlisted against their will and cannot even comprehend the basic military commands? Yet, around this raw, disparate bunch hang scarlet and gold banners heavier with honors than the colors of any other regiment; on paneled walls, mystic relics and the names of heroes testify to courage, loyalty, and long traditions.

The motley squad of improbable soldiers from seven different countries forms the weekly intake of the French Foreign Legion. Now, they are standing in the museum and crypt of the regimental headquarters at Aubagne in the South of France listening to a German sergeant-instructor haranguing them about the Legion.

The previous week, a dozen miles away in Fort Saint-Nicolas at Marseilles, these men sold their civilian gear and traded their identities for a Foreign Legion name. They have their own secret reasons which no one, not even the colonel, can question. For the young German it might be wanderlust or the romantic appeal of the Legion; the Italian and several others have probably joined to forget somebody else's girl or their own wives; the Belgian accountant exudes the smell of embezzled funds; the giant Cuban is obviously putting an ocean between himself and the Fidel Castro regime. Like every legionnaire they are starting from zero in somebody's old denims, boots, and forage caps to construct a new life.

"Straighten up, you lot. Stomachs in—chests out. Now listen hard. La Légion Étrangère was founded in 1831 by Louis Philippe, King of the French, for service outside France. It has always been an elite unit of the French Army."

As a legionnaire with thirteen years' service, the German NCO might be permitted some historical license. In fact, the Legion surfaced almost accidentally out of the backwash of European upheavals in 1830. The revolution that replaced Charles X with the frock-coated bourgeois king, Louis Philippe, also filled Paris with a wrack of dissidents who had risen vainly against their masters in Belgium, Germany, Italy, and Poland; in the French capital, bombs and broken glass reverberated as hungry mobs joined disbanded mercenaries to ravage and loot shops or public buildings. "So they wish to fight," murmured the war minister, Marshal Joseph Soult. "Then let them bleed or shovel sand in the conquest of North Africa." Intrigued by the notion, the king signed a leaf of War Office notepaper to create the Foreign Legion on March 9, 1831.

An elite unit! Indeed, it started life as an untameable rabble, fit only to toil with labor battalions around Algiers. Given a chance to fight the Berbers, it fumbled and fled so shamefully that French generals smartly foisted the Legion onto the Spanish royalists in the Carlist Civil War. Even in this campaign the men acquitted themselves anything but brilliantly, turning to slaughter each other like some demented reptile bent on suicide. France had to salvage the survivors, enroll them in a new Legion, and give them a second chance in North Africa.

> "As legionnaires, never forget that your regiment can boast of having a king, four royal princes, one French president, and one prime minister serving with its colors. Four marshals of France were proud to have commanded legionnaires. One of them started just like you—in the ranks. But don't get any ideas from that."

Not until 1837 did the Legion make its mark. Under Captain Saint-Arnaud, who later became a marshal, it spearheaded a French army and pried open the great stronghold of Constantine in eastern Algeria to prove to dubious generals that men who lived badly could fight and die well. From that moment, for a century and a quarter, the Legion never stopped fighting in North Africa. Who counted the battles, or the dead, against Abd el-Kader and his Berber fanatics? When he departed, some new messiah would keep legionnaires trekking over crags and dunes to pacify an area bigger than western Europe. With another commander, Maurice MacMahon, who later would be President of France, they snuffed out the Kabyle revolt, ambling through fire from 5,000 muskets without returning a shot to take the fortification of Ischeriden for the loss of one officer and eight dead. From the mountains, they strode into the Sahara, penetrating its forbidden oases and opening up a new French empire. And, after Algeria, they turned and tackled another foe in another country—Abdel Krim and the Riffs of Morocco. There was always some enemy, whether Berber, Riff, Chleuh, or Fell. Legionnaires made little distinction between them. Their politics was the Legion. A man had his liter of rough, red wine (*pinard*) to fuel his long marches into the North African wilderness, or as he called it, the *bled;* he had his comrades, each aware that the other, too, had an unspoken secret, all of them alienated from their families and their countrymen and by their role from the people of their adopted country. They had their own stern religion and the monastic discipline of the corps for which they had contracted to fight and to die.

North Africa and the Legion molded each other. The rugged Atlas and Aurès mountains, the infinite, eye-searing Sahara sands seemed to impress themselves on the faces and bearing of these men just as deeply as they imprinted their presence on the country by constructing their square, white forts, their palm-fringed roads, their barrack towns like Sidi bel-Abbès. But this land, which they came to consider part of their birthright, became, ironically, the theater of a Legion tragedy the moment France conceded Algerian independence claims. The crack First Paratroop Regiment rebelled and seized Algiers, defying President Charles de Gaulle and France to hand over *their* country. No Frenchman could comprehend such a revolt; no one but a legionnaire could understand the feelings of these rebels and the schizophrenia with which the Legion quit North Africa in 1962.

To the Camp de la Demande, beside the sleepy town of Aubagne, they ferried the symbols of their history, disinterring their more illustrious dead to bury them in Provence. On the parade ground stands the massive Monument aux Morts, hewn from pink Saharan granite by legionnaires and transported from Sidi bel-Abbès. The museum is full of African souvenirs. From its walls, the familiar image of the legionnaire stares out—face framed in white kepi and Saharan neckcloth, body in loose, desert battle dress. This archetype of the recruiting poster, hero of the Beau Geste blockhouse and the Riff campaign, possibly reminds the older recruits of Gary Cooper, Ronald Colman, and other celluloid braves who have smudged the real portrait of the Foreign Legion. For, if the legionnaire became synonymous with the sun and sand of Africa, he perhaps wrote his most glorious pages elsewhere.

> "We have fought on four continents, in more than thirty countries, in battles such as Barbastro . . . Zaatcha . . . Sebastopol . . . Magenta . . . Puebla . . . Tuyen Quang . . . Dahomey . . . Vimy Ridge . . . Djebel Badou . . . Narvik . . . Bir Hakeim . . . Dien Bien Phu . . . Algiers."

To the new boys, these names resonate like distant bugle notes, signifying no more than exotic sound. Their eyes wander over the mementos of these campaigns: the saddle bits and spurs of a disgraced Legion hero, a Marshal of France named Achille Bazaine; the ceremonial ax and chased-silver pipe that belonged to an African pagan king called Behanzin; the Manchu flintlocks and sardonic Chinese masks from Tonkin; Prince Dmitri Amilakvari's kepi, riddled with the German shrapnel that killed him; the plaque containing the thirty-four citations for bravery won by three Hungarian NCOs who joined together and died in Algeria in the same week.

Brave, bizarre, or brilliant figures confront each other at every two paces. Tharsile Bernelle, the colonel's lady who shared the hardships of the Carlist War and is reputed the only woman ever to strike terror into legionnaires; the bullheaded General François de Negrier, who summed up his military philosophy in one ominous phrase, which still greets the rookie as he enters the regimental barracks in Marseilles: "You legionnaires are soldiers in order to die and I am sending you where you can die." Poets like the American, Alan Seeger, and the Swiss, Blaise Cendrars. General Paul Rollet, the father of the modern Legion, who carried its monastic principles so far as to wear no shirt under his rough twill uniform and to hold his cuffs and collar together with elastic. And the only woman ever to join the Legion, Susan Travers, daughter of a British admiral, whose courage made even the toughest legionnaires feel like cowards.

> "This is the tassel of the fourth company of the 13th Demi-Brigade." The segeant points to a ragged pennon. "A sergeant risked his life to recover it after Dien Bien Phu."

Ah! Dien Bien Phu. That, some of the recruits have heard or read about. The greatest colonial defeat in history, wasn't it? More than 1,500 legionnaires died and another 4,000 were taken prisoner by the Vietminh. The sergeant, however, appears to consider it neither a defeat nor a humiliation. When these recruits look harder at the museum, they will discover that it represents as many combats lost as gained; they may then begin to understand that the Legion can be sacrificed or suffer martyrdom. It does not admit defeat.

That, and the other myths of the Legion, sustained the French colonial empire in the Far East for nine bloody years after the war. Most legionnaires who fought at Dien Bien Phu were Germans, former Wehrmacht men who had enlisted from prisoner-of-war camps. Who but the Legion could have enrolled such men, some from hated SS units? Who could have set French people cheering these ex-conquerors as they marched along the Champs Élysées before embarking for Indochina? Who could have converted these soldiers to the point where they stood and died for somebody else's empire already lost?

In this corps, myth and mystique run strong. Ask any officer or NCO where they have their center and he will answer in one word: Camerone.

"This is the most famous officer in the Legion—Captain Jean Danjou. With two officers and sixty-two legionnaires, he held out against 2,000 Mexicans in the farmhouse of Camerone on April 30, 1863."

If anything, Danjou looks the antithesis of a hero. The painting depicts a man with a placid face, balding head, quiet eyes. Yet, it was Danjou who decided that his company would fight to the last man rather than lay down its arms; who made each legionnaire swear to die before giving up a dilapidated mud and straw farm in a deserted, unmapped hamlet of no military value. Only a handful of his men survived, though that mattered less to the Legion than the spirit with which the soldiers fought. During that eternal day, not one of them thought of breaking his oath. Few of those legionnaires were French. What did France's dream of a New World empire mean to German, Belgian, Dutch, and Italian mercenaries? What did they care about a Mexican squabble? No, they died because they had given their word to the captain and the Legion.

"This is the only thing left from Camerone. It is the hand of Captain Danjou."

In the crypt, like some relic of a Christian saint, Jean Danjou's hand lies inside a miniature coffin of carved wood and glass. A closer look reveals that the hand has been fashioned from wood. Danjou lost his left hand several years before Camerone and had an artificial limb made to enable him to stay with the Legion.

"On the anniversary of Camerone, the hand of Captain Danjou is paraded before the First Foreign Legion Regiment by a distinguished former legionnaire. The story of Camerone is read to the men by an NCO."

A similar ceremony takes place in every unit wherever the Legion serves: after the homage and the recital of their credo, legionnaires celebrate their "saint's day" in their own way—with as much *pinard* as they can drink. Short of murder, no offense is considered grave enough to go uncondoned on April 30 and May 1.

"Looking at you bunch, I don't suppose it will ever happen, but one of these days you may understand what Camerone is all about," mutters the sergeant as he marches the men out of the museum.

These recruits will leave for Corsica and six months' training before being drafted to Jibouti in French Somaliland, to Madagascar, to Mururoa, the atom-test atoll in the Pacific, or back to France. By then, most of the twenty will have become legionnaires the hard way, shaped by discipline and the rough camaraderie of the regiment into crack troops. One, or perhaps two, will never see the end of the training course but will buy his release with a bullet or a length of rope, for the suicide rate runs higher in the Legion than the French army will ever acknowledge. Another half dozen will flit in and out of the guardhouse, permanently rebelling against authority, either victims of a persecution complex, barrack-room blues, or just playing the army game. Those who make genuine legionnaires will view this regiment as their family and fatherland. They will fight and die for it, and will not hang up their green tie and white kepi until they have done fifteen years. They will comprehend the bizarre ritual of Camerone and why everything comes back to this combat. They will know why the Legion never mentions defeat and accepts victory merely as a resting-halt between one battle and another. They will appreciate why American legionnaire William Moll asked for his ashes to be buried in the crypt and will realize why, in a small graveyard in Provence, in the place of honor beside General Paul Rollet and Prince Christian Aage of Denmark lies Legionnaire Heinz Zimmerman, who won no honors or rank but died for his regiment.

That is the Legion.

THE DAMNED DIE HARD

ONE

*When you've blue'd your last tosser
On the brothel and boozer,
And you're out on your ear.
You hump your bundle to the quay,
Pick up a ship and stow away
To be a legionnaire.*

The recruiting officer gave no more than a glance at the bull-necked young man in the uniform of an infantry quartermaster sergeant. He ran an eye over the letter from the colonel of the 37th Line Regiment authorizing his transfer, then picked up his service sheet. François-Achille Bazaine, born at Versailles on February 13, 1811. Profession: grocer's boy. (He looked better than that!) Eighteen months' service with a clean sheet and quick promotion to sergeant. A cut above the riffraff he had seen that day. The captain indicated a cubicle where an army surgeon was sweating to thin the long queue in Chaumont Town Hall. The doctor wasted no time on Bazaine. "Fit for service," he shouted. The young soldier returned to scribble his name on the enlistment document. That afternoon of August 6, 1832, Bazaine borrowed a horse and began the long ride through Dijon and Lyon to Toulon and the Foreign Legion draft for Algiers.

At twenty-one Achille Bazaine saw the Foreign Legion as his only road to glory. By rights he should have been wearing the uniform of a cadet at Saint-Cyr, the military academy, or studying law or medicine; he had, however, squandered those chances in failing his Polytechnic examination. And no one knew why. His tutors found him brilliant, though one or two showed uncanny prescience when they described him as sly, turbulent, and lazy. Was it some unconscious protest against the desertion of his father, Dominique Bazaine, who was working in Russia and living with another woman? Or against the intrusion of his so-called patron, Baron Roger, whom many took for his real father? Whatever the reason, Bazaine failed, and instead of emerging as a potential officer or member of the rising bourgeoisie, landed behind a grocer's counter. Rebelling at this mean existence, he enlisted as a volunteer for the conquest of North Africa, only to be handed a musket, a blue tunic, and red trousers, an enormous shako and five hundred days of grinding parades in Auxonne barracks. There, he heard about the new foreign regiment formed by King Louis Philippe for overseas service. It must surely see action in Algeria. Bazaine took the step that would make him the most popular of French soldiers, and eventually the most reviled in the history of the French army.

A babel of Swiss and Germans, Poles and Italians, were also thronging new depots in eastern France: officers enrolled because France refused them citizenship and the regular army snubbed them; men joined for their *soupe* and the chance to grab some of the fabled treasures of Africa. Behind them pressed the hungry and jobless, the vagrant and felon. To recruiting officers it seemed that every French mayor viewed the new Legion as an asylum for their most undesirable characters. Soon more than 5,000 men were straggling to Toulon and Marseilles to embark for Algiers. Fortunately the seven Legion battalions contained a hard core from the old national regiments that had served Napoleon and the Bourbon kings. Swiss and Germans from the Hohenlohe Regiment buttressed the first three battalions, Spaniards the fourth, Italians the fifth, Belgians and Dutch the sixth, and Poles the seventh.

Algerian generals stared incredulously at the tatterdemalion army shambling into its barracks. "They'll never make soldiers," muttered the commander in chief, General Bertrand Clauzel. Watching a draft disembark at Oran, French author Camille Rousset shared this view. "A real masquerade," he wrote. "To clad this mob, which comprised men of every age from sixteen to sixty and over, we appeared to have scraped the bottom of army supplies to procure the oldest rags. They were a bizarre sight that would have delighted a circus crowd. But, their heads high, their banner before them, their drums beating to the rhythm of the famous war chant, 'La Parisienne,' they proudly paraded through the crowded city streets." Their discipline proved as rough as their garb: they spoke their own national languages and had imported their prejudices and quaint regimental customs. In September 1831, the arrival of the Polish battalion drew this comment from a staff officer. "The first day, thirty-five men were missing at evening roll call. The day before yesterday a whole company got drunk and beat up its officers. We jailed the lot, except two men who are going before a court-martial."

Algiers, the fabled paradise, soon turned sour for the new legionnaires. In high-necked blue tunics, immense shakos on their heads, they roved the casbah; its maze of mud slums repelled them; local food poisoned them; Arab and Kabyle women glowered through their veils; Eastern diseases, like dysentery, cholera, and syphilis filled their ambulance tents; worst of all, they had to drink fiery, native arrack since the French brandy went only to crack regiments. And the great African adventure? Was that a mirage, too? They wanted none of it and everybody spurned them. Hundreds deserted. Those who stayed drank their scanty pay, then ransacked the Arab liquor stalls and beat up their owners; when the Arabs vanished, the battalions turned on each other to settle national quarrels. A German, after all, was worth five Poles, or ten Spaniards or twenty Italians. Bad blood between the battalions grew to such a pitch that the Legion was losing more men in feuds than in fighting troops. General Clauzel solved the problem by dispersing the regiment around Algiers, Oran, and Bône and handing them picks and shovels. Thus, they had achieved the lowly status of criminal labor battalions, building blockhouses and outposts for French troops.

Ironically, they showed they could create as well as destroy. Across a fever swamp and over flinty hills between

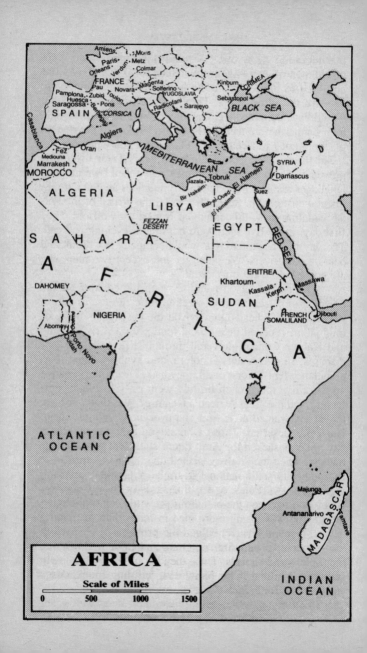

Douala and Boufarik, in two months the Swiss Second Battalion engineered, to Clauzel's amazement, a highway forty miles long. They even added frills, lining what became known as the Legion Causeway with poplars, wells, and fountains. And they had their first taste of fighting. In April 1832, as a German battalion was clearing a blockhouse at Maison Carrée, on the outskirts of Algiers, it was attacked by the El Ouffia tribe. Throwing down their picks and shovels, the legionnaires picked up muskets and swords and beat off the Arabs. But as soldiers they had a long way to go. Their first commander, Colonel Stoffel, a Swiss veteran of the Napoleonic Wars, tried to beat discipline into them with the flat of his saber and the lash; he soon gave up, returning to France muttering blackly into his spade beard about legionnaires.

Such was the unit that Sergeant Achille Bazaine had joined. He must have appeared an odd legionnaire, for he stood aloof from the carousing and scuffling in the casbah and was critical of drunks and brawlers. His battalion commander, Colonel Joseph Conrad, a little, crinkly haired Alsatian, took an instant liking to the new NCO. In the Legion, Bazaine had at last found the father he had missed in his childhood; he began to take soldiering seriously, smartening his drill and baggy appearance. While fellow NCOs were sowing havoc in the wineshops and brothels, he toiled through military manuals and presented Conrad with defense plans for Bône, the seaside fortress. With Conrad's backing he rose to sergeant major and, within eighteen months of joining the Legion, became a second lieutenant. At the beginning of 1835, Conrad wrote to Achille's mother, "Your son, who is also mine if only by adoption, is such a worthy young man and has such fine prospects that, despite his youth I have just proposed him for the rank of lieutenant. . . ."

The Legion mess reflected the turbulence in its ranks, and Bazaine shared the concern about the future of his regiment. Three colonels had come and gone in as many years, defeated by this polyglot crew with raffish manners. One of them, Colonel Michel Combe, might have succeeded. A hard taskmaster with a knife-blade nose and flowing side whiskers, Combe had followed Napoleon into exile at Elba and captained his guard at Waterloo. But could he drum discipline into the Legion? He despaired of men who fought their own civil war when not attempting to desert. Why, they resisted even a simple innovation like quickening their march from the rustic eighteenth-century pace of eighty steps a minute to Napoleon's 115 a minute. (The French never did manage to alter the Legion's Saxon stride and still have to place it at the rear of every review rather than throw their whole army out of rhythm.) Colonel Combe fulminated and fretted just as much about the officers who defied him—Captain Johan Albrecht Hebich, for instance.

Hebich, a temperamental Swabian nobleman, distinguished himself by his drinking and brawling. Discipline to him meant laying his saber across a legionnaire's rump; for good measure, he upbraided his fellow officers in crude German. No one thought of calling his bluff; the dueling scars on his face testified that he had survived too many bloody encounters. Combe loathed him. A man who could scarcely put two French words together and could not command a detachment of canteen women! For his part, Hebich made no secret of his contempt for the Legion. After the skirmish as Maison Carrée, he announced loudly in the mess, "Your Legion is full of thieves and robbers. As for its soldiers, I wouldn't use their mustaches and beards for gaiter straps." Combe urged the War Ministry to chase Captain Hebich ignominiously from his regiment. "He is drunk, undignified, brutal, unjust to his inferiors, arrogant and rude to his superiors; he is a lazy malingerer who refuses to do his duty," the colonel wrote.

Only Conrad, for whom courage transcended and excused everything, interceded for the German. "His men like him and he has been a good soldier," he pleaded.

"We cannot tolerate a man who lives like that," Combe replied.

"Is it how a soldier lives that matters?" Conrad said quietly. "Isn't it how he dies?"

Combe had overlooked the German's powerful friends at court, among them Louis Philippe, for whom Hebich had done a service. It was Combe who went. His successor, Colonel Joseph Bernelle, determined to make or break the regiment. An officer with a strong theatrical touch, Bernelle put his faith in spit and polish and the knout, and after a few months of crowded cells and corporal punishment, it did seem that legionnaires might make some sort of soldiers.

While Bernelle was trying to purge and tame the Legion, the Algerian War had taken another turn. The French conquest had begun like some comic operetta, with Hussein, the dey of Algiers, swatting the French consul with his fly whisk during a financial wrangle. The French, who had seized the city in 1830 with an army of 37,000, contented themselves with occupying coastal towns like Oran, Bougie, and Bône, leaving the wild Atlas and Aurès mountains and the fringes of the Sahara to the Berbers and Arabs. Now these tribes had a new leader. Though only twenty-four, Abd el-Kader had proved himself a skilled general, with a fiery tongue that preached Koranic religion and rebellion against the infidel French. Soon western Algerian tribes were hailing this descendant of the Prophet Mohammed as Amir of Mascara; they swarmed behind his green burnoose, a Koran in one hand and a sword or musket in the other. In Paris, society hostesses raved about this handsome and romantic young sheik; the Algerian generals regarded him with mild amusement. What did such a boy know about war? They would hunt him down and destroy him and his myth. They entrusted the task to General Camille Trézel, who was persuaded by his friend Bernelle to use the Legion.

In the third week of June 1835, Trézel's column, 2,500 strong, straggled out of Oran. Hampered by heavy wagons, it labored over dusty trails and rock-strewn hills and plowed through swamps. Two Legion battalions formed the advance and rear guards, their Poles and Italians sweating in blue greatcoats under a hundred pounds of equipment. In front of them flitted the red burnooses of Abd el-Kader's horsemen, taunting them, luring them eastward into the swamps of Moulay-Ismail. There, on June 26, as the column floundered, the young Amir struck with 6,000 cavalry and 1,300 infantry. From the hills his mounted troops surged in waves, charging into the scattered Legion ranks. A panic-stricken bugler blew the retreat instead of the charge. The legionnaires had little alternative but to fall back into the cover of a thick forest. For a day they stood off cavalry and infantry charges while their wounded piled up among the trees. Trézel saw only one way to save his column from extinction—withdrawal through La Macta Pass. Pulling the men together, he placed the wounded in wagons and began slowly to retreat. As they reached the pass a sirocco blew up; clouds of searing sand enveloped the long train of men and wagons as it groped toward Macta. In the choking heat, men collapsed while others broke rank.

And Abd el-Kader was waiting. Through the swirling sand he charged with his lancers while his infantry poured plunging fire into the ragged army. It was slaughter. The moving pall of sand, the crash of lances and musket fire, the suffocating heat spread panic, which sent the men screaming and running from the hellish defile. Italian legionnaires, who were covering the retreat with the wounded, scattered and fled.

But for Colonel Conrad no one would have survived. Hoisting his red cap on the point of his sword, he rallied two Polish companies and rode full tilt at the tribesmen. Behind him Bazaine spurred his horse, swinging his saber at the tangle of native cavalry butchering the legionnaires. A musket ball hit him in the right forearm; he transferred the sword to his left hand and kept plying it. The giant Hebich had bullied his company together to support them. Muttering curses and insults about *"dieses verdammte Regiment,"* he was blazing away with a long musket and using it as a club at close quarters. Above the battle din, mortal screams reached them. As the sandstorm cleared they saw, to their horror, Arab women dragging their comrades from the ambulance wagons and mutilating them. The Poles yelled in vain anger as one of their favorite officers was held down, emasculated, and decapitated before their eyes. What could they do? When Trézel reached safety with the remains of the column, Conrad drew them off. More than 250 dead lay on the battlefield; another three hundred men fell to marauding cavalry before the broken army reached Oran that night. To crown their chagrin legionnaires learned that the heads of their fallen comrades, exhibited on lances, decorated the streets of Mascara and the Amir had gained several thousand more recruits.

That night Conrad came to Bazaine's tent to look at his

wound. Removing the Cross of the Legion of Honor from his own chest, he pinned it to the young lieutenant's tunic. "Until you get the one you merited today," he said. The colonel wrote to Bazaine's mother, "Yes, madam, your son acquitted himself like an angel in the two battles with the Bedouin on June 26 and 28. Although wounded in the right arm by a bullet, he continued to do his duty and helped to keep the company in order. Since Achille is one of the small number of companions with whom I am pleased, I have proposed him for the Legion of Honor and I am sure that this will be warmly supported by General Trézel." Bazaine got his Cross, the first ever given to a legionnaire from the ranks.

Individual bravery did not, however, efface regimental shame. Macta was fought all over again that night. Enraged by the desertion and the treatment of their wounded, the Poles attacked and killed more than twenty Italians. Realizing that such national strife would tear apart his regiment, Bernelle decided to scrap national battalions. Henceforth, the battalions would be mixed and every legionnaire would learn French. To Bernelle goes the credit for fusing the nationalities and creating the esprit de corps that sustained the Legion; but it was Macta that wrought the transformation that neither Bernelle, Combe, nor Stoffel could ever have achieved through discipline.

Abd el-Kader's victory nevertheless confirmed what Clauzel and other generals had whispered: "They'll never make soldiers." Had they not turned tail before the Bedouin! A month later, when Paris ordered them to dispatch the Legion to Spain, no general officer demurred. Bernelle, Conrad, and other senior legionnaires contested Louis Philippe's decision. Paris gave them a dusty answer: "Any officer refusing this new engagement will lose his rank without compensation. Any NCO or legionnaire who leaves before his engagement is finished will be treated as a deserter." So the King was handing his Foreign Legion over—lock, stock, and barrel—to help an infant queen put down a rebellion that seemed of no concern to France. Or was it?

The Spaniards had adopted their time-honored custom of resorting to civil war to decide who should misgovern them. The Carlist Civil War was meant to determine which of two despots should assume the throne left vacant by the pitiless reactionary Ferdinand VII in 1833. The King had altered the male law of succession, making Isabella, only child of his fourth marriage, the Queen of Spain. His brother, Don Carlos, claimed the throne. As inevitable as the civil war was European involvement. The Austrian chancellor, Prince Metternich, who was no liberal, dubbed the infant queen the "revolution incarnate." That was enough for Lord Palmerston, the peppery British foreign secretary. A British Legion of 10,000 men sailed to support Isabella. Seeing himself outdone by the British, Louis Philippe handed over his Legion to the child queen and the Regent Maria Cristina.

Fattened with new contingents from France, the Legion sailed for a campaign that all but ended its career. At Palma, where they had to lie in quarantine with fifty cases of cholera in their ranks, Bernelle seized the chance to shuffle the nationalities and reform the battalions. On August 17, 1835, the legionnaires disembarked at Tarragona, striding through its tight streets with bugles and fifes playing "Riego's Hymn," the anthem of Spanish liberalism. *"Vivan los Extranjeros! Vivan los Argelinos!"* the crowd roared; rose petals fluttered among shakos and blue tunics. Behind the band rode Colonel Bernelle, surrounded by a strange detachment of broad men in leather aprons bearing axes on their shoulders—the colonel's new bodyguard of Legion sappers, formed to impress his presence on the Spaniards. But it was the person following them who caught the crowd's imagination—a dark, long-faced woman attired in an officer's shako, blue tunic, and black-striped trousers. *"Quién es esta mujer?"* the Spaniards asked.

No legionnaire could have trusted himself to answer that question politely. Tharsile Bernelle, the colonel's lady, terrified them—perhaps the only woman ever to halt the legion in its stride. From her buggy she bowed regally to the throng as though the Spaniards had come to welcome her personally. His officers blamed Bernelle for saddling them with his wife. The poor man had no choice; he might bluster and bully in the mess or the parade ground; in his home he bowed and scraped. Everyone but Bernelle realized that he had married a shrew. Tharsile, fifteen years younger than her husband, made the most of it. As one officer put it:

> *"Madame Bernelle has decreed that*
> *Handsome lads get an officer's hat."*

She made no secret of her amours; mostly, they appeared as promotions on regimental orders. Fortunately for Bazaine, he had Conrad's support, for his jowly face and bulky, peasant figure would never have elevated him to captain while Tharsile reigned; she preferred dashing, fine-boned figures like Captain Thadeus Horain, who quickly became Bernelle's chief of staff and Tharsile's lover. Madame Bernelle flirted with Conrad; his snub rankled so much that it led to friction between Bernelle and his most senior officer. The Legion mess, which grumbled about the five Bernelle relations at its table, soon lost patience with the lady. Legionnaires, too, gave her a wide berth. That, or hear her favorite phrase dinning in their ears: "Eight days in the cells!"

It was no war for a woman. The Spaniards stayed true to the macabre ritual of their civil wars, each side bent on outdoing the other in cruelty. From Catalonia, Navarre, and Aragon, more than 20,000 Carlist mountaineers had armed themselves for a guerrilla struggle. Bernelle had to split his Legion into separate battalions to combat their hit-and-run tactics. At Pons, in the Catalonian hills overlooking the Segre River, Captain Bazaine had to hold out for a week with 120 men against 3,000 Basque and Navarrese troops. Conrad arrived just in time. But soon, Conrad would no longer help him. Though commanding the Legion after Isabella had made Bernelle a general, he found that Tharsile was still choosing even his officers and NCOs. He might have responded to the lady's advances, but in the words of a Spanish observer, "Conrad is too brave an officer to flatter a woman who merits a dozen lashes an hour." In disgust, the Alsatian returned to France.

In midwinter, when northern Spain lay under snow and ice, Bernelle received orders to march to Pamplona to aid General Espartero's drive against Carlist strongholds in the Pyrenees. For two hundred miles the legionnaires slogged through icy blizzards, their feet sinking in the snow and thick mud of the Ebro Valley. Neither the Cristinists nor the French had considered supplying them with food, let alone winter equipment; they begged as they went and, when that failed, they stole or pillaged. Men dropped out to die of exposure or fatigue or dysentery; the mutinous were flogged or shot. Only one person seemed to revel in these desperate conditions. Madame Bernelle, flanked by her handsome sappers, riding her buggy in full legionnaire uniform, still vented her explosive temper on the regiment. First to rebel were her mules; they suddenly reared; the bearded pioneer driving them lost control; Madame Bernelle and her maid landed in a pool of mire, their legs in the air, their dresses pinned by heavy trunks. "Eight days in the cells," Tharsile screamed before they freed her. The sapper escaped the punishment. Where were the cells on that march?

At Pamplona, the tired and hungry men were thrown straight into the fighting on a fifty-mile mountain line. Fragmented into companies, they bivouacked where they fought, on the icy ground. The Carlists seemed determined to destroy these impudent foreigners. "Muchachos, go for the French officers' epaulets," their leaders cried. During those long winter nights Carlist officers or NCOs would filter through the lines. "On the other side we have food and warm clothing, and Don Carlos pays us well," they would whisper. Who could blame those who listened and slipped over the mountain?

Their red and yellow epaulets, red pantaloons, and blue jackets made legionnaires prime targets for the Carlist cavalry. In April 1836 at Zubiri, a day's march west of Tirapegui, two companies of Navarrese lancers swooped on a section of battalion scouts, scything them down with sabers and lances. Only one legionnaire stood on his feet, Sergeant Samuel Berset, a barrel-chested young Swiss. With one shot he brought down and killed El Rojo, the renowned cavalry commander; with no time to reload his Napoleonic musket, he parried charge after charge with its bayonet and stock. When his battalion arrived to scatter the horsemen, Berset still remained on his feet. He had received fifteen bayonet thrusts, two of them deep, two saber cuts, one lance wound, and two bullets in the ribs. Bernelle promoted him a subaltern on the spot.

Winter, and the spring and summer combats, had left gaps in the Legion ranks. Desertions, too, had taken their toll. And France, it seemed, had forsaken its latest regiment. Bernelle badgered the War Ministry with petitions: for their six months' pay in arrears, for new recruits, for decorations, for promotions. "You seem to forget," replied the French army command, "that the Legion belongs to Spain and therefore the French Government cannot accede to your demands." The men began to grouse and discipline suffered. Bernelle fell back on harsher punishment. Drunks got twenty-five to fifty strokes across the buttocks, more humiliating than a month in the cells.

Legionnaires accused Madame Bernelle of inflicting this treatment on them. She had now become Queen Isabella III, or the Queen of the Legion. A Spanish officer, writing to his commanding general, said of her, "There's no one who doesn't murmur against that lady; the soldier, the officer, the Frenchman, the foreigner, the friend, the indifferent man. Everyone, without exception, detests and despises her. No one can deny that her presence in the corps will be one of the coming causes of the downfall of the Legion." In Pamplona and Saragossa, Tharsile now flaunted her various lovers; the younger Legion officers had the blond hair, the blue eyes, straight noses that pleased her so much. The joke ran that she rationed the cannonballs to sell the surplus and keep herself in style.

Bernelle was too busy tussling with his government to notice his wife's foibles and their baleful effect on the regiment. Had France deserted them? What had happened to their pay? Why no official protests about the Carlist atrocities? Finally, Paris lost patience with the petulant colonel and relieved him of his command. He, his wife, and Captain Horain left for France. Relief at their departure turned to dismay when the new man arrived. Colonel Lebeau looked and behaved like Don Quixote; he sported a Comédie Française hat bought from an actor; his trousers barely covered his knees; huge spurs jangled from down-at-heel boots; a Turkish scimitar dangled from a frayed rope around his waist; his cape appeared to have survived the retreat from Moscow. Which it had. He cannot last, the legionnaires thought. Colonel Lebeau regarded the starving, surly men and felt likewise. Within a month he had gone and the Legion got back its real leader, Colonel Joseph Conrad.

Conrad was the first true legionnaire colonel, the model for so many others. The men adored him. Hadn't he tamed the regimental shrew? He had what the African veterans called *baraka* (good luck) which appeared to confer on him an almost mystic invulnerability to shot or shell. Who but Conrad would have carried nothing but a cane into battle! The Spaniards dubbed him El Bravo del Caballo Blanco—the white-horse hero. On the longest march he would ride the column quipping with the men in five languages. Such a man could have led legionnaires anywhere. Ironically, he led them to their destruction. What had Bernelle bequeathed him of the 4,000 men who had landed in Spain? Two battalions, two squadrons of lancers, and one artillery battery; men in pitiful clothing, their feet wrapped in rags, who had to beg their bread from the Spaniards. Conrad met the same apathy as Bernelle when he appealed to Paris. The colonel and his new chief of staff, Captain Achille Bazaine, noted that more than eight hundred legionnaires had deserted to the Carlists. "They now have their own Legion," a Spanish staff officer commented to Conrad. "It's more than we'll have soon," he replied. To keep the men in food and clothing, Conrad spent his own pay and savings, depriving his wife and family of money.

Still, they had to fight, in a winter more rigorous than the previous. North of Pamplona, Conrad chased Carlist guerrilla bands without ever catching them. At the end of winter, however, the Carlists emerged—in strength—from the Sierras de la Pena and Guara. Action would stop his men rebelling. With General Irribaren's Cristinists, Conrad joined the pursuit. On a freezing March night the two Legion battalions bivouacked at Larrainzar, a small village dominated by twin peaks christened Las Dos Hermanas— The Two Sisters. Conrad spotted something that had escaped the Spaniards: a Carlist attack from one of those peaks would prove fatal for him and Irribaren's army. He posted one battalion on the slope, then called Captain Johan

Hebich. "Take your company on to the hilltop. If you're attacked defend it to the last man."

Some officers protested. "Hebich! That loudmouth! He's no solider. He'll let us down." Conrad stifled the protests.

Hebich and his company scaled the wooded slope and began to knock loopholes in a crumbling shepherd's dwelling. Hardly had they finished when 2,000 Carlists swarmed from the woods and attacked them and the First Battalion. Their weight forced the battalion downhill. Now only Hebich stood between the Carlists and the defenseless Legion. The Carlists charged, but could they budge Hebich? Sitting astride a rock, he calmly picked off man after man and met others with the bayonet. For two hours, in pitch darkness, he directed his company's defense of the vital post, giving Conrad time to climb the hill with the Second Battalion and beat off the attack. Captain Johan Albrecht Hebich, the insufferable German with perhaps the worst record of any Legion officer before or after him, had saved the Legion. That battle neither modified Hebich's behavior nor his contempt for everyone in general; but now Hebich could get drunk, curse legionnaires, insult fellow officers without anyone remarking the fact. Except perhaps to say, "Well, you know Hebich. He's one of our characters."

Under Conrad, young Bazaine was learning his trade. He shared the colonel's frugal rations, his tent, and his gloomy prognosis about the Legion. Bazaine gave his hero all his affection and from him he learned soldiering in the hard-bitten manner of the Grand Army. When in doubt you charged, for the closer to the enemy the lighter the losses; a finely honed bayonet was worth a hundred bullets; no commander should ever look over his shoulder to see if his men were following. What did they do about that other aspect of leadership—morale? Ill-fed, ill-clad, and unpaid men did not fight well. General Irribaren could only shrug and point to his own ragged ranks and empty kitchens. The next battle would bring them Carlist plunder. Many legionnaires did not wait but stumbled over the frozen sierras to join an army that at least fed its troops. Bazaine had the difficult task of supplying and moving the two battalions, lancers,

and guns with the Cristinist army when his men were on the
point of mutiny.

Outside the old town of Huesca they ran into a superior
Carlist force. Passively the royalist troops sat while Conrad,
on his white horse, with his red cap on a cane, led charge
after charge into the thick enemy columns. Bazaine rode to
ask Irribaren for support only to find the general dying from
a lance thrust; he had to gallop back to Huesca to help salvage the remnant of the Legion. In terms of Carlist dead,
those three days of fighting could count as a victory; but the
Legion had lost 350 men out of their total strength of 1,200.
Conrad quit the battlefield exhausted and in tears. Bazaine
heard him mutter, "If they're going to let the Legion die,
then it will die bravely."

What had Conrad meant? What was he brooding over
as he led the shard of his Legion down the Aragon road to
the next town, Barbastro? His ribald jokes with the men
seemed to Bazaine an attempt to conceal his desperation, his
fatalism. Only eight hundred men remained of the proud
force that had landed at Tarragona two years before. A battalion, but only in name. A tattered mob that marched and
fought like so many marionettes because the next town
might mean food and wine and shelter and, if they were
lucky, women. France had spurned them and Spain had almost finished them. Conrad's expression became more and
more martyred. Had he made up his mind that he and his
Legion would die soldiers' deaths?

They had a new Spanish commander in chief, General
Oraa, a braided idiot with a predilection for serenading the
enemy with his brass band, then charging impregnable positions. At the end of May 1837 he outdid himself by
bivouacking his army in an olive grove west of Barbastro in
the path of the Carlist army, led by the Pretender himself. At
midday on June 1, Don Carlos fell on the Cristinists, who
recoiled, leaving Conrad and his legionnaires to take the
shock. Salvos of cannonballs scattered the legionnaires
among the splintering olive branches; the grove filled with
dust and the smell of burned powder and scorched flesh.
The men were ready to join the fleeing Spaniards when
Conrad, cap on cane, pulled them around. He might have re-

treated honorably. The thought never occurred to him. He turned the battalion to face the enemy.

There, in the sunlight filtering through the smoke-filled grove, the Legion imagined it was confronting many of its own phantoms of the past two years. They gazed at the blue tunics, red pantaloons, red and yellow epaulets—their own mirror image. The Carlist "Legion"! Eight hundred of their own deserters. From the Carlist side, the German soldier Baron von Rahden watched the clash. "I have never seen, throughout my rather hectic military career, neither before nor after, a battle as bloody as the one I saw there. During the combat the soldiers recognized each other, they called each other by their own names, they questioned each other—then shot each other heartlessly." With no time to load and fire, legionnaires and renegades crashed into each other, using bayonet and broad saber; they clubbed each other with rifle butts and olive branches; they kicked and punched. Anything to kill. The olive grove became a writhing, screaming mass of wounded and dying as Poles settled old scores with Italians, Germans with Belgians or Dutch or Swiss. Jubilant Carlist officers stood by, watching the Legion of foreigners committing suicide like some demented scorpion stinging itself to death. In the thick of the fight were Conrad and Bazaine, the little Alsatian flitting from one company to another trying to rally them. Foot by foot, however, the Legion was ceding ground. As a last desperate effort Conrad stuck his cap on his cane. *"En avant,"* he shouted. As he rushed forward, Bazaine saw him stagger and collapse; a musket ball had caught him in the forehead. Carlist legionnaires pounced on the body of their old colonel, but Bazaine and four sappers hacked their way through them. Lifting Conrad's slight figure, Bazaine bore it through the grove. Placing the dead colonel on his horse, Bazaine rode to the highway, where he handed the body to a lieutenant. His eyes full of tears, he turned and galloped back to rescue the shreds of the regiment from the olive grove.

"Is Old Fritz all right?" the legionnaires demanded.

"He has gone back to have his wound dressed," Bazaine told them.

"That one won't die," said one man, and went back to the battle.

At nightfall the survivors groped and stumbled away from the carnage among the trees. The Carlists had lost all but 160 of their 875 legionnaires and most of those left were wounded; Bazaine could count only 130 of his battalion. As so many senior officers had predicted, the Legion had destroyed itself. At Berbegal, where those men who could still march learned that Conrad had been killed, they threatened to attack the Cristinist Royal Guard, whom they accused of deserting them and therefore murdering their colonel. Bazaine had to muster the officers to prevent this massacre. On June 3, Bazaine formed a guard of sappers and lancers around the coach containing Conrad's body; with a drum tapping the Legion's deliberate stride, they made for Huesca, then followed the Gallego River to Saragossa. There, on a burning day, in La Seo, the great medieval cathedral, they buried Conrad with full military honors. One hundred legionnaires had borrowed spruce uniforms from other units; many of them, tough veterans of Macta, Tirapegui, and Barbastro, wept as the crude coffin slid into the Moorish sepulcher wall. A legionnaire with a broken arm nailed the plaque bearing merely the name and dates: *Colonel Joseph Conrad: December 8, 1788 to June 1, 1837.* To many it seemed they were immuring the soul of the Legion with him. Captain Achille Bazaine wept, too. From that moment he resolved to give neither affection nor trust to any other man; but, as in so many things, he would forget or fail his promise.

Bazaine led the legionnaires back to Pamplona. From there, he wrote to his mother, betraying his emotion about Conrad's death in faltering phrases and illegible scrawl. "You must know of the great loss I suffered in the last engagement. The death of my general has affected me profoundly. I am suffering and I need to see my family. I escaped many dangers in the last battle. Never have we had such a bloody fight. Anyway, I did my duty right to the end, I saved his body on the battlefield, I made them render him a king's honors at Saragossa and Pamplona. It remains now to fulfill my duties to the family and I shall fulfill them even if it is painful for me. Adieu, dear mother. Pardon me for speaking only of my general, but my heart is still full of him and the circumstances of his death were horrible, and being on my horse, in my arms, I was covered with blood."

Though Barbastro had finished it as a fighting force, Maria Cristina refused to disband or repatriate the Legion; neither did she pay nor feed it. Bazaine had to trek to and from the Cristinist headquarters in the Plaza del Castillo, wheedling provisions for his men. At that moment he was contemplating quitting the Legion; it had too many evil memories; he had lost Conrad, his *beau idéal*, and the regiment was disintegrating daily. To save the men from involvement in the Pamplona mutinies, he moved the debris of the Legion to Saragossa before joining the staff of the French war commissioner. Bazaine found himself a posting to a French infantry regiment; but before long he would begin to pine for the Legion and want to rejoin.

Just over two hundred legionnaires had collected at Saragossa. Left to themselves, they could have disbanded, but something other than military discipline kept them together: the quarrels that had riven the rival battalions ceased, and with rough camaraderie the men and their women handed around their meager rations and shared the winter hardships. Even the Spaniards had to applaud the dignity and bearing of the broken French Legion. On December 8, 1838, Madrid finally sanctioned the departure of the two companies. They had sixty-three officers, of whom twenty-nine were French, 159 NCOs and legionnaires, with only twenty-five Frenchmen. On New Year's Day, 1839, they gathered in the Plaza del Pilar, a column of battered men with seventy-five mules to transport their women and children. The fifes and drums struck up. *"Marche,"* shouted an officer. Hoisting Louis Philippe's frayed banner before them, they stepped out north. Six weary days later they pleaded for food and permission to rest one day at Jaca, the last town before the frontier; the military governor ordered them out. So they stumbled on, into the Canfranc Valley, following the tumbling Aragon River, climbing 5,500 feet to the Somport Pass. It took five days to cross the snow-bound Pyrenees; the men scrounged enough wood to make a campfire, enough food to keep them alive. When, finally, they limped into the mountain village of Pau, the French inhabitants stared at the curious convoy, wondering where it had sprung from, what it had done.

Captain Johan Albrecht Hebich might have enlightened them had he spoken enough French. So might Lieutenant Samuel Berset had his Zubiri wounds not opened and festered on the long march. Would it have meant anything? That they had left more than 4,000 of their dead in towns and villages and battlefields whose names signified nothing? That they had fought for principles that neither the Spanish Queen nor the Pretender would ever accord? That they had left Conrad, their colonel and the first hero and martyr of the Legion, in a church wall in Saragossa?

Yet, this was France and they were legionnaires. The old Legion had died by its own hand. *Quién sabe?* The new Legion might turn out better. The recruiting office in Pau town hall seemed to magnetize them. Almost to a man they lined up to re-enlist. That night Lieutenant Samuel Berset sewed back his sergeant's stripes. They all had to begin again with their old rank. To the legionnaires it was as though the Spanish nightmare and men like Conrad existed only in their minds.

TWO

You'll find mates from all over,
From Milano and Hanover,
No one like the others.
Some peers and some pimps
Who've washed up like shrimps
With the legionnaires.

Some strange figures passed through the Legion depot
in Pau, on their way to Spain and Algeria, but few as colorful as Lieutenant Arnaud-Jacques Leroy. In his thirty-six
years he had posed as officer and gentleman, playboy, ad-
venturer, guerrilla fighter, fencing master, commercial trav-
eler, actor, and singer. For Leroy the disastrous and
disgraceful end of each career merely marked the beginning
of a fresh and more glorious exploit that would redeem his
future and his fortune. Now he was chancing his arm with
the Legion. From a well-to-do Paris family, Leroy had entered Saint-Cyr to emerge with distinction and join a crack
hussar regiment. In 1822 he suddenly resigned, leaving a
mass of gambling debts and several enraged husbands. Sur-
facing in Greece, he fought for that country's independence,
acquitting himself bravely at the siege of Modon. Then he
made his way back to France and sought a commission in
an infantry regiment. Instead of his guerrilla experience in
Algeria being used, he was placed on a draft for the West
Indian island of Martinique. When his regiment sailed from
Marseilles, Lieutenant Leroy had failed to report; he was ordered to be arrested and imprisoned as a deserter . . . if they

could find him. His ship had put out from Brest to land him in England. Leroy's fine tenor voice charmed Regency salons, but the language and fencing lessons he gave could not support him in the style of a buck. Again, pursued by tradesmen and cuckolds, he fled to Belgium. In Brussels people remembered Arnaud-Jacques Leroy as a stage actor with a light touch on the piano and at the card table.

In 1830, Leroy stole back to France, which forgot or forgave his early misdemeanors and handed him back his commission. This time he did set out with his regiment to chase the rebel Duchess of Berri, whose supporters were trying to claim the throne for her son, the Duc de Chambord, grandson of Charles X. The duchess was caught and jailed at Blaye Castle, and Lieutenant Leroy became one of her guards. His fine-boned face, his romantic ballads, his prowess on the guitar impressed the lady; her chief jailer, Colonel Thomas Robert Bugeaud de la Piconnerie, also took a liking to the dashing lieutenant, perhaps the luckiest encounter in Leroy's life. Bugeaud, a brilliant soldier and the most rough-tongued deputy in the National Assembly, had spent long years in the wilderness for his Bonapartist leanings; now the new king had singled him out for high office.

No sooner was the duchess released and Bugeaud back in Paris than Leroy fell from grace again. He tried desperately to be a gentleman: ran up debts at the best card tables; flirted with society hostesses; challenged the right people to duels. He succeeded only in appearing a well-bred scamp. Instead of advancement, he found bailiffs at his door with the threat of a debtor's prison. At that moment his wife, Laure, died. Leroy took off once more, this time for the Legion and the Carlist War. Was it the prison threat? Or depression at his wife's death? Or Bugeaud's advice? Leroy never provided the answer; nor did the Legion press him. When he arrived in Pau the French Government had grown weary of the Spanish adventure. Leroy was given a Legion company, the promise of the first vacant captaincy, and dispatched to Algeria. Had the military surgeon examined the new lieutenant he might have gone no further than Pau, for he was suffering from an incurable heart disease.

Writing to his brother on the eve of his departure, Leroy said, "How I'll fight when I get the chance. With me it will be all or nothing." He would win the Knight's Cross of the Legion of Honor or perish in the attempt. He had misgivings about this Legion. "What a droll regiment . . . superb men, but the scrapings of every nation, an amalgam of every state, of every profession, of every social calling who have come to join one another and many of them to hide. Germans, Prussians, Dutchmen, Belgians, Italians, Spaniards, Poles, Greeks—we have a bit of everything, but the Belgians and the Dutch, then the Germans, are in the majority."

Leroy found the French army licking its wounds after the rout of 20,000 men before Constantine, the Kabyle mountain citadel in eastern Algeria. On October 1, 1837, another 20,000 men had gathered for a new bid, among them a battalion of legionnaires. "Constantine must bring me something," Leroy wrote to his brother. "The troops are fine and well-disposed, but are too heavily equipped to obtain success. Every soldier carries twelve days' rations in bread, biscuits, rice, salt, with coffee and sugar to replace wine."

For five days, in rain and hail, the column plowed over barren wastes and up goat tracks dragging seventeen siege guns, which sank to their axletrees in mud. When the minarets of Constantine floated above the mist, Leroy understood why the first assault had failed. The massive, crenelated citadel sprouted from a dizzy, chalk pinnacle with 1,000 feet of gorge plunging on three of its sides. Only from the craggy plateau of Koudiat-Aty could the French hope to attack. There, however, the Kabyles and their Turkish masters had concentrated troops and guns. The punctilious commander, General Sylvain Valée, would attempt nothing until he had breached the walls. For five days his troops lay in the mud under incessant blizzards, watching cannonballs bouncing like peas off the walls. Men died from dysentery, cholera, and exposure; their hungry animals perished, to be eaten by the starving troops. Captain Leroy implored his chiefs to gamble on a frontal assault. He would lead it.

Finally, with a hole big enough to take a platoon, General Valée agreed to attack on October 13. Behind the gun emplacements, the troops massed. The Legion would charge into the breach in companies, each doubling across

the 120-yard stretch as Louis Philippe's son, the Duc d'Aumale, signaled with his white lace handkerchief. Crouching
behind the cannon, Leroy's legionnaires recognized their
old colonel, Michel Combe, who would lead the attack with
Colonel Lebeau. "We're certainly not superstitious," Combe
murmured. "A Friday, a thirteenth, and a year with an odd
number."

The guns ceased; the beat and hiss of rain came from
the steaming cauldron around Constantine; the lace handkerchief fluttered. Seconds later, Combe and Lebeau were
scrambling over the mound of rubble into the breach. The
handkerchief fluttered once more. Captain Leroy crossed
himself. Death or the Legion of Honor! Raising his saber, he
sprinted for the gap, followed by Sergeant Major Doze,
Sergeant Pietri, and Corporal Mohlenfel, a German from the
old Hohenlohe Regiment. Leroy could not believe it. Their
cannons had failed! Through the curling smoke, he glimpsed
yet another wall ringed with Turks and Kabyles who sprayed
him and his legionnaires with fire. Leroy described the
scene: "We arrive at the top of the breach. . . . At that moment there is a terrible explosion. . . . The tumult gives way
to dead silence. Those driven back by the force of the blast
seize on anything for support . . . their sabers, their comrades, the left-hand wall. Those on top of the breach wipe the
dirt, the dust, the powder from their eyes and choke for several seconds. But then we all see the most horrible sight . . .
the lucky ones with their limbs intact run down the breach
toward the battery, screaming. Hearing those lamentable
cries, I wonder that those who flee do not drag behind them
the whole column thronging into the breach."

The legionnaire colonels, Lebeau and Combe, realized
that a powder magazine had detonated behind the wall, finishing the job their guns had started. *"En avant,"* they cried.
As Combe charged, two musket balls struck him in the chest.
Turning, he walked slowly back to the battery. "How goes
the assault?" the Duc d'Aumale queried. Combe explained.
"But you, Colonel, you're wounded," the prince said. *"Non,
monseigneur,"* Combe replied. "I am dead." He died the following day in the ambulance tent, watched by a wounded
captain whose name was Certain Canrobert.

On the breach everything was standing still; cannon

and musket fire pinned the legionnaires behind the debris. Leroy could sense defeat—for himself a personal, permanent defeat. He leaped over piled French and native dead; against the pall of dust and gunpowder his frail figure stood in silhouette. *"A moi, La Légion,"* he bellowed. "With the bayonet, *mes enfants.* It's nothing but shot." His dazed company fumbled after him through the great hole and into Constantine. The labyrinth of narrow, twisting streets rang with musket fire. Leroy led them up one alley and down another; they ran, blindly, through the market scattering Turks and Kabyles like rats in a maze. A mob, armed with spears and scimitars, halted them. Doze and Pietri picked them off, then lunged after Leroy with their bayonets. Behind them swarmed French and native troops, chasing the will-o'-the-wisp figure of the legionnaire captain. Within two hours the strongest fortress in Algeria had capitulated. No one could credit it, least of all Captain Leroy, who had unlocked its defense.

With that one action Captain Arnaud-Jacques Leroy, playboy and actor, lifted himself onto the stage of history; he chided himself for not receiving the wound that would confirm his courage and ensure his Cross. But, as he wrote, "My soldiers have proclaimed me brave with great shouts. . . . Our Legion has immortalized itself. Our reputation is such that every regiment compliments us and we have taken our place at the head of the army." Constantine had indeed effaced the evils of Macta and Spain; generals no longer grimaced at the mention of legionnaires. Leroy gained his medal. So did Doze and Pietri. Though Mohlenfel and three hundred legionnaires lay in a mass grave beneath the citadel walls.

Where now for this restless, hungry character? As far as his spirit and weak heart would carry him. At Djidjelli, a fortified port east of Algiers, he swam ashore and sabered his way into the casbah. There he watched his best friend, Captain Thadeus Horain, a former lover of Tharsile Bernelle, die slowly from a spear thrust. Here, too, Captain Johan Hebich fought his last battle. Wounded for the twelfth time in his short Legion career, the German retired to France with little gratitude and a pittance of a pension. "I alone seem to be respected by the bullets and I am almost

sorry," Leroy wrote. He nearly died of fever, however, and
they shipped him into a hospital in Algiers. His patron, Marshal Bugeaud, who had become its governor general, had
some sound counsel for the impetuous Leroy. His saber had
done enough; now he needed a more imposing name and
powerful friends. In 1840 the official journal announced that
Captain Arnaud-Jacques Leroy would henceforth assume
the name and title of Captain Leroy de Saint-Arnaud. With
his Cross and the noble particle adorning his name, how
could he fail this time?

The fall of Constantine had set Abd el-Kader on the
move again, the young Amir contending that the French had
broken their treaty with him by seizing the Kabyle stronghold. With an army of 25,000 cavalry and infantry, armed
and equipped from his own arsenals, he began to raid
French garrisons, even threatening Algiers. General Valée
decided to wrest the principal towns from Abd el-Kader and
garrison them. Among these was Miliana. On June 8, 1840,
a column 1,200 strong entered the smoldering arsenal seventy miles southwest of Algiers. The Arab chief had quit
Miliana without fighting, but had gutted and fired the town.

The Miliana garrison comprised a French infantry battalion, the First Battalion of the Legion, and five guns.
Colonel de Illens commanded the post; in charge of the Legion and his second in command was Adjutant Major
Achille Bazaine, who had rejoined the Legion after a year in
France. From the first days, Bazaine, the supply officer,
wondered if they could survive until the relief column arrived in September. Even if they could hold out against
thousands of tribesmen, would their skimpy rations? They
began to rebuild the derelict town, patching the walls with
baked clay and constructing outposts on the slopes around
it. But within days Abd el-Kader had struck, leaving them
with twelve dead and thirty wounded. Within weeks the cattle they had brought for fresh meat were dying for want of
fodder; the men were dropping from dysentery and heatstroke. By mid-July the mosque could take no more patients
and they were burying a half-dozen men a day. Bazaine had
to ration "monkey," as his legionnaires dubbed their tinned
meat.

"If we had some baccy, *mon capitaine*," the legionnaires grumbled.

Bazaine and the regimental surgeon noted that smokers deprived of their tobacco succumbed more quickly than others to heat and disease. An Arab smuggled in tobacco, but only once; they watched burnoosed warriors torture and behead him in full view of the post. The pharmacist tried the smokers on vine leaves, which only made them sick. Salt, too, ran short and they spun out the supply by mixing it with saltpeter. On August 1, when Abd el-Kader rode out of the hills, no more than four hundred men could stagger to the walls to beat off the attack. Disease had already accounted for more than two hundred men, with another five hundred sick.

Bazaine and de Illens often had to carry the sentinels to the outposts; once there, the men sat through their stint, rifles on laps, staring out over the plain, their eyes mirroring its monotony, their minds its remoteness. The Berbers fell on one outpost in early August; of its eight men only three could stand. The others sat, firing blindly. To save them from death or torture, Russian Legionnaire Georgi dashed out of Miliana with three men. They killed seven tribesmen with bayonets and hunted the remainder. Their reward—a thimbleful of brandy to wash down their hardtack and "monkey."

Men slept with rifles strapped to their arms, and trained savage Arab dogs to give the alert. The Arabs infiltrated the posts, naked, knowing that dogs never bark at a nude man; they oiled their bodies to wriggle free if attacked. Often a stone, wrapped in a paper bearing the signatures of corporals and sergeants who had deserted from other outposts, would land in the town. "Friends," one document said, "Twelve hundred Europeans are serving with Sultan Sidi Abd el-Kader. The food is good, healthy, and plentiful. They always have money. When you join us you will be given a horse and its harness and you will be feted by everyone. But bring your arms. You will be well paid for them. The camp is three miles from Miliana, following the river toward the setting sun." Who, in Miliana, felt strong enough to walk three miles? No one deserted.

Men did, however, run amuck, turning to stab madly at

their comrades with bayonets; some walked around like
zombies, seeing and hearing nothing; a few lay in a rigor-
like death. One legionnaire dug a grave—his own. Bazaine
asked if the surgeon could treat this madness. "It's not in my
book," the man replied. "Know what they call it? *Le Cafard*." These demented men really believed that a *cafard*, or
black beetle, had invaded their bodies and was gnawing at
their minds. Thus began the myth of the *cafard*, this beetle
that legionnaires blame for everything from a drunken orgy
to murder or desertion. In Miliana the *cafard* thrived in the
heat and the crowded, insanitary ambulance wards.

Abd el-Kader kept up his raids, though convinced that
the three hundred men still standing would soon join those
in the mosque or the graveyard and the town would fall
without his firing a shot. But, on August 7, an Arab and his
wife slipped over the garrison wall. Abdullah, he called
himself, though he confessed to being a Piedmontese legionnaire named Valentino, whom the Arabs had taken prisoner some time before. He would carry a coded message to
Marshal Valée in Algiers. "The man's a deserter," de Illens
said. "You still have to trust him," Bazaine insisted.
Valentino flitted away with a piece of paper. Even with
luck, could he march seventy miles through the Arab lines
to deliver it?

They gave him up after a month. Now their 150 men
paraded like tramps, with feet bound in strips of bullock
hide. Too weak to dig graves, the garrison cremated its
dead. The men had no duties; they cleaned their rifles,
honed their bayonets, and kept one bullet in their tunic
pocket for themselves. Every day another unfortunate comrade was tortured. The tribesmen would stake him to the
ground, lacerate his body, pour honey into the wounds, and
leave him in the blazing sun as ant meat. When the screams
stopped, these victims were dying of thirst. On September
21, Valentino returned. General Changarnier, the most resolute and able commander in Algeria, had started with a relief column.

Changarnier had to bulldoze his way through thousands of tribesmen to reach Miliana. Not until October 5 did
the garrison sight his dust and a patrol breaking away to run
the gauntlet into the town. Major Maurice MacMahon rode

in with a message telling them to hold on. MacMahon was shocked by the state of the defenders. Of the 1,200 more than eight hundred had died, mostly of disease; only one hundred men were fit to march.

Miliana marked the first meeting of Bazaine and MacMahon. For more than forty years their careers would cross, conflict, or collide until one would die, exiled and disgraced, the other honored and lamented by the French nation. They marched around the garrison together, the grocer's boy who had risen from the ranks and looked like a plowman beside the polished Saint-Cyrian who could trace his descent from the tenth-century Irish king, Boro Brien, who could boast of fourteen MacMahons killed in French service and who secretly regretted the fall of the Bourbon dynasty.

The folly of Miliana provoked an outcry in Paris. Society ladies no longer considered Abd el-Kader as a burnoosed version of Byron; Marshal Thomas Robert Bugeaud was sent out to destroy him once and for all. This irascible, pock-marked little man transformed the Algerian War—and the Legion. No more static garrisons or lumbering wagons or heavy guns. He stared, aghast, at legionnaires sweating in shakos, high-necked tunics, and woolen trousers, staggering under one-hundred-pound loads. Henceforth, they would wear light uniforms and kepis with neckcloths. They would exploit Abd el-Kader's own methods, raiding his livestock, destroying his crops. They would build, too. Towns for native and European settlers with roads to link them and outposts to keep the peace. Bugeaud began the real colonization of Algeria, despite opposition from generals who disliked this upstart who had risen from the Grand Army ranks. Changarnier showed his disrespect by flouting orders. Bugeaud, who had Irish blood and an Irish temper, berated him.

"I've been fighting for six years in Algeria and believe I have some experience," snapped Changarnier.

"Frederick the Great had a mule that took part in six campaigns—it came back a mule," Bugeaud replied.

His tactics succeeded. His flying columns hounded the sultan's troops until, finally, in 1844, Bugeaud and a large force caught his army at Isly and in one day smashed his

power. Three years later Abd el-Kader would hand over his
sword and begin his exile. By a strange twist his great-
grandson and namesake would join the Legion just under a
hundred years later to fight first in Indochina, then against
the FLN in Algeria.

By now it had become an honor to command the Legion, this strange babel of mercenaries who never sat out a
battle. In 1844 the distinction fell to Colonel Maurice
MacMahon, who inherited the usual collection of Germans,
Swiss, Poles, Belgians, Dutchmen, plus about one hundred
Carlists who had crossed the Pyrenees after their defeat and
forty Englishmen who had fought in Spain with General de
Lacy Evans' Legion. How would the polished aristocrat
cope with such a bunch? His first shock came when he entered his quarters in Algiers to find his batman drunk with a
gang of barrack mates—on the proceeds of the new
colonel's kit. MacMahon might have had him shot; instead
he let him cool his heels in the cells and took him back. The
legionnaires gave the colonel full marks.

Within a few months Colonel MacMahon was marching his regiment against the mountain fortress of
M'Chounech, which the Arabs called the Constantinople of
the Aurès Mountains and believed impregnable. Astride a
steep cliff at the end of a goat track, the rich citadel had already defied two infantry battalions that had rushed the
heights. As MacMahon studied the position nearly 1,500
men had their heads down among the rocks, trapped by fire
from the bastion and its outer trenches. Two relief columns
had ended up with them. Only MacMahon's two Legion
battalions remained. "Can I count on you, Colonel, not to
follow the example of the others?" the young Duc d'Aumale
asked MacMahon.

"I shall lead them myself, sire."

"No, I should like the honor of placing myself at the
head of your legionnaires," said the prince.

MacMahon hesitated. To have the youngest son of
Louis Philippe killed while commanding his legionnaires
would hardly help his promotion prospects in Paris. But already the prince was removing his gaiters in front of the
First Battalion. MacMahon summoned a gangling, eagle-

nosed captain called Louis Espinasse, renowned for his reckless courage. "Take the shortest route and scout it for the battalion," he ordered. Halfway up, Espinasse spotted four hundred Kabyles, the advance guard of another thousand, slithering down to take the prince and the battalion from the rear. Doubling back, he picked up the right-flank company and led it into the Berbers' path. To decoy the tribesmen, Espinasse clambered on a ridge and gesticulated; a volley caught him on the chest and thigh, dropping him behind a rock. But his company had gained cover to ward off the attack. Everything descended on them—musket and cannon fire, avalanches of rock. Espinasse lay there, cursing legionnaires who wanted to transport him downhill. He knew these men—they would die over him if he stayed. Two more bullets hit him, in the chest and arm. As he fainted from blood loss, he saw the battalion moving through and the blue greatcoats swarming into M'Chounech. He opened his eyes the next day to find the Legion of Honor shining on his chest, pinned there by the Duc d'Aumale.

Two years with the Legion taught MacMahon much about soldiering. Men who lived badly did not necessarily die badly; legionnaires whose service books read like police court files, who rebelled against barrack duties and fatigues, fought like tigers in the African *bled*. Spaniards marched and fought all day on their beef-hide shoes with no more than a few mouthfuls of water and a mess tin of *soupe* to sustain them; no one could touch the Germans for stolid discipline. And his forty Englishmen? A quaint bunch who gobbled their eight days' rations in four, then staged a sit-down strike. Rather than leave them to the Arabs, MacMahon disguised native *goums* as Berbers and had them make a mock attack on the English legionnaires; soon they saw through the trick and were as mutinous as ever.

On those columns a man could die so many ways: by bullet, sword, or lance; by crucifixion in the sands when he dropped out. In the mountains the men froze to death; in the dunes they died of thirst or heatstroke. MacMahon's legionnaires once ran into a sirocco that felled several hundred men with heatstroke. Army surgeons were rare, and the Legion considered itself fortunate to have Captain Ridzech, a

former cavalryman of Polish descent. He had a rude hand
and one cure-all: bleeding. He bled seventeen of the sun-
stroke victims. Not one survived. In MacMahon's presence
he then carried out as crude a post-mortem as any in medical
history. Grabbing an ax, he split a legionnaire's skull. What
this piece of medical research taught him, Ridzech never di-
vulged. He made the other victims drink several spoonfuls
of ether and rubbed more on their bodies. To a man they recovered. MacMahon thought his own phial of ether saved
his life in more torrid moments.

For every Constantine, every M'Chounech, the Legion
fought a hundred battles that never made print. "Walk the
track, but make the road," Marshal Lyautey said fifty years
later. When not marching and fighting, legionnaires were
plying pick and shovel, sledgehammer and crowbar on
roads and outposts, each like another, with thick, square
walls, watchtowers, and sentry ledges and billets as cheerful
as a monk's cell. Life was the return of the column that had
disappeared over the horizon three months before; in between, nothing but guard duty and fatigues, relieved by the
occasional foray against dissident tribes. No books or newspapers; for news and gossip they relied on the "Arab Telephone," which left nothing unsaid. When camp chores were
done, the Germans dreamed about cold beer and sang nostalgic songs—*"Ich habe mein Herz in Heidelberg ver-
loren."* The Spaniards gambled all night; the Poles and
Russians argued about the last or the next revolution. And,
when the legionnaires had drunk their ration of brandy or
absinthe, the talk turned to women—those they had run
from or who had run from them. Most had joined the Legion
to forget. Forget what? Some had forgotten even that. How
could they remember in those monotonous and melancholy
posts? There Monsieur le Cafard was king, seizing the most
tranquil man with the desire to kill, or desert, to wander into
the hills or dunes and keep wandering, to load his rifle, fill
the barrel with water, and blow off the head that hurt so
much with the thoughts and dreams he could not stifle.

Lieutenant Thomas Landsdowne Parr Moore was luck-
ier than most. Khamis outpost lay one hundred miles from
the coast, even if the wild and bare Ouarsenis Mountains
hemmed it in and hid hostile tribesmen. He had cheap and

abundant drink, and in his Legion company he could argue
with a cardinal's nephew, a Frankfurt banker's son, a high-
court judge's favorite boy. But what was Moore, eldest
child and namesake of the great Irish poet, godson of
Byron, doing in Khamis? The Comte de Castellane, who
spent several weeks with the Legion garrison, wanted to
ask, but the tacit rule forbade anyone prying into a legionnaire's past. Moore impressed him as a gifted man who
might have made his name as a poet or novelist had it not
been for the bottle and his wild, unstable streak. Moore did
talk about India, where he had fought before pitching up
with the Legion; some scandal had forced him to give up
the commission his father had bought him. In his slight,
tenor voice, he would sing some of his father's Irish
melodies until breathlessness and a dry cough forced him to
stop. "She Is Far from the Land Where Her Young Hero
Sleeps," was his favorite, but he sang another with great
feeling—"The Light of Other Days."

> When I remember all
> The friends so linked together
> I've seen around me fall
> Like leaves in wintry weather,
> I feel like one
> Who treads alone
> Some banquet hall deserted,
> Whose lights are fled,
> Whose garlands dead,
> And all but the departed!
> Thus in the stilly night
> Ere slumber's chain has bound me,
> Sad memory brings the light
> Of other days around me.

Why had Moore applied to Louis Philippe to commission him in the Legion? Why the forgotten post? Moore's
billet yielded Castellane one clue—the portrait of a beautiful woman that he would pick up absently. The flush on his
cheeks would burn brighter as he talked about home and the
eventual reunion with the woman he loved. Was she married or had she jilted him? Castellane never discovered. He

had to quit Khamis, which came under siege during the last
spasm of Abd el-Kader's bid for Algeria. When he returned
to relieve the Legion, he found Moore emaciated, coughing
blood, and prematurely aged. They strapped him to a mule
and he left with the column at the beginning of February
1846. He would rest in Algiers for several days before embarking for England. He never reached Algiers. Castellane
believed that he died on the road of TB; however, the Legion records state that he was killed in a tribal raid on February 6, 1846. That combat, like so many others the Legion
fought, went unrecorded; no one has ever unearthed Thomas
Moore's grave.

Wherever they marched, in the mountains or desert
fringes, the legionnaires left Biscuitvilles, so-called because
they stocked hardtack and tinned stew. In autumn, 1844, two
companies under Major Manselon dragged their feet through
the Ouled-Ali gorge; before their tired eyes a marvelous
country opened. The distant Thessala Mountains hung in the
sun-hazed sky like a tattered, bleached djellabah; the fore-
ground of low hills sloped into a plain stippled with palms,
acacias, and dwarf pines. The two hundred men marched on,
banging with rifles at woodcocks for their evening *soupe* and
rounding up a stray sheep. Beyond a clear river they spotted a
huddle of Arab huts around the saintly tomb of a marabout.
The saint had been known as Sidi bel-Abbès, or Lord, the
Happy One. Manselon marked it as a Biscuitville site; his
men slaughtered and ate the stolen sheep and lay down with
hyenas and jackals crying in their ears. Next day they began
to build; soon they had a church, a school, and, finally, a
small barracks; they planted crops and constructed dwelling
houses. By the early 1850s, when Colonel Achille Bazaine
came there to command the Foreign Legion, the town of Sidi
bel-Abbès was taking shape and its name was as well-known
as Oran or Constantine.

Neither Abd el-Kader's surrender in 1847 nor
Bugeaud's colonial policy brought peace. The marshal had
set up Arab bureaus, staffed with French officers, to administer the conquered territories and supervise native chiefs.
Reforms meant taxes, which many Arab chiefs refused to
pay. In the summer of 1849, at Zaatcha oasis, Sheik Bou-
Zian hunted the young Arab bureau representative back to

Biskra empty-handed. Thus began a revolt that would cost hundreds of French lives. For Zaatcha, which its people called the Garden of Allah, had been turned into an almost impregnable fortress; its thick palm groves concealed traps and trenches; its minarets, mosques, and casbah, shimmering over the pink sand, contained arsenals, blockhouses, and 6,000 well-armed men. Bou-Zian, the former Algiers water carrier, had drilled and indoctrinated them to resist the French. "No infidel will ever pollute Zaatcha," he cried.

To teach this impudent rebel a lesson, Colonel Jean Carbuccia plowed south with two Legion battalions and one African unit.

Zaatcha looked easy. Carbuccia barely broke stride to probe its outworks before barging into the assault. The legionnaires put one foot into the palm groves, which immediately erupted. Only three men reached the moat, where their bodies floated as Carbuccia sounded the retreat. Some thirty-two of his men had penetrated Zaatcha—the unlucky ones. Retreating legionnaires caught their agonized yells as Bou-Zian's women tortured them.

News of the infidel defeat brought every tribe for fifty miles around into Zaatcha, including one of Abd el-Kader's former chieftains with 4,000 men. Bou-Zian snubbed the French, who offered him terms. A fresh force of 4,000 men, led by General Emile Herbillon, tried again on October 4. But Zaatcha still held. Sappers began to trench through the palm groves. Men fell to Bou-Zian's snipers while hundreds of the entrenched troops collapsed from dysentery caused by drinking foul water. On October 20, Herbillon tried once more. Artillery slotted a hole in the wall for the Legion and two line companies broke into the citadel. Half of them finished dead on the pile of rubble.

From the ramparts the Arabs taunted Herbillon's troops; at night they stole out and captured sentries for the next day's sport. Legionnaires had to witness the torture of their comrades, stripped naked and bound to a post in full view of their camp. The women, with shrill screams, excelled at this game, emasculating, blinding, and beheading. Starving dogs were loosed on the prisoners to tear them to pieces. The Garden of Allah had become a hell; the sand vibrated in the heat of the day and scintillated with frost at night. Finally, a dumpy little man with puffy cheeks rode in with a new column. Colonel Certain Canrobert, former Legion officer and friend of MacMahon and Saint-Arnaud, always led from the front. He fixed the next assault for November 26.

At dawn two batteries opened up, cutting a swathe through the palm grove, gouging a great hole in the walls, and pounding minarets and mosques while Canrobert, with the legionnaires, darted in at the head of the assault. Dead clogged the breach and the palm grove. Berber women, more bloodthirsty than their men, crept out to butcher the wounded in the gardens. But in two hours Canrobert had planted the tricolor in the highest tower of the fortress. Sappers began to demolish the honeycombed casbah to allow legionnaires to use rifles and bayonets on the fanatics who hid there.

"Where is Bou-Zian?"

An Arab bureau spy, planted in the casbah, indicated his house. Three shells ripped open the wall; sacks of gunpowder destroyed one side and the roof. From the rubble stepped a green-burnoosed figure with blue eyes and a wispy black beard. His hand clutched a Koran. "I am Bou-Zian," he said.

Later that morning Colonel Canrobert was resting in his tent when a sergeant nudged him awake. Canrobert choked. Before him, on three pikes, were the heads of Bou-Zian, his son, and his religious teacher. The Zaatcha revolt, which had cost 1,500 lives, was over.

Major Achille Bazaine settled quickly into his new job as head of the Arab bureau in Tlemcen, near the Moroccan frontier. It suited a Legion officer, this old Roman town with its twenty different nationalities, its bazaars, casbah, synagogues, Christian churches, and mosques. Like the Legion, it squabbled; the Arabs complained about the Jews and they about the Gentiles while the Spaniards quarreled with everybody. Bazaine enjoyed the role of interpreter, judge, tax collector, and intelligence officer; and the Arabs admired him—this corpulent man who would stop to sip sticky tea with a stallholder, listen to his plaint, quote an Arab or Koranic proverb that, though it left the problem unsolved, won him respect. In Tlemcen, Bazaine acquired the Arab traits of patience, resignation, and cunning. An Arab could read your thoughts, so his heavy-lidded eyes and pudgy face assumed a mask betraying nothing. Under his direction Tlemcen became a model for other Algerian possessions, and, in 1848, Bazaine's superiors showed their gratitude by promoting him to colonel. French officers found the new colonel a quiet man; for a legionnaire he had an unusual aversion to drinking, gambling, and visiting the local brothels. He lived frugally in his office in the citadel until Señora Tormo arrived from Murcia to set up an inn. Bazaine moved in as her first boarder. The inn soon resounded to the clatter of sabers and stamp of feet as officers persuaded the vivacious señora to show off her flamenco dancing. Then the youngest of her three daughters, Soledad, would jump on the table and sway and drum her feet to the rhythm of her mother's castanets and a thrumming guitar. In that inn Bazaine fell in love. He was thirty-seven and Soledad, at seventeen, a slip of a girl. But Señora Tormo gave her blessing; Colonel Bazaine, after all, virtually ruled Tlemcen. However, the colonel was in no hurry to get married. Soledad must finish her education. Out of his meager pay, Bazaine sent her to school in Oran, sixty miles from the dubious society of Tlemcen. When he considered her education finished Bazaine applied to the War Ministry for permission to marry. Such requests must go to the general officer commanding the district, said the ministry. And Brigadier Maurice MacMahon, an unromantic hero, assumed a lofty attitude. What a notion! A French colonel marrying the daughter of a Spanish innkeeper whose background and establishment seemed, to put it kindly, unsavory. Too many colonels blighted their chances by hasty marriages. MacMahon went as far as to hint that Soledad might be counting on the impressive death rate among Legion officers to collect a widow's pension. At this Bazaine lost his temper; the two officers had a stand-up quarrel that finished with Bazaine returning to Tlemcen, still a bachelor.

The colonel was still determined to marry Soledad. MacMahon, a devout Catholic, might view the girl differently if she graduated from a French convent. So he enrolled her at the Sacré Coeur in Marseilles, where for three years she studied French, read her Bible, prayed, and played the piano for the nuns, who discovered that she had

innate musical ability. Who now would take her for the girl
who had danced for green-turbaned zouaves and legionnaires in a shabby quarter of Tlemcen? However, Bazaine
was a full colonel and commander of the Foreign Legion before he had the courage to make a second application to
marry. Not until 1854 did his request reach the War Ministry. This time there was no MacMahon to object. Bazaine
married Soledad in Versailles, his birthplace, then crossed
the Mediterranean to bring her to Sidi bel-Abbès. They had
no time for a honeymoon, for the events that had shaken
France in the six years that he had wooed Soledad now
caught the colonel and the Foreign Legion up in a strange
adventure.

Leroy de Saint-Arnaud had been anything but idle. On
a white Arab thoroughbred, his black and white silk
burnoose carefully deployed to show his colonel's epaulets,
he had earned himself a ruthless name in Algeria for his
methods of "pacifying" tribesmen. Scandal still shadowed
him. In 1845 he caused an uproar in Paris by sealing up five
hundred men, women, and children in the Dahra caves of
the Aurès, then burning and suffocating them. He wrote,
complacently, "I had the apertures to the caves hermetically
stopped up. I made one vast sepulcher. No one went into the
caverns; no one but I knew that, under there, were five hundred scoundrels who will never again slaughter Frenchmen. . . . I have done my duty as a commander and
tomorrow I would do the same over again; but I have taken
a disgust to Africa. . . ."
   Such a man and such a conscience impressed certain
people in Paris. Marshal Bugeaud, for instance. And the
cryptic figure of Louis Napoleon Bonaparte, biding his
chance to make himself ruler of France. In February 1848,
when the Paris streets rose against Louis Philippe, the con-
scientious colonel was on leave in the capital. Bugeaud gave
him a brigade, with orders to clear the mob from the streets.
The rue Richelieu ran with blood as Saint-Arnaud charged
with his cavalry into the crowd. "I shall never allow myself
to be dominated by the streets," he wrote. Louis Napoleon
took note; when he became President of France and was

casting around for senior officers to transform the republic into an empire, he lighted on this raffish, ruthless brigadier.

Saint-Arnaud became the new war minister. The frail figure still was impressive; but now because of the cold, marble eyes, the blasé, insolent face, and his attitude. He was a condemned man, a gambler prepared to risk everything on some fantastic last throw. He had made the conversion from monarchism to Bonapartism with no misgivings; he was prepared to kill a few hundred more wretches to make his prince-president an emperor and himself a marshal. With him he had Canrobert and Espinasse, both good legionnaires, their eyes, too, on a marshal's baton. On December 1, Saint-Arnaud mustered more than 40,000 troops in the capital ready to cope with trouble when Paris read the proclamations ending the republic and opening the way to the Second Empire. Barricades foundered before his troops, but mercifully few people dared to challenge Napoleon and his heartless general.

Could even Napoleon trust his war minister? After the December plot the prince placed 200,000 francs on his study mantelpiece; the man he had made a Marshal of France pocketed the bundle of banknotes to pay his debts. Wasn't a revolution worth that? The scandal broke, the chief accusation coming from General Louis Cornemuse, head of the Paris army. Saint-Arnaud challenged him to a duel. At dawn on March 7, 1853, they met in the Tuileries Gardens. What chance did the fifty-six-year-old general have against an old fencing master? Cornemuse's death did not muffle the scandal, but at least it had removed the main witness. From his exile in Guernsey, Victor Hugo had coined a new name for Saint-Arnaud: he was the cold-blooded jackal. Names had never meant much to Saint-Arnaud. Except one. His own.

THREE

There are lawyers and quacks,
Judges, counts and boot-blacks.
A few solicitors.
Even priests who don't shame
To give God our nickname,
Among the legionnaires.

When the wooden-walled troopships furled their sails
in the Dardanelles in July 1854, legionnaires crowded the
decks to admire the Roman and Byzantine outline of Gallipoli. The more curious questioned their NCOs. Why are
we fighting the Russians? And why with the English, after
two hundred years of strife? What are we doing with the
Turks as allies when they are enemies in Algeria? The
NCOs knew no more than the legionnaires; they doubted
even if their commander, Colonel Bazaine, or their commander in chief, Marshal Saint-Arnaud, could supply the
answers. Indeed, the Crimean War would baffle historians
and turn out to be one of the blackest farces of the nineteenth century. Tsar Nicholas I had begun the chain reaction by appointing himself Protector of the Holy Places in
Palestine. Fearing that Russia would grab most of the splintering Ottoman Empire, Britain threatened war. Napoleon
III dreamed up several dark motives for allying himself
with England: no Catholic could stand aside and see orthodox priests administer the holy places; no Bonaparte could
forget the retreat from Moscow; no new emperor could ignore the prestige of a good war, well won. The combined

English and French navies sailed with 60,000 men to the mouth of the Black Sea.

But the war seemed to have eluded them. Having destroyed the Turkish fleet and marched into the Danube provinces, the Russians turned about, crossed their own frontier, and appeared ready to listen to peace overtures. "The worst has happened," wrote Saint-Arnaud. "In running away, the Russians have stolen a good chance of victory." *His* victory, of course. Peace would have robbed the French commander of the chance to die gloriously, for Leroy de Saint-Arnaud knew he was dying. General MacMahon, who visited him in Paris to beg a division in the coming war with Russia, found a gaunt figure vomiting at his desk in the War Ministry. His doctor, Jean-Louis Cabrol, had told him the worst. "I have four months at the most," Saint-Arnaud gasped to MacMahon. "Just time to beat the Russians in Turkey."

While London and Paris debated about where to fight and why, the army landed at Gallipoli among a squalid huddle of slums housing Turks, Armenians, Greeks, and Jews. To heighten the misery, the French put ashore several cases of cholera, which ran like a lit fuse through the army; within weeks thousands were dying.

At last they heard about the battlefield. It would be Crimea, the tag of land on the north coast of the Black Sea. But what did London or Paris or Saint-Arnaud or Lord Raglan, the British commander in chief, know about Crimea? They had no large-scale maps, no naval charts.

The armies sailed for Varna, on the east coast of the Black Sea, taking with them their cholera—and Madame Soledad Bazaine's piano. For Soledad had pestered Bazaine into bringing her to the war for her honeymoon. She could help nurse the wounded, she said. Legionnaires crated her piano at Bel-Abbès, saw it on the ship at Oran, and were now ferrying it across the Sea of Marmora and through the Bosphorus to Varna. Toiling waist-high in water to bury the dead, the men heard Mozart and Chopin melodies tinkling from the crowded base hospital. In Paris the beautiful Madame Bazaine became as famous for her recitals to the cholera victims as Florence Nightingale for her hospital work. The Empress Eugénie sent Soledad a personal note commending her courage.

Meanwhile, Saint-Arnaud and Lord Raglan were wrangling interminably and incompetently about the invasion site. Literally carried to the conference table, his feverish eyes glittering like the Constantine medal on his chest, Saint-Arnaud declaimed his strategy.

Beside his elegant figure, Lord Raglan looked shabby in his floppy hat and silk muffler; his right sleeve hung empty, for he had left his arm at Waterloo, the last battle the British had fought. The ghost of his old chief, Wellington, seemed to hover over him, for he continually referred to the enemy as "the French." To spread the confusion, the new war correspondents relayed these secret deliberations to Britain and France; a British staff officer asked one group of pressmen for their papers only to discover they were Russians! Did it matter? *The Times* and *Frazer's* magazine seemed better informed about allied strength and plans than the two leaders, though it must have disconcerted the Russians to read about their own forces and dispositions in the same issues.

Sebastopol, the great naval base, was the obvious target, but Saint-Arnaud and Raglan were still arguing when the French embarked on September 5. They would have continued the tiff, but Saint-Arnaud was too ill to leave his flagship, *Ville de Paris*, and the one-armed Raglan could not climb up the ship's ladder. The British would have no other landing place than the Old Fort, several miles west of Sebastopol. Hadn't *The Times* predicted the place and date a week before? Indeed, the Russians read this tidbit, but sensing a trap had concentrated their army on every other beach in Crimea. So not a soul contested the landing in the glowing dawn of September 18. The five hundred ships filled the sea, their masts like matchsticks on the horizon. As the 60,000 men, 2,000 horses, and hundreds of field guns were beached, Cossacks on the skyline waved their hats; the English officers bowed in return. With equal courtesy, the Russian governor of Eupatoria received the troops. He fumigated their formal surrender summons, however, and begged them to observe the quarantine regulations.

General Canrobert supervised the French landing. The

previous night on the *Ville de Paris*, Saint-Arnaud had suffered one more crisis and had exclaimed, "What will become of the army when I'm gone?" Canrobert felt the moment had come to break the seal of the letter Napoleon had written in his own, neat hand. Saint-Arnaud read the document. In the event of the commander in chief's death, the command will devolve on General Canrobert. On the beach that evening of September 18, the tubby general was convinced that they had seen the last of Saint-Arnaud. Suddenly he glimpsed two red spahi burnooses flashing behind a white, plumed hat. No! Saint-Arnaud and two aides. "Ah! How lovely it all is," Saint-Arnaud cried. "And to think they didn't want to come here." That letter appeared to have stirred a new fire in the man. The next day, as the army marched east through rolling vineyards and olive groves, he was chasing hares with his spahis and grumbling that the British were never on time. Having arrived with little food and no tents, the British were weary and hungry. But already in the hilly country near the Alma River they had sighted the advance scouts of Prince Menchikov's army of 40,000. That night Saint-Arnaud and Lord Raglan held a hurried conference. At dawn they would roll up the Russian flanks and rout them with a frontal assault.

The French were swarming toward the Alma just after daybreak before the horrified Saint-Arnaud realized that the British had not stirred. "They must have their English breakfast and a bath," grumbled General Emmanuel Wimpffen at his side. Saint-Arnaud galloped over to rouse Raglan. Though he could hardly sit upright on Nador, his white Arab, he cut a striking figure. His head adorned with a plumed, cocked hat, he sported every medal he had gained on his braided marshal's uniform. But he and his men had to breakfast before Raglan appeared, hitching his Waterloo saber around his rumpled pantaloons and silk shirt. It took the British three hours to form ranks. Saint-Arnaud rode along the lines. "Hurrah, the British," he shouted in his best English. "Now is the moment to charge. The French are on the move. Follow me. Forward."

Military textbooks mention the Alma as a cautionary tale. The British, dimly recalling how they had licked

Napoleon forty years before, pointed their regiments in
dead-straight ranks on a collision course, hoping to bleed
and die better than the enemy; the French, too, remembered
their hit-and-run triumphs in Algeria and let each commander muddle through; and the Russians were obsessed (as
they had been since 1812) with one strategic idea: retreat.

When at last they moved, Canrobert asked Saint-Arnaud for orders. Stabbing a dramatic finger at the heights
opposite, Saint-Arnaud explained, "With men such as you,
I have but to point to the enemy." In any case the French
had not waited for orders: baggy-trousered zouaves and
red-cloaked spahis broke and rushed across the river and
scrambled for the hills beyond. Surfing along in the middle
of this mob, Canrobert was bowled over by a cannonball
and only just survived under the feet of his own men; in
vain he tried to check the rabble. At that moment Bazaine
and his legionnaires appeared, marching as though on parade. "Ah, my brave legionnaires," shouted Canrobert, who
had served no more than two months with the Legion. "Set
the others an example at the right moment." Not to be
eclipsed, Saint-Arnaud, who had opposed sending the Legion to Crimea, took up the cry. "Forward, the elite battalion," he bellowed. With three commanders leading them,
the legionnaires drove like a solid wedge into the Russians
massing on the heights, then clung to the ground they had
won.

On their left, the British were falling like reaped corn.
From the high ground Canrobert observed the brilliantly
sunlit massacre, enthralled. Sir Colin Campbell trotted at
the head of his Highlanders, who, with wailing bagpipes
and muskets crashing salvos in unison, strode over their
dead into redoubts bristling with guns; Coldstreams and
Grenadiers formed a perfect line of scarlet tunics and black
busbies as they slow-stepped through a hail of rifle fire.
"As though they were in Hyde Park," Canrobert mused.
"Or doing some intricate square dance." Indeed, years later,
the marshal watched Queen Victoria, in a geranium-red
dress, dancing a quadrille with Prince Albert at a Paris ball.
He remembered the Alma. "The British fight as Victoria
dances," he said to himself.

British coolness and French fury finally chased the

Russians off the Alma hills. Some 6,000 Russians were killed or wounded; the British lost 2,000, the French 1,500. Now Sebastopol lay open. Surely Raglan and Saint-Arnaud would strike north to the Perekop Isthmus and isolate the base! So convinced did Prince Menchikov feel that he pulled out his main force from the base and headed north, nearly blundering into the British, who were making for Sebastopol days late. No one had maps. The Russians trekked, full-circle, for a whole day to land up confronting the allied armies before Sebastopol. They realized they could garrison and defend the base. The second act of the farce had begun.

"We have beaten Agamemnon and the siege won't last as long as the siege of Troy," Saint-Arnaud wrote modestly. He had achieved his dream. He had time to pay tribute to his old regiment, the Legion, by upgrading all its officers before they carried him, dying, on board the ship for home. They buried him near Napoleon I in Les Invalides.

The Crimean winter set in. Allied artillery and mortars ripped into houses and green-tiled churches, into the huge barracks and arsenal; from battlements the Russian guns replied, showering the entrenched soldiers with shrapnel and frozen mud. Raglan and Canrobert argued with increasing bitterness over tactics and strategy. During truces to collect their dead, Russian and French officers would shake hands and swap cigars before returning to the battle. The British, who had bled too freely and were living miserably, dispensed with such gallantry after the Alma.

Chivalry had never bothered legionnaires. While their officers were entertaining the enemy, they stole into no man's land to strip the Russian dead of their long gray coats and sheepskin jackets and the purses attached to their thighs. They augmented rations in the time-honored way, by scrounging or stealing; the more dutiful remembered Canrobert's injunction to pay for everything and left a brass button or an empty cartridge case. They bartered anything for brandy. On a freezing day General Canrobert inspected Bazaine's regiment. The sight of one legionnaire who had sold his boots to buy brandy and was parading in black-leaded bare feet nearly melted the fiery French commander's mustache wax. Forgetting that he had once captained a Legion company, he berated them as thieves, scoundrels, murderers, and tramps. What were down-at-the-heel noblemen and even a prefect of the Rome police doing in *his* army!

Bivouacking on the right flank of the Legion were the 23rd Royal Welsh Fusiliers and their regimental mascot, a magnificent billy goat called Dai. A present from Queen Victoria, the goat had won a citation for its cool conduct at the Alma. Two legionnaires coveted Dai, not for his *sang-froid*, but his fleecy coat. One night they crept over and poisoned the pride of the Welsh Fusiliers. When Dai had been buried with solemn ceremony in Inkerman cemetery, the legionnaires dug up the coffin and skinned the luckless animal. A tanner and tailor finished the job and the legionnaires tossed for the thick hide jacket. The man who won was wearing it when a major from the Fusiliers approached him.

"That's a fine jacket," he commented.

"C'est assez bien," muttered the legionnaire, trembling in case the murder and body snatching had been discovered.

"Must keep you warm," the major went on. "Tell you what—I'll give you twenty pounds for it."

Twenty pounds! A whole wagon of brandy! The major walked off, garbed in the skin of his own regimental mascot.

After a final set-to with Raglan, General Canrobert handed over the command to General Aimable Pelissier, a crusty, iron-handed soldier. That spring General MacMahon arrived to lead a division. Bazaine took a step up to brigadier. Soledad had set up a home for her husband behind the lines, piano and all. But she seemed to sow strife between Bazaine and his chiefs. General Forey accused Bazaine of deserting the trenches to spend the night with his wife. When Pelissier scotched the indictment, he and Soledad became firm friends. More than that, some officers hinted. The choleric old firebrand suddenly rediscovered a youthful poetic impulse and developed a passion for

Mozart and Chopin, as well as a patronly interest in Bazaine's career, which kept the new brigadier at the front. Those nights, Soledad would dine with the commander in chief in his quarters and perhaps partner him in a two-step or a waltz. Other evenings, Pelissier would hitch the only coach in the Crimea (captured from Menchikov) to a horse-artillery team and drive to Soledad's modest house to turn another page of Mozart and keep her company until "lights out." The new electric cable hummed with his Emperor's behests to finish the war; but Pelissier seemed in no hurry.

Finish it they must, however, before another winter destroyed the allied army. Raglan had died of cholera, and General Simpson had assumed his command. A full-scale autumn attack was mounted on the two outer forts of Sebastopol, the Redan and Malakov. While the British left hundreds of dead beneath the Redan without advancing much, MacMahon stormed Malakov. As the battle seesawed, Sebastopol literally heaved as its arsenals and mined forts detonated one after the other; the base and the allied fleet in the bay rocked with the explosions. But now MacMahon's pennant fluttered over Malakov. Fearing that this fortress would vanish in a pall of gunpowder, General Simpson sent an aide to ask MacMahon if he was staying on the hill. "Here I am, and here I stay," retorted MacMahon. Fortunately, the cable igniting the powder charges was faulty.

They might have crushed the fleeing Russians, but Pelissier was tired and Simpson said he would wait to learn the Russian plans. Queen Victoria cabled, somewhat tartly, that she "was tempted to advise a reference to St. Petersburg for them." The allies entered the smoking ruins of Sebastopol on September 10. General Bazaine commanded the occupying troops, mostly legionnaires. What the Russians had left, the legionnaires destroyed, with the pent-up fury of the year in which they had begun to hate the name of Sebastopol.

Bazaine was chosen to give the *coup de grâce*. With a mixed French and British force, he sailed to Kinburn at the mouth of the Dnieper and seized the naval fortress with a frontal landing. It was worth another star and another medal; and General Pelissier, a thoughtful man, took care of Soledad while her husband was winning new honors.

A futile war, followed by a flimsy treaty that had no lasting effect. More than 300,000 men had died, among them 1,625 legionnaires and seventy-two of their officers. "Let's get back to real soldiering," said one of the Legion officers, yearning for the sun, the hot sands, and the rich wine of Algeria.

FOUR

No spit-an'-polish or army bull
For men like us, whose only school
Is somebody's war.
It's battles, bordels and bistrots,
But dammit, this is comme-il-faut
For a legionnaire.

At Sidi bel-Abbès their German bandmaster, Wilheim, greeted the Crimean veterans with a new march. They did not much care for it. True, the opening fanfare rattled like musket fire. But the refrain! What did Wilheim think they were? Missionaries! His march sounded like a revivalist hymn. It had something, though. Legionnaires began to hum or whistle the new tune with the fifes and trumpets of their *clique*. A few men tried to weld verses to the air, but gave up. Not until 1870 would some wag jot down a parody of Wilheim's hymn and call it *"Le Boudin."* Why a black pudding as the Legion symbol? They did nickname their knapsack blankets sausages, and the men gobbled the blood sausage they got as a special treat. The anonymous versifier came down rather hard on the Belgians for their late entrance during the Franco-Prussian War.

Hey, we have black pudding, black pudding,
For the Alsations and the Swiss
And the boys from Lorraine.
But the Belgians must give it a miss
For being the last in the line.

To the strains of *"Le Boudin"* the Legion marched out of Sidi bel-Abbès in the second week of June 1857. Marshal Jacques de Randon had gathered 35,000 men to crush the Kabyles once and for all in their own wild Djurdjura Mountains. The tribes in this craggy amphitheater of hills had defied fifteen expeditions and were still raiding and looting even to the fringes of Algiers. In their mountain fortification of Ischeriden more than 20,000 men had taken an oath to slaughter the infidel French. To beat this army on its own ground would be a gamble. Failure could put the Algerian conquest back twenty years. Randon split his force into four divisions. Leading the one incorporating the two Legion battalions was their old commanding officer, General MacMahon. They came in over the 5,000-foot plateau to the west of Ischeriden.

The Kabyle army lay five miles away, but it might have been five hundred yards. In the sapphire clarity of the African morning, MacMahon could count the tribesmen massing behind rocks and trenches, could pick out their long muskets glittering in the sun as they gestured to the French to dare attack. MacMahon studied the terrain. Two miles of open ground and 1,000 feet to climb to the fortress; in between, a deep ravine and two rocky outcrops on which sat more than 1,000 armed Kabyles. June 24 promised to be a bloody day.

Brave and elegant Brigadier Charles Bourbaki led his zouaves and French infantry down the slope and over the ravine. The Kabyles waited, silently. Bugles blared and the blue and white columns surged onto the flinty escarpment; suddenly they swiveled and buckled under the barrage of fire; men pitched into each other as they tumbled down the sheer cliff. One brigade of MacMahon's division was gone, blocked in the ravine.

On the plateau MacMahon sent for Major Paul Mangin, commanding the Second Battalion. "Can you take those trenches?" he queried. Mangin nodded. What legionnaire did not consider himself worth ten of Bourbaki's zouzous? Mangin spurred his white Arab horse into the ravine. As they snapped home their bayonets, the legionnaires mocked the zouaves. "Is Sidi Mahomet [the sun] too hot for you?" . . . "Hope you didn't dirty your nice, baggy

pants sliding down the hill?" They threw down their knap-
sacks, but even with 1,000 feet of back-breaking cliff before them and a hot sun on their backs they kept on their
greatcoats. Who could trust thieving zouzous?

The bugle notes of the *Boudin* blew. *"En avant,"* Mangin shouted, and put his horse to the slope. No orders. Who
needed them? The legionnaires followed Mangin and his
horse, bent almost double on the steep cliff-face. Volley
after volley met them; Mangin's horse skidded and reared,
but stayed upright; the legionnaires marched slowly, as
though to Wilheim's slow melody. Not one answered the
fire. Stop and fire, and they would never reload. Old cam-
paigners, they realized that you counted fewer dead the
closer to the enemy. If Mangin and his horse had fallen . . .
But on they went.

Up and over the crest. Mangin now bore down on the
entrenched Kabyles, saber glinting. Behind him came the
first company, Captain Mariotti leading. He fell, but as
the tribesmen ran to finish him, Sergeant Mori, with legionnaires Pietrovitz, van Leyden, and Coulman, drove
through them with their bayonets to grab Mariotti. In half
an hour the battalion had cleared the trenches; the Kabyles
were scampering up the mountain to spread panic among
the red-tiled houses of Ischeriden. With the fall of the
town, the Kabyle dream of driving the French into the sea
evaporated.

Randon and MacMahon had stood marveling at the
unspoken scorn of these legionnaires who had walked
through the strongest fortification in North Africa. The Caid
of the Beni-Yenni tribe shared their incredulity. "The Longcoats forced us to forsake our barricades," he told the
French leaders. "Without them you would never have
gained our defenses, and we were about to destroy you. But
when we saw the Longcoats climb to take our positions
without even firing back at us, we fled. But say, who was
the devil incarnate who rode at the head of the Longcoats? I
fired at him. All of us fired at him. We saw our bullets raise
the dust around his white steed. But still he came on. Would
you reveal his name to me that I may keep it in my heart?"

Mangin's battalion had lost only one officer, though
three were wounded. Eight legionnaires had died and

eighty-seven were wounded. A dark-haired young German
called Gerhardt Rohlfs had come through unscathed and
won the Legion of Honor. Later he would make his name
exploring the Sahara. One of the wounded was Sergeant
Mori; his courage had created a personal problem. Randon
wished to add the Cross of the Legion of Honor to the military medal he had won in Crimea; but at that time no man
could wear the white cross under any but his real name.
Mori hesitated between anonymity and the Cross. Then
from his knapsack he produced papers that proved he was
Prince Mori-Ubaldini, a former priest and member of the
oldest and richest nobility in Florence. He would soon leave
the Legion to fight for Italian independence, but, like so
many others, would be lured back.

The officers of the Second Regiment in their mess at
Saida knew that, when Colonel Granet Lacroix de Chabrière
called for champagne, the parades were over. The colonel, a
gentleman of the old school, with high-domed brow and
gray muttonchop whiskers, raised his glass. *"Vive l'Em-
pereur—à bas les Autrichiens,"* he said. It was May 1859.
His regiment would sail from Oran to help wrest Italy from
the Austrians and proclaim its freedom. Only the announcement that the Emperor would personally lead his troops dis-
mayed the officers. "We'll roll the Austrians up over the
Lombardy Plain," Napoleon said grandly at Genoa.
Younger officers at that conference noted with amazement
that the Emperor could not read a map; but then neither
could many of his senior generals.

In fact, the army of 140,000 had to ford rivers and
ravines and plod painfully through olive groves and mul-
berry orchards; its guns and supply trains clogged the narrow roads. As usual, the legionnaires marched in the
ditches, caked in dust from gun carriages and cavalry. The
Austrians retreated before them. Only at Novara did a spy
whisper to Napoleon that they might stand and fight on the
Ticino River. He deployed MacMahon's corps near Magenta to draw off the enemy while he and the main army
crossed the river. But on June 3, everyone believed that the
Austrians had again bolted. That evening Lieutenant Laurent Zédé, the youngest officer in the Legion, dined with

General Louis Espinasse, commanding his brigade, and his own chief, Colonel Chabrière. "They've given us the slip," said Espinasse. Chabrière agreed, but took out his full-dress uniform for the next day's battle, just in case.

On June 4 the two armies, groping for each other, suddenly collided near Magenta. Northwest of the town, MacMahon had taken Bernate and swooped on Buffalora. But his left flank crumpled and recoiled before cannon fire and cavalry charges outside Magenta. Only Colonel Chabrière, with his two Legion battalions, stood firm. "No retreat," he cried. "Keep the sunny side of them. Down sacks and charge." As he spurred his horse, a bullet hit him in the chest. Sergeant Major Victor Maire, whose son would later make a great career in the Legion, ran to pick him up. *"Mon colonel, mon colonel,"* he stammered. Chabrière gazed at him, then whispered, "Shsh . . . listen . . . I must tell you something." He sat up and cried, *"Vive la Légion,"* and fell back, dead.

In reserve, behind the first two battalions, stood the third, commanded by Colonel José Martínez. Holding his own battalion in perfect formation with his bull voice and bad French, Martínez led them down the railway line that led to Magenta. MacMahon was cutting through to Magenta when word reached him that legionnaires were fighting in the main square. "The Legion in Magenta," he said. "The affair is in the bag." The Legion still spilt its blood before MacMahon's corps arrived to force the Austrians to retreat. No one had picked up points for good generalship that day, when the two armies had blundered into each other like blind elephants, and the soldiers did the work. Napoleon never appeared (his army had bogged down outside the town) but he rode in style through Magenta, pausing to create General Maurice MacMahon a Marshal of France and Duke of Magenta.

Legionnaires celebrated by running wild in the quiet market town, sacking and looting its shops and cellars. Fearing an Austrian counterattack, Martínez had the *Boudin* sounded. "The troops were too busy looting the wine cellars to bother with bugle calls," said Zédé, who tried to round the men up. The subaltern found some of them floating in the wine vats the next morning—dead. When he came to hand out cartridges, no legionnaire needed more than nine to make up his regulation fifty. "And this after a battle in which they left a fifth of their comrades," he thought. "Proud soldiers, these."

The Austrians retreated west, the French fumbling after them. To their left the Italian Alps, snow-tipped; to their right the lush Lombardy Plain. On June 22, Napoleon halted at Chiari, west of Lake Garda; informants whispered that the Austrians had crossed the Mincio and were fleeing for home. French forward units thought otherwise. Young Zédé spotted dust clouds approaching and suggested to a staff officer that the Austrians might be returning.

"Nonsense," the officer said. "Cross and fight with their backs to the river? Never!"

"But the dust . . ."

"No buts. What age are you, anyway?"

"Twenty-two."

"They shouldn't trust these jobs to young cubs," the officer muttered and rode off to console the Emperor.

MacMahon's equerry had to rouse Napoleon the next morning to announce that the two armies had again clashed. "Where are they?" Napoleon asked. "Solferino," they said. Around the small town some 400,000 men had met head-on over a fifteen-mile front. More than 700 Austrian guns and 520 French pounded at each other's lines; nearly 40,000 cavalry were drumming across the plain at each other. Around Solferino Tower white-coated and blue-coated bodies were piling higher and higher; at the cemetery General Bazaine was leading his division as Conrad might have led a Legion battalion—from the front. ("I was lucky enough to get through without losing any bits of myself," he would say.) A bullet grazed him, lodging in his saddle. They took the cemetery, lost it, took it again, lost it—terrain had ceased to matter that day. Only the slaughter.

As the afternoon wore on it seemed that the two armies would exterminate each other. The legionnaires fought off yet another attack; the French had retaken the cemetery; the Austrians had once more seized the tower. At five o'clock, above the din of cannon, came a louder rumble: a whipping wind drove a dust pall over the battlefield; lightning ripped across the sky. Suddenly the whole battlefield was awash;

the soldiers raised their faces to drink some of the deluge. To both emperors on the field the thunderstorm seemed a providential signal to stop.

Neither side had won. The French counted their dead and wounded, 12,000 of them; their Italian allies had lost another 5,000; the Austrians admitted to 13,000 casualties. And Napoleon had merely nudged the Austrians out of one Italian province. He rapidly signed a peace treaty and went home to ponder another fanciful scheme. This time he had his eye on Mexico, which would serve as a bridgehead from which to control events in the New World. He did not intend to use the Legion, but its officers grumbled so much about their exclusion that finally, almost fatefully, the Emperor consented. The Legion sailed for Vera Cruz and a campaign that would change its whole history.

FIVE

For that strutting dummy on sentry-go
Outside the palace of So-and-So
You don't much care.
In the Tonkin scrub you're more at home
Than square-bashing in some barrack-town,
If you're a legionnaire.

At the approach of the Legion column, buzzards scattered like shrapnel, though they still planed expectantly in the torpid sky over the small Mexican hamlet; coyotes that had been sharing the feast slunk into the bush to watch and wait. As Colonel Pierre Jeanningros reconnoitered the western edges of the ruined village with his men, a boy emerged from the tangle of cactus and mesquite bushes. "It's Lai, the drummer of the Third," someone shouted. Casimir Lai was barely recognizable, barely human. A stiff rag of shirt hung over his body, with blood from a chest wound still oozing through it; lance wounds festered on his arms and thighs; his right arm hung useless; his lips moved but he could not speak. An officer forced some weak coffee mixed with rum over his throat. Even then, Lai could only babble over and over in his Italian accent, "I . . . I'm the only one left of the Third."

Twenty-nine hours have passed since the Third Company of the Legion marched out of Chiquihuite down the Fever Road, which the legionnaires have guarded since arriving in Mexico a month before. Its mission: to meet and protect a wagon train bringing 4,000,000 gold francs, supplies, and munitions from Vera Cruz to the French army besieging Puebla, the key to Mexico City on the high plateau.

Late at night, on April 29, 1863, an Indian spy bursts in on Colonel Jeanningros to inform him that a strong Mexican column, led by Colonel Francisco de Paula Milán, means to seize the convoy between Soledad and Chiquihuite. Who can Jeanningros spare? Even the Third Company, which he calls off guard duty, has nearly half its strength in hospital with yellow fever, black vomit, and Mexican *cafard*, caused by drinking too much pulque or mescal; his three battalions are scattered along the sixty miles of the Torrid Zone, from his command post at Chiquihuite to Vera Cruz. Who, for instance, could lead the Third? His adjutant major, Captain Jean Danjou, immediately volunteers himself. Jeanningros hesitates. The most important convoy since the Mexican campaign has begun! Danjou is a "*brave*." Algeria. Crimea. Magenta. But maybe he has been too long on desk work and with Legion survey detachments. Also, he has lost his left hand while firing a signal pistol that burst. "I would like the honor of leading the Third," Danjou insists. Jeanningros can only concur.

At one o'clock in the morning the company starts its march from Chiquihuite; in single file, the three officers and sixty-two men pick their way over loose scree, through stunted trees and thick ferns; only the squawk of a parrot or a macaw or the clink of ammunition boxes and mess kit on their two mules interrupt the silence of night. They know this sinister route, having traveled it from Vera Cruz, where the Legion landed. The trail plunges to the Atoyac River, runs through Paso del Macho (Mule Pass) to Camerone village, and finally to their rendezvous at Palo Verde (Green Wood). A trail littered with the shards of previous convoys, with animal carcasses picked clean, with French graves dug deep against the coyotes.

Mexico! What promise it had held! A land of snow-tipped volcanoes and purple mountains, of flashing streams and dazzling flowers; its men were friendly, its women dark-eyed and hot-blooded. Less dedicated legionnaires dreamed of gold in the sierras or wet-backing across the Rio Grande into the promised land of America. What was the reality? Torrid country where swamp alternated with

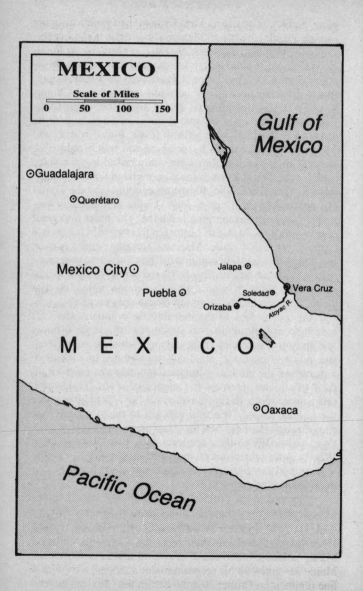

jungle, where men vomited what looked like coffee grounds and died without warming the bores of their Minie rifles, where vampire bats bled their mules and horses to death. A savage, hostile population, and women who shrank from *Los Bandidos Extranjeros*. A milky firewater called pulque, which made absinthe taste like nectar; and *aguardiente* and mescal on which not even *le cafard* would feed. And beans, beans, beans! Nor did they rightly comprehend why they had come. Of course they had their own version:

Once upon a time there was a Mexican President, too old and thick to notice that his young wife was shacked up with a caballero called Marmón, who first pinched the wife, then the job. But a wicked Indian character called Juárez hunted Marmón, who then went to a Swiss banker named Jecker and wrote an IOU for a good many millions that he never saw and some more that he did. With the money, he had a go at Juárez, got a bloody nose, and ruined Jecker. Now, Little Emperor Nap had a brother, the Duc de Morny, always short of a few sous. Morny bought Jecker's IOU for next to nothing and coaxed Nap to snuff out Juárez so that he could recover from Marmón the money he'd never coughed up.

The Sphinx of the Tuileries had, however, a more grandiose scheme. Money served merely as the pretext for Napoleon's mystic design to turn Mexico into the center of a Latin empire in the American hemisphere, to further French interest and destroy United States hegemony. His Mexican emperor would be Archduke Maximilian, the pliant younger brother of Austrian Emperor Franz Joseph. The Great Thought of the Second Empire would materialize while the North American states were tearing each other apart in the Civil War. The three Legion battalions were part of a French force of 40,000 that would secure the throne for Maximilian.

At 1:15 A.M., Danjou's company fords the Atoyac some six hundred feet below Chiquihuite and moves toward Paso del Macho. With them marches Corporal Philippe Maine, a burly, broad-faced man with a walrus mustache. Maine has given up his sergeant major's stripes, won with a line regiment in Crimea, to take part in the Mexican adventure. That day he will witness so much fire and gore that he will not discuss Mexico and speak of his company until twelve years later. "A good company, ours," he will say. "The Third of the First in army terms, it was rightly considered one of the best in the Legion."

Danjou, for instance. A quiet man with fine features and scant blond hair. Not the hero type, but a soldier through and through. The only officer of the three to graduate from Saint-Cyr. To enter the army he had defied his father, who was forcing him into the hatter's business he ran in Chalabre in the Pyrenean foothills. He might have quit the Legion when he lost his hand, but he had someone fashion for him a wooden replica that allowed him to ride a horse and keep his saber arm free. Maine is impressed with Danjou's flair for sizing up situations and barking precise orders.

Second Lieutenant Napoléon Vilain has come up through the ranks. In his middle twenties, he looks no more than a boy under the floppy sombrero that has replaced the kepi in Mexico. The other officer, Second Lieutenant Clément Maudet, has the stamp of the former Legion sergeant major. Tough and resolute, he did well in Crimea and at Magenta.

Just after 1:30 A.M. Paso del Macho. The Legion detachment under Captain Saussier turns out to greet Danjou's company. Saussier looks at them dubiously. "Take some of my grenadiers," he suggests. Danjou shakes his head. "If you're in trouble, I'll come running," says Saussier. No one doubts it, for Saussier is already a legend. The Third clatters across the wooden gangway into the scrub.

Behind Danjou marches Sergeant Major Henri Tonel, the company heavyweight and, at five-feet-ten, its tallest man. Not even the Legion, where fat men are rare, has trimmed his paunch; not even Mexico has stifled his booming laugh. Tonel, a one-time actor, and Sergeant Vincent Morzycki are the jokers. Morzycki, a former student of Franco-Polish parentage, is perhaps the most intelligent of the NCOs and certainly its fittest. Who else? Tall Victor Catteau, one of fifteen Belgians. Young Johan Reuss, at seventeen one of the two babes who had lied about his age.

Today he will fire in anger for the first time. He is one of the thirteen Germans with Danjou.

And Sergeant Evariste Berg. There's a funny one. A dandy, even in the scant blue tunic and cotton pants they wear here; he seems to spend more on mustache pomade than the company on pulque. From a well-heeled family in Reunion Island, Berg had been a lieutenant in a crack zouave regiment. What is *he* doing humping his sack with the Legion? There's Lai, the Sardinian drummer; Leon Gorski, the Pole; Ulrich Konrad, the captain's German orderly; eight Swiss, two Spaniards, a Dane, a Dutchman. "A good company, ours, the Third of the First."

Paso Ancho. Fruit bats flap overhead. Nearly dawn. At first light they make out a derelict hamlet, a casualty of the guerrilla war on the Fever Road. Danjou's hand-drawn map tells him it is Camerone. The shell of its hacienda still stands, though sun and rain have eroded the adobe shacks on either side. The legionnaires give it no more than a glance as they plod on to Palo Verde. "Juice [coffee] in half an hour," somebody says.

Palo Verde. A scrubby clearing with no cover. Fifty guerrillas would finish his company. Danjou posts lookouts and sends a detachment for water. "We halt here for a rest, then reconnoiter," he tells his lieutenants. "Can we drum up some juice, *mon capitaine*?" the legionnaires ask. Danjou nods. In ten minutes the big coffee pots are simmering, the men are breaking out their hardtack. Suddenly a lookout signals. Danjou follows the pointing finger. A score of Mexican cavalry on the skyline. *"Aux armes,"* he cries. The coffee pots are kicked over, the mules loaded, and five minutes later the company has taken to the bush to protect itself against cavalry charges. Danjou remembers Jeanningros' injunction: the convoy must get through at any cost. He must probe the enemy strength. Turning, he doubles back toward Camerone. As they reach the ruined hacienda a shot rings out and a legionnaire falls wounded. On Danjou's order, the company splits, flanking and searching each shack and the main building. Nothing. They press on.

But the shot had been a signal. Half a mile through the hamlet several hundred Mexican cavalry are massing to charge; they drum toward the legionnaires, who form into a square. Thirty rifles let fly, then another thirty; the horses rear and plunge, trampling men on the ground. As the Mexicans regroup, Danjou looks at the hacienda. In the open he'll be crushed; there, he might hold out long enough for Saussier to relieve him and save the convoy. He staves off a second charge, then barges through the cavalry into the old farmhouse of Camerone.

Those attacks have scared off their mules, which carried their provisions. And their water. The men have neither eaten nor drunk since one o'clock. Scarcely inside the high walls when a volley from the one solid building drops two more legionnaires. The Mexicans have beaten them to it. Detailing men to cover the snipers at the windows, Danjou posts his small force around the walls and surveys the hacienda. With the enemy in the main building, he has only an old stable in the opposite corner; facing this, he has a breach to protect, and on the west side two gaping doorways, their doors long vanished. Using stones and planks, the legionnaires barricade the breach and gates. Sergeant Morzycki sprints across the courtyard and claws onto the red-tiled roof of the main building. "They're all around us," he shouts.

"How many?"

"About eight hundred."

The Mexicans have gone strangely quiet. At 9:30 a staff captain rides up waving a truce flag. Captain Ramón Laine calls to Morzycki. "You're outnumbered. Why be killed? Surrender, and Colonel Milán promises to spare your lives." Morzycki relays the message to Danjou. "We'll die rather than surrender," the captain shouts back.

The truce flag drops, the signal for a Mexican attack. Bullets whine through the gates and breach, kicking up dust spurts, ricocheting from the walls; the Mexicans storm the openings, but move so awkwardly in heavy leather chaps that the legionnaires pick them off in dozens in the corral. "Make each bullet count," Danjou tells each man. He remembers their thirst. "The wine, Konrad." The batman brings the captain's liter of French wine that he has carried from Chiquihuite. Solemnly, Danjou dispenses it, giving each man one sip out of his glass. As though it were some sacred communion, he makes them swear on oath. "You promise me to die rather than surrender?" Each answers, *"Oui, mon capi-*

taine." . . . *"Ja, mein Kapitan.* . . . *"Sí, Sí, capitán."* Just before eleven o'clock Danjou is crossing the corral to visit a barricade; the men watch him clutch his chest and fall; Vilain darts to pick him up, but Danjou shakes his head. He tries to whisper something, writhes, and lies still.

Now, no more thought of surrender. Vilain, the wavy-haired boy, assumes command. For the second time the Mexicans offer terms. *"Merde,"* yells Morzycki from his rooftop perch. How the sergeant survives no one knows; his face black with powder and rage, he fires at everything as bullets clink off the tiles around him. Only forty men are left in the corral. Young Reuss has fought his first and last battle. And Jean Timmermans, the baby of the company. Corporal Adolfi Delcaretto and Ludwig Rohr, Peter Dicken and Charles Dubois—they have all kept their pledge. Sergeant Jean Germays falls. Drummer Lai runs to drag him into the stable. "No, boy, I'm done for—here, take my rifle." Tonel blocks a rush at the breach and he, too, drops. *"Courage, mes enfants,"* his voice booms. "You know the order—to the death." And the remaining men stare, mesmerized, at the blood drying and steaming in the corral dust. And they remember their swollen tongues.

Midday. A long bugle note. "That's Saussier. He'll get through hell to us." Lai is listening to the deep drum beats. "They're Mexican drums," he says. Morzycki confirms it; he sees more than 1,000 Mexican infantrymen approach. For the third time Milán proffers surrender terms. In legionnaire language Morzycki tells him what to do with them. The Mexican infantry press around the farmhouse and, an hour later, a dozen more legionnaires lie dead. Corporal Maine watches Lieutenant Vilain cross the corral; in the center he spins around and falls dead.

"At that moment [Maine will say later] a horrible and profound sadness came over us all. The heat pressed on us; the sun struck from the white walls of the courtyard, searing our eyes. When we opened our mouths to breathe we seemed to inhale fire; the leaden air vibrated; even the dust spurts from bullets appeared reluctant to leave the ground and rose in lazy spirals. Overheated by the sun and our firing rate, the rifle barrels scorched our hands like glowing spits.

So intense was the heat in the furnace of a redoubt that we
watched the dead bodies decompose before our eyes."

Friedrich is down . . . and Bertolotto . . . and Hipp.
They have taken several of the enemy with them. The Mexican wounded implore the Virgin or curse God; they cry,
they plead for water. The legionnaires lie silent. "The poor
souls fear they will reveal our losses and give the enemy
heart," Maine thinks. His own tongue fills his mouth, his
lips are cracking; in the heat and din, his temples throb like
the sunlight in the dust; he feels his mind wavering. Before
his eyes the wounded drag themselves on their bellies to lick
the blood pooling in the courtyard; others contort their limbs
to suck the blood from their own wounds. Anything to blunt
their maddening thirst.

Lieutenant Maudet, the old sergeant major, has taken
charge. "You know what we have to do," he growls to the
handful of men still alive. Yes, they know. For how much
longer? Berg still holds the northern gate, standing alone
now, his face scorched with powder, his eyes bloodshot.
Whatever his past, he has kept his word to Danjou and the
Legion. Morzycki, finally driven from his dangerous perch,
lies alongside Maine, counting his last cartridges. At the
breach, corporals Karl Mangin and Heinrich Pinzinger and
two legionnaires, Gorski and young Hippolyte Kunasseg,
signal that they, too, are running out of shells. Another Mexican rush carries them away. Maine witnesses Berg being
engulfed by Mexicans. Only the outhouse still resists. Now
there are six out of the sixty-two men and three officers.

Maine senses something drop on his shoulder and
glances around. Morzycki's eyes stare at him. Morzycki, the
witty . . . Morzycki, the brave . . . "Morzycki is dead," he
croaks to Maudet.

"Bah," the lieutenant retorts. "Another one. It'll soon be
our turn." He rams another cartridge home and keeps firing.

Maine rummages in Morzycki's pockets. Only two cartridges. They count their ammunition as they do the last
minutes of their lives. Maine has four more bullets to fire.
("Since that morning I had never for one moment lost my
head or my spirit. Suddenly I felt I was going to die.") Before his eyes passes a procession of images: he is playing
with his school chums at Musidan, his birthplace in the

green hills of Perigord; now he lies wounded in the Crimean mud; a general is pinning a medal on him for his part in the Little Redan assault; he is removing his stripes to join the Legion as a second-class private and hears that he will go to Mexico. . . .

Will he leave his bones in this old shack with no thatch on its roof and hardly any walls? He looks around him. Besides Maudet there are Victor Catteau and Laurent Constantin and Gottfried Wenzel, the square-faced Prussian. What can they do? The Mexicans have filled the corral and stand only a yard or two from their barricade in the yawning door of the stable. Dust and fumes hang in the torpid air. Each man has one cartridge left. Maudet's raucous whisper reaches them: "Charge your rifles. You will fire on command, then we will charge with the bayonet. You will follow me."

Everything goes quiet and still; even their wounded have ceased to moan; the four men in the stable wait for Maudet's order.

Maudet springs to his feet. "Take aim," he shouts. "Fire!" The four legionnaires stumble after him, loosing off their remaining shots and pointing their bayonets. A burst of Mexican fire deafens Maine and sets the air trembling. At that moment Legionnaire Catteau throws himself in front of Maudet, grasping the officer in his arms and falling, riddled with bullets. Maudet drops, too. Miraculously, Maine, Constantin, and Wenzel stay on their feet.

A Mexican officer of French origin, Colonel Combas, knocks away his men's bayonets with his saber. "Gentlemen, you must surrender," he calls.

"If you leave us our arms and equipment and look after our lieutenant," Maine replies in Spanish.

"Talk French or my men will think you're Spanish and massacre you," Combas whispers. He leads them through the troops to where Milán and his staff are waiting. "What!" says the Mexican chief. "Is this all that's left of them?" Combas nods. *"Pero, no son hombres, son demonios."* (But they're devils, not men.)

Two officers and twenty-nine men had died in the hacienda. Maudet died several days later in a hospital. Even though Milán treated the prisoners and the wounded like heroes, few of the fifteen wounded survived their exposure to the grilling sun and no water. The majority of the nineteen prisoners did not come through the Mexican campaign. Returned from captivity, Berg and Maine became officers. A year later Berg died of wounds in Orizaba Hospital. A duel with a fellow officer, they said, though no one ever proved this. Maine quit the Legion to reappear in another regiment as a captain in the Franco-Prussian War.

And the Mexicans? They had lost some three hundred men, killed and wounded, and had no heart to attack the convoy, which, in any case, had sought safety at Soledad. During that day the legionnaires had fired 3,000 rounds of ammunition, of which one in ten had found a human target. Most of the fatal and grave wounds were in the head and chest, which testifies to their marksmanship.

As soon as the fighting had stopped, news of the Camerone tragedy spread. To Colonel Jeanningros at Chiquihuite rode an Indian messenger who babbled of a massacre; the colonel gathered a detachment and sent a message, rolled in a cigarette, to a company below Palo Verde instructing it to rendezvous where Danjou had first sighted the Mexicans.

But what came over Jeanningros himself? In a day of heroes and martyrs, he emerges as a bumbling, hesitant, and . . . cowardly figure. He might have reached Camerone that evening, but chose, instead, to camp at Paso Ancho, three miles west. The next morning he marched past Camerone, ignoring the bodies already shredded by buzzards and coyotes and decaying in the heat; he picked up the company at Palo Verde and strode through Camerone again, halting only when Drummer Lai stumbled from the bushes. Lai's stuttered account must have left the colonel in no doubt about the resistance that Danjou and the Third had put up. Yet he backtracked and hid in the bushes, fearing another Mexican attack. Only the protests of his officers and legionnaires forced him to return and bury the dead. Not until two o'clock did they dig a mass grave and place the martyrs of Camerone in it.

As the burial party worked, a legionnaire picked up something lying in the courtyard: the wooden hand of Jean

Danjou. It would become the most precious relic of the Foreign Legion.

Who would have believed that Captain Danjou, the quiet, diffident soldier of almost mystical devotion, would symbolize the heroism and self-sacrifice of legionnaires? That Camerone, a *débâcle*, would come to be celebrated in the Legion like Good Friday? That Danjou's grave face would take pride of place in the Legion mausoleum over its more colorful captains? That his wooden hand would mean more than the standards, heavy with honor, that surround it in the chapel?

April 30 is the sacred day in the Legion. The parades look like religious rites wherever the Legion serves; the sole reminder of Camerone, the small, wooden hand, is borne by a distinguished former legionnaire to the Monument aux Morts to be saluted by the First Regiment while an NCO intones the legend of Camerone. No legionnaire can smirch his service sheet on Camerone Day.

Yes, a defeat. But one from which the Legion learned much about the anatomy of courage and loyalty. The Legion knows that martyrs make the faith just as faith makes martyrs. So Camerone sits at the center of legionnaire faith. What man, swearing his oath to the Legion, indoctrinated with the heroism of those sixty-five men, could ever think of retreat or defeat!

Later that year the Legion had better news: one of their own, General Achille Bazaine, had taken over command in Mexico. Since the summer of 1862, Bazaine had proved himself, commanding one of General Elie Forey's divisions. At Jalapa he scattered 20,000 Mexican cavalry with 4,000 men; at Puebla he broke the siege and opened Mexico City to Maximilian by chasing 6,000 Mexicans off the San Lorenzo heights with half that force. Napoleon rewarded him with over-all command. In his turn Bazaine pulled his old unit out of the badlands and convoy duty and gave them some real soldiering. Mexican mountain and desert lent themselves to Algerian tactics. Powerful mobile columns from Bazaine's mixed army of 14,000 Frenchmen and 7,000 Mexican loyalists chased Benito Juárez and his guerrillas into the scrub and cactus deserts north of Monterrey.

Whereas Forey had malingered for six months between
Vera Cruz and Mexico City, Bazaine purged the country of
Juarists in six weeks.

In May 1864, Maximilian and his empress, Carlotta,
drove from Vera Cruz to Mexico City, escorted part of the
way by a Legion company. On June 12, Bazaine's wedding
day, the commander in chief rode beside their carriage into
the capital. Bazaine had one regret: Soledad could not be
with him. She never would be again.

What Bazaine gleaned of his wife's tragedy is not
known. His face, an impassive Arab mask, and his hooded
eyes revealed none of his feelings. For the first time Soledad
had not accompanied him to war, begging to stay in Paris
until he had settled the Mexican campaign. Gossips, whom
Bazaine never heeded, might have whispered the real reason: she had fallen in love with a worthless man who had
another mistress, a spiteful woman who had made something of a name with the Comédie Française. The impulsive
Soledad wrote several love letters, which Ma'mzelle Nitouche—as she was nicknamed—discovered. One day a letter arrived for Soledad. Horrified, she read that the woman
had collected her love letters and posted them to Bazaine in
Mexico, marked personal. Almost out of her mind, Soledad
rushed to Empress Eugénie, imploring her to stop the mail
boat and seize the letters. Bad weather prevented the Emperor's launch from intercepting the steamer; when Soledad
learned this news she poisoned herself.

When the letters arrived Bazaine was campaigning in
central Mexico, at Guanajuato. His staff officer, a lean long-
bearded colonel called Henri Willette, opened the packet
and read the letters. One by one, he burned them. Bazaine
was his hero and victory in Mexico was worth more in Willette's view than two treacherous women. His general had
toiled too long for his baton to falter now. A week later the
cable arrived announcing that Madame Bazaine had died.
Bazaine broke down when his nephew rode north to give him
the news. Six years of penance before he could marry
her . . . then the Crimea . . . Italy . . . their plans to make a
home in Mexico . . . and when he became a marshal . . . Now
she was dead. For months he brooded, though he did not
spare himself or his troops. Some say that he never learned

the real story; others, that he only read it when Ma'mzelle Nitouche spiced her memoirs with Soledad's tragedy.

For eight months Bazaine virtually ruled Mexico, and even his opponents conceded that the railways and posts ran on time and bandits left travelers alone. The general's biggest millstone was Maximilian, who appeared less concerned with founding a solid government than with establishing a Hapsburg court. The practical soldier pointed out—half a century before the Mexicans themselves admitted the fact—that the country's future lay with its own population, including the downtrodden Indians. Bazaine's views earned only resentment from Maximilian and the French ministers. Napoleon recognized his achievements, however, and made him a marshal in 1864. To celebrate, he snuffed out the last pocket of resistance in the country. Oaxaca, in the south, had been held by Porfirio Díaz since the beginning of the campaign. The city lay behind twenty miles of fortifications, defended by 10,000 men armed with artillery and American rifles. In blue and white burnoose, Bazaine led Legion and French infantry units through breaches punched by his guns and cleared Oaxaca, taking 8,000 prisoners and fifty guns for the loss of fifty men.

On his return from Oaxaca, Bazaine started courting again. María Josefa de la Pena y Barragón resembled the young Soledad—she was seventeen, slender, dark, vivacious, and penniless. Bazaine, a paunchy fifty-four, with stubby legs and a puffy, triple-chinned face, ignored the sniggers and the gossip. Now, he had the best of sponsors— Napoleon and Eugénie, Maximilian and Carlotta. When Bazaine and Pepita were married in the private chapel of Mexico City cathedral, Maximilian offered them the ornate Buenavista Palace as a wedding present.

Soon rumors were flying. Pepita had not married Bazaine for his looks. Had not her uncle been President of Mexico? She meant to make Bazaine viceroy and later Emperor of Mexico, in place of the effete Maximilian. The whisper ran that Bazaine was secretly consorting with the Juarists to stage a coup d'état. Even the French ministers accused Bazaine of playing a double game.

But did Bazaine really contemplate taking Maximilian's place? As a soldier, he realized that he could never hope to hold Mexico when the American Civil War had ended and battle-hardened American troops were concentrated along its frontiers: He had also received coded instructions from Napoleon at the beginning of 1866 to withdraw slowly from Mexico. France was concerned about the cost of the fiasco; Napoleon, worried about the growing Prussian menace, wanted his army back intact; and the American Secretary of State, William Henry Seward, was demanding the evacuation of his forces. No, Bazaine knew that France had lost the Mexican gamble. To the eccentric Carlotta he had to prevaricate, but to Maximilian he spoke more bluntly, warning him that without French troops he was doomed. He also had to resort to every military and political ruse to disengage his 40,000 men without stirring rebel forces into action, which would cost him lives. All this Bazaine accomplished. If his campaigning had been brilliant, his painless withdrawal south through Mexico City to Vera Cruz was masterly. By January 1867 all but a handful of French troops had embarked.

Maximilian refused Bazaine's final offer to escort him to the ship and safety; behind lace curtains in his palace he watched the marshal and the last Legion detachments leave. Already Carlotta had rushed to Europe to plead with Napoleon to keep his army in Mexico. The Emperor was deaf; the Pope could do nothing for the demented woman. Despair drove her mad; she never realized that Maximilian, the reluctant emperor, had been caught and shot at Querétaro. She would live in her own mad world for another sixty years.

The Mexican adventure ended tragically for most of those who took part. Bazaine arrived at Toulon to a deserted quay; but, ironically, Napoleon's snub endeared the marshal to the public and the press, who were tiring of the Second Empire. As it turned out, Bazaine might have finished less of a villain had he been less popular.

SIX

It's fifteen years in a hard billet
Unless you cop a lucky bullet,
Fair and square.
You could become just jackal-meat
If you weren't one of our elite.
A legionnaire.

In their whitewashed Beau Geste forts, legionnaires gleaned the news from camel- and mule-supply columns and flickering heliographs. "War declared on Prussia, July 19." In Sidi bel-Abbès and Saida, officers interrogated each other. What does the Legion do? Its charter banned operations in France, though surely not while the country was struggling for survival. Napoleon, however, stuck to the letter; he had another reason for ordering his Legion to stay where it was. It had too many German legionnaires, and who could ask or trust Germans to fight against their own kin? So the Legion, reduced to 3,000 men after its bloodletting in Mexico, busied itself on fatigues and helped French *colons* to control locust plagues that summer of 1870. They heard the sober news from France. A superior Prussian army had trapped and crushed MacMahon at Worth on August 6. Alsace had gone. Nevertheless, the bulk of the French army still battled on; they had the African generals like Canrobert, Bourbaki, and old Changarnier. And Bazaine. France was pinning her hopes on him and his army in the Metz fortress. But Bazaine, outnumbered and outgunned by four to one, could only sit there waiting for a miracle. What could a French army of 300,000 do against 1,200,000 men? What could bickering generals, schooled on tribal conflicts, do against a well-drilled, mobile Prussian army? The cannon of Magenta and Solferino sounded thin against the massed batteries of new Krupp guns. Before he left for Lorraine, Bazaine had listened to the Paris mob smashing the Prussian Embassy windows and crying, *"A Berlin."* The same mob that had voted against conscription. "We are heading for a disaster," he confided to a friend. Now, in response to political pressures and street slogans, the mortally sick Emperor had chosen Bazaine, the youngest of his marshals, to save France. Fearing that retreat on Paris would bring down the Empire, he had instructed Bazaine to withdraw no farther than Verdun.

Krupp Gun

Was Verdun any stronger than Metz? Bazaine thought not. Anyway, when he tried in August to move his army of 130,000 men along the Verdun road, its snail's pace so shocked him that he returned. German cavalry and artillery would pulverize him in the open. Let them break their teeth on Metz, and maybe MacMahon, with his new army of Chalons, would come to his relief. In two battles, Rezonville and Gravelotte, Bazaine did inflict heavy losses on the enemy, leading his army in Conrad's style; his bulky figure, spurring his chestnut, jinked through cannon fire, his white kepi bobbed now among the Lancers, now the infantry. His generals tut-tutted. A Marshal of France behaving like some foot-slogger! They would complain, too, that he could have saved France by attacking the wobbling Prussian divisions at Gravelotte. For Bazaine it was the lion's mouth and an honorable massacre; he turned back to sit under the sodden clouds over Metz and wait for MacMahon.

MacMahon never came. Instead, on September 2, the Germans released hundreds of prisoners, who brought the bad news. MacMahon had blundered into the Prussians at Sedan; after three days of fighting, the Emperor had handed his sword to the Prussian King. His young son was Emperor, his Empress the Regent. Only Bazaine's beleaguered force stood between France and defeat. And Bazaine, as a legionnaire, had witnessed too many such sieges to doubt the outcome.

Threatened by the German advance, Paris was playing its traditional game: making and breaking dynasties. The Third Empire lasted three days before Empress Eugénie fled into exile at the Marine Hotel, Hastings. The Third Republic rose in the perfervid image of the French Revolution. "Not an inch of our territory, not a stone of our fortresses," cried Jules Favre. A dumpy little lawyer, Leon Gambetta, soared out of Paris in a balloon to drum up a popular army at Tours. France was finally taking the war seriously.

Still, no one thought of the Legion. Some former legionnaires were already doing their bit. Old General Joseph Bernelle, over eighty and a widower for many years, offered his services only to receive a polite refusal from the War Ministry. Nevertheless, someone had to cope with the thousands of foreigners queuing at recruiting depots. Swiss and Belgians, English and Americans, even a few Chinese, wanted to fight the Germans. Astonished recruiting officers noted that more than 1,000 Germans had offered their services. A small, fine-featured youth enrolled as a sergeant; the captain at the depot recognized him from their Saint-Cyr days as Prince Karageorgevitch, who later became King of Serbia. Before she fled, Empress Eugénie signed a decree authorizing the formulation of these men into a foreign regiment in France.

German volunteers were packed off to Algeria to the Foreign Legion; the others gathered at the Recollets Barracks in Tours, more than 1,500 men drilling without arms or uniforms. In one respect only did they resemble the parent Legion: they caroused, they beat each other up, wrecked shops and bistros. The mayor of Tours demanded the expulsion of this rowdy Fifth Battalion. On October 10, in the light of bivouac fires, they were handed uniforms, kitbags, and old Minié or Chassepot rifles that few knew how to use. They would help the defense of Orléans that Gambetta was organizing. Led by Major Victor Arago, son of the famous physicist, they arrived at Orléans the next day to be told by the townspeople, "You've come to get your share, too."

They had no time to eat their midday meal before a shout went up: "The Uhlans, the Uhlans." In fact, a Bavarian regiment was attacking the town. Kicking over their cooking pots, the legionnaires straggled down the street to meet the enemy. A burst of fire from a church knocked over a score of his men before Arago could organize and place them in barns, ditches, vineyards, and behind trees. While he was directing them—too nonchalantly, perhaps—a bullet hit him in the head. The Bavarians rushed from the church to grab his body, but Lieutenant de France de Tersant and a section of legionnaires drove them back at bayonet point. They carried Arago, dead, into a butcher's shop.

"No retreat," shouted Captain de Villeneuve, who took over the battalion. So, for six hours, these rookies held off a crack regiment. One sergeant knocked down eighty Bavarians with his Chassepot rifle; another legionnaire, a Belgian named Joseph Feront, accounted for another thirty with a similar weapon. There and then, the awkward squad were taught how to load, aim, and fire. No one had issued orders; no one expected any. The men stuck to their posts, unaware that they were covering the retreat of the main Orléans army across the Loire. At 6:30 that evening they were still clinging to the Bannier district, house by house. A colonel galloped up to Lieutenant de France. "Sound the retreat," he said. The subaltern pointed to their only bugler, lying on the pavement, his instrument to his lips—killed, sounding the charge. It was too late to retreat; the Prussians were advancing from the south and the legionnaires found themselves wedged between the two forces. "Surrender," a Prussian officer called. "Never," Villeneuve replied. In a few minutes, Prussians and Bavarians were shaking hands over a pile of bodies.

At seven o'clock the shreds of the battalion crossed the Loire. Lieutenant de France counted the survivors; of the 1,500 only 180 could stand, and many of them were wounded. Of the twenty-two officers he alone remained.

The day the Fifth was holding the Orléans streets, the first boatload of legionnaires arrived at Toulon. "Good God! More Germans," exclaimed the mayor, and thrust them into quarantine. The Legion had, in fact, sifted the Germans out of its ranks. At Orléans it incorporated the few survivors from the Fifth with new recruits; it took up positions with General d'Aurelle de Paladine's army in a final bid to seize the town. As they drilled, the legionnaires heard the incredible news of October 28. Bazaine, one of them, a legionnaire, had surrendered Metz with 130,000 men, 1,400 cannons, and vast stocks of ammunition.

"He's sold us out," the troops muttered.

"No—not Bazaine. He'd never do that," the legionnaires countered.

"Why, he even stopped the regiments burning their standards," someone said.

To that the legionnaires had no answer. Nor to the rumors that Bazaine had secretly negotiated with Bismarck to make himself master of France after the armistice; nor to the idea that Bazaine had kept his army intact to quell the riots that would follow the country's collapse. Gambetta hammered home the treachery of Bazaine. "Metz had capitulated," he trumpeted. "The general on whom France counted, even after the Mexican expedition, has robbed the country during its peril of more than 100,000 defenders. Bazaine has betrayed us. . . ." Bazaine suffered the fate of generals who win every battle except the last; he found himself branded as Napoleon's lackey and Bismarck's accomplice. If only he had resisted another week. . . .

For, incredibly, France counterattacked at Orléans on November 9 and routed General von der Thann's army. Legionnaires spearheaded part of the attack by Gambetta's army of 100,000. This victory might have turned the war had Gambetta not split this force and given the Prussians time to mass reinforcements. Again the Legion covered the retreat over the Loire. In blizzards of sleet and snow, with trees cracking around them, they left 2,600 of their 3,600 men in those forests. Men froze to death on their feet, and not even mortal wounds bled in that cold. With an infusion of new recruits from Brittany, they joined General Bourbaki's eastern army; at Sainte-Suzanne, west of Montbeliard, they astounded a French general by walking straight into and through a German battery and annihilating the gunners. They watched Bourbaki's army retreat across the Swiss frontier to lay down its arms.

The Year of Disaster had not yet finished for France—or the Legion. Half-starved during the seige, angered by Metz and armistice rumors, the people of Paris had risen on October 30, and troops had to rescue the government from the Town Hall. On January 28, Bismarck and Jules Favre signed an armistice convention to allow a newly elected Assembly to vote for peace or war. The February elections returned a monarchist majority that ratified the peace and Bismarck's heavy exactions: Alsace, part of Lorraine, and 5,000 million francs reparations. Republican Paris, which wanted to pursue the war, simmered; the sight of Germans goose-stepping through the capital, Bismarck's final condition, sent mobs to the barricades. The city had its National Guard; Montmartre bristled with cannons; a group calling themselves The Commune incited the city to revolt. They began by shooting two generals sent by Prime Minister Adolphe Louis Thiers to disarm the National Guard. Thiers replied by raising an army under MacMahon to crush the revolt. On April 1 more than 1,000 legionnaires arrived to join this army. The next day they attacked the barricades in Courbevoie, a suburb. "No quarter," Thiers had ordered. It was as bloody as Orléans; the legionnaires used the bayonet; the Communards fought back, and even handed the troops poisoned food with a smile. Along the Seine the Legion battled; at Neuilly they rigged barricades with pianos and bedsteads and, between times, looted and burned houses. When Thiers opened the gates of Paris, legionnaires cleared the great avenues around the Place de l'Étoile and moved into the heart of the city. MacMahon's shells and Communard kerosene bombs set whole boulevards ablaze and ravaged the Île de la Cité, even threatening Notre Dame. The legionnaires moved through the fire, up onto the Montmartre heights, to clear the gun positions and break the right flank of the Commune army.

As cannon pounded the streets and houses, the Communards seized hostages. The Archbishop of Paris and several of his priests were shot before troops could save them; the diehards set the Tuileries and the Town Hall alight and contested every street. In the barge basin and slaughterhouses of La Villette, the legionnaires lost scores of men trying to dislodge tough dockers with the bayonet and grenade; in the public park of Butte-Chaumont they had to face the National Guard, armed with new rifles and artillery. Bloody Week ended under the walls of Père Lachaise cemetery, with the Communards making a last stand. In those seven days the Legion lost more men than at Magenta. For the Legion the Franco-Prussian War had started with fatigues; it finished the same way. Picks and shovels in their hands, the legionnaires had to clean up Paris before embarking for Algeria in June 1871.

Bazaine had watched the final convulsion of the war from Switzerland, where the mounting campaign of vilification reached him. He drew the promise from Thiers to hold an inquiry into Metz; published in 1872, it blamed Bazaine for almost every defeat France had suffered. The National Assembly ordered an investigation into the surrender. Once more it found against Bazaine. By now his ally, Thiers, had resigned, leaving Bazaine's fate in the hands of the new President of the Republic, Marshal MacMahon. Bazaine was brought to trial before a military court, accused of capitulation of a fortress and surrender in the field.

The trial began at Versailles on October 6, 1873. Bazaine seemed loath to defend himself. Why had he negotiated with the enemy, offering his army as a police force after the peace? He had no government to advise him, Bazaine replied. "My sole director was my conscience," he said. He had surrendered to avoid useless loss of life.

Did he have anything to say in his defense? He lifted himself up. "I have graven on my chest two words—Honor and Country. They have guided me for the whole of my military career. I have never failed that noble motto, no more at Metz than anywhere else during the forty-two years that I have loyally served France. I swear it here, before Christ."

Before the assembled guard, General Pourcet, the state prosecutor, read the sentence. "The council unanimously condemns François-Achille Bazaine to death and military degradation."

"My first punishment," Bazaine murmured. "I am ready—shoot me now." However, the court had strongly recommended mercy. The decision lay with MacMahon. Pepita stormed into his office. "Are you going to have my husband shot?" she shouted at him. "There may be a reprieve," MacMahon muttered. The government wanted to banish Bazaine for life; MacMahon insisted on life imprisonment, though he softened, and commuted this to twenty years. Bazaine wrote to thank his fellow legionnaire, though added, tongue in cheek, that he might have let his feelings run away with him. It was an academic concession for a man nearing sixty-three.

Bazaine celebrated New Year's Day, 1874, in the citadel of the Île St. Marguerite, notorious as the prison of the Man in the Iron Mask. Pepita soon tired of its grim routine and took their son to France; only Colonel Willette stayed to look after the man he had served since Crimea. His door was locked in early evening, his letters censored, his friends watched. In any case they seldom returned once they had tasted the prison fare. Bazaine began to wonder if he could swim the mile to Cannes beach and flee into Italy. When a new war minister hinted at cropped hair and a prison garb for the former marshal, Pepita exploded. "They want to turn him into a convict. Well, they'll see." They began to plot his escape.

First, Pepita took her cousin Señor Alvarez Rull to the island. As they stood on the battlements with the prison governor, she cried suddenly, "My wedding ring! It's fallen. Go and find it, Alvarez." Accompanied by the governor, the young man climbed down the sheer cliff and retrieved the ring. "The water's not deep here," said the governor. "We'd have found it even had it dropped in." Alvarez took note. That spring the craggy rock welcomed a bizarre figure from Bazaine's past. Captain Doineau had been convicted for the murder of an Arab chief in Algeria; Bazaine had interceded with the Emperor on his behalf and Doineau had never forgotten it. Now in charge of the Monte Carlo gasworks, he thirsted for something more spectacular. He would act as courier. Through Doineau they fixed the night: August 9.

While Bazaine and Willette were growing tomatoes to hide the hole they had pierced in the marshal's room, Pepita was busy. She and Señor Rull went to Genoa, masquerading as the Duke and Duchess of Revilla, and hired Captain Cechi and his launch, the *Baron Ricasoli*, for a sail to Cannes. At the Croisette they went ashore to pick up an old manservant, Pedro. In fact they asked a boat-hirer to rent them a rowboat so that they could look at Sainte-Marguerite from the sea. The man took one look at the thunderclouds and choppy sea and refused. When he turned his back, the couple grabbed a boat and rowed furiously for the island.

In his prison, Bazaine had finished dinner; he and Willette slipped onto the terrace and fastened, with an old croquet hoop, their flimsy lifeline around a gargoyle; the end was tied around Bazaine's heavy body. Bazaine did not even glance at the three-hundred-foot drop or the flimsy rope of luggage straps and clothing strips; unhesitatingly, he swung out in the dusk. From their boat Pepita and Rull spotted his silhouette, which disappeared. "He's killed himself," Pepita cried. But no. Bruised and sodden, Bazaine had reached the water's edge and minutes later lay gasping under their tarpaulin, his hands dripping with blood. Captain Cechi might have wondered about Pedro, the Duke of Revilla's manservant. But these Spaniards! Two hours later Bazaine stepped ashore in Italy.

With their passion for reconstructing crimes, the French police sent a fifteen-year-old cabin boy down Bazaine's escape route. He failed to make the descent, in daylight. The press clamored that MacMahon had abetted his old comrade, but those who knew the President dismissed the notion. Doineau and Willette served several months in prison for their collusion and the Bazaine case became a forgotten mystery.

To Bazaine it seemed that Spain was the only country in which he could spend his exile; they still remembered his part in the Carlist War and Queen Isabella's son had just been proclaimed king. By midsummer 1875, the old soldier had settled in Madrid, where Isabella had arranged lodgings in the Calle Hortaleza. In these spartan rooms he toiled slowly on his book, *Episodes of the 1870 War and the Siege of Metz*; it appeared in 1883 with a dedication to Queen Isabella, which ended: "Her very humble and very devoted servant, François-Achille Bazaine, Ex-fusilier of the 37th Line, Ex-superior officer of Spanish service, Ex-Marshal of France, a refugee in Spain from 1874." The book made little impact. France still blamed him for its humiliation. Bazaine himself continued to hear Gambetta's words ringing in his ears: "*Bazaine a trahi. . . .*" August, September, and October, the black months of Metz, saw him sleepless, reliving his tragedy.

The last years he spent alone. Pepita did not like Spain and took the children to Mexico. Bazaine, who had been accused of selling out to the Germans, could no longer pay his lodgings and moved to miserable rooms in the Calle Atocha. His suits were threadbare but clean, his boots worn but well-polished, and he still marched erectly. He had to cook for himself, and allowed himself only one luxury: a few small cigars each week.

On September 20, 1888, he was found dead in his lodgings. At seventy-seven, his heart had given out. Only one Frenchman joined the funeral procession to the San Justo cemetery: his priest.

MacMahon, the aristocrat with whom Bazaine seemed fated to quarrel, survived him by five years; Paris gave MacMahon a funeral that choked the wide boulevards for hours. Canrobert, last of the Legion marshals of the Second Empire, was buried like a prince in 1895.

The Foreign Legion, which has never felt obliged to accept the French view on anything, still honors Bazaine. In its museum there exists almost no trace of MacMahon, of Canrobert, of Saint-Arnaud. Bazaine, however, has his own corner, adorned with his battered kepi, the bits and pieces of the harness he used at Rezonville and Gravelotte, and the Cross that Conrad pinned on him after Macta. The Legion

may have its misgivings about the role Bazaine played at
Metz, but it knows that courage is not a mask that a soldier
can wear or discard at will. It pays tribute to Bazaine's
courage. Conrad would have agreed with that view.

SEVEN

No, not with our mates, they don't.
They're buried right, with sacrament
And prayer.
Two bits of wood to bear his name.
What odds if it is a sham?
He's a legionnaire.

Many legionnaires would rather have crossed the waterless Tanezrouft Desert than march under Colonel François de Negrier. Some of them tried, and died. For the colonel was a flinty man, as sharp as the glass "daggers" legionnaires picked up when lightning fused rods of Sahara sand together. An apt name, de Negrier. "White slaver by name and nature," the men muttered, though well out of the colonel's hearing. For his part, Negrier appeared to consider legionnaires a nameless bunch who came with no questions and asked to kill or be killed. Whichever did not worry him. His own family tree had been riven by two Napoleons and by a few French kings on either side. When he came to command the Legion in 1879, his legend had preceded him. At Saint-Cyr he had killed a fellow officer in a duel. Trapped in Metz with a thigh wound, he refused to sit out the siege, riding off with bogus hospital papers. When two Uhlans stopped him to examine his papers, Negrier coldly shot one, wounded the other, and galloped off to resume the war in Brittany. Legionnaires conceded him one thing: he would trek to Timbuktu and back to save one of *his* men.

Negrier's arrival coincided with the rise of yet another

Arab messiah, Bou Amama. Using the ancient formula of Koran and flintlock rifle, he roused the tribes south of Tlemcen and harried Legion posts. To match this tribal cavalry, Negrier created mounted companies. He dismissed horses since they ate too much and camels for they ambled more slowly than a fully kitted legionnaire and they detested Europeans. What about mules? Headstrong legionnaires and stubborn pack animals ought to suit each other. So, companies got fifty mules, one for every two men. Every hour a whistle blew, and the marching and mounted men changed places. That way Negrier could force-march a battalion fifty miles a day for weeks.

Negrier gave himself no rest until he had run Bou Amama and his followers into Morocco. So impressed was the French prime minister, Jules Ferry, that he handed Negrier a promotion to brigadier and a new assignment: Indochina. Old and young legionnaires remembered long afterward the night they presented arms in farewell to General François de Negrier; few Spanish bistros came through unscathed as they toasted his departure.

Once in Tonkin, Negrier sent for a Legion volunteer battalion. Surprisingly, more than 1,000 men went down; some were too raw to know about the colonel; the majority were just bored with barrack life and fatigues. When they arrived in Haiphong in November 1883, General de Negrier greeted them with a classic military welcome. "You legionnaires," he barked, "are soldiers in order to die, and I am sending you where you can die." He had not changed.

French influence in Indochina dated from the establishment of Jesuit missions in the sixteenth century; political and trade ties were established over the years. In 1858, however, the French had to use force to stop the massacre of Christian priests and converts. Three eastern provinces, Cochin-china, became French colonies. In 1881 the murder of two French traders gave Jules Ferry the pretext for conquering Tonkin; the new republic intended to redress in the Far East the influence it had lost to Britain and Germany in Europe, Africa, and the Near East. Ferry envisaged Indochina as a great French possession and General de Negrier as the man to grab it. However, Negrier had to reckon with China, which regarded Indochina as a vassal country;

the Empress had ordered the Black Flags, armed pirate bands, to help throw the foreign devils out. In 1883 these marauders, who plundered on both sides of the border, had found a spirited and able commander in Liu-Vin-Phuoc, who occupied fortified towns along the main rivers.

In the Hanoi Delta the new country was already casting a strange spell over the legionnaires. Life moved with the slow tempo of the Red River to the peal of Buddhist temple bells. They might miss the rough, full-bloodied *pinard* and their forays in the red-light quarter of Bel-Abbès, but native *choum* (rice alcohol) was a consolation. And the women! Who could compare the exquisite, graceful, and compliant *congaï* with the whores and *moukères* of Algerian towns. Their eyes and minds soon lost the memory of wild mountains and limitless horizons and adapted to the brilliant greens of jungle and paddy fields, the bright, noisy bazaars. General Negrier did not, however, allow them much time to imbibe *choum* or dally with *congaï*. Herded onto French gunboats, they sailed from Haiphong to Hanoi to begin operations.

Most of the 5,000 French troops were ferried up the Red River; as usual, the Legion marched, squelching thigh-deep through paddy fields or cutting through tangled jungle. Their first mission: Son Tay fortress, thirty miles upriver on the ancient Mandarin Road to China. On December 16 the gunboats opened up, but they and the troops made little headway against the 20,000 Chinese in the stockaded fort surrounded by a ten-foot moat. Algerian Rifles and French Marines slithered and halted before the great gates. Negrier then pushed the Legion through, but even this faltered. From the leading company sprang a giant sapper in leather apron, wielding nothing but his ax; he leapt the moat, clawed over the bamboo spikes and through a breach blown by guns. Grabbing a black standard from the astonished Chinese, he waved it aloft, shouting, "Long live Belgium—long live the Legion." The rest of the battalion scattered the Chinese with their bayonets. The Belgian sapper was Corporal Minnaert. "Had you waved the Tricolor and cried, 'Vive la France,' I would have given you the Legion of Honor," said Admiral Courbet as he pinned the military medal on his chest. Joined by another Legion battalion, Negrier turned east to route 20,000 Chinese regulars at Bac Ninh. Following this, the Chinese recognized the French protectorate of Annam and promised to withdraw their troops. German Brière de l'Isle, commander of the expeditionary force, started to garrison the empty forts of Lang Son, That Khe, and Cao Bang near the Chinese border, and Tuyen Quang on the Mandarin Road.

The peace did not last. At the end of June six hundred men were caught and massacred by Chinese as they marched to occupy Lang Son. Three warlords from the Yunnan, Kwangtung, and Kwang-si provinces had led powerful armies over the border to seize the Tonkin forts. By autumn their advance guards were encircling the three hundred legionnaires and a company of Algerian Rifles at Tuyen Quang. General de Negrier decided first to settle the border posts.

His small force of 3,500 included 1,000 legionnaires who had already given him an Annamite nickname: General Maulen-maulen (Double quick). Brière de l'Isle was General Man-man (Dead slow). Again, Negrier was experimenting with animals to speed his column. He found water buffaloes as dangerous as Black Flags, and gave them up when several legionnaires were gored; no one could manage elephants, which were too cumbersome anyway. The Legion would march. Through jungle thick with bamboo and creeper they had to hack their way; everywhere along the writhing valley to Lang Son, the Chinese lay in ambush, falling on the column with long knives or picking men off with their Manchu muskets. They had nothing to learn from the Kabyles about torture, even adding a few macabre refinements. Legionnaires kept a last shot for themselves; the death of a thousand cuts amused nobody.

On February 13, 1884, the Legion bulldozed into Lang Son, the most powerful fortress on the Chinese border. This was what they had come for, they thought, looking at the city with its thriving market, its dainty, doll-like women, its stocks of rice wine and *choum*. Before they had dumped their packs, assembly was sounding. Where now? "China," someone said, incredulously. Within three weeks General "Maulen" had them charging through the Chinese Gate and into Kwang-si Province.

Of his 3,500 men, no more than half remained; the Legion now numbered only seven hundred men. In front of them, massing on the slopes of Bang-bo, lay a Chinese army of 6,000, entrenched and backed by guns. A lesser man would have waited for fresh troops. Negrier feinted a frontal attack and flung the legionnaires in from the left flank.

They seized Bang-bo, but only for a day. Now 20,000 Chinese had gathered behind the first army, and even hard-headed Negrier realized the folly of sacrificing his column; for the first time he took a backward step, leaving 350 dead legionnaires on the misty hill. The weary and hungry men grumbled that they needed rest. Negrier silenced them. They still had battles to fight. Haiphong had sent him 1,700 fresh men, which decided him to face the Chinese on the Kilua Plain; he trained his guns on the valley, placed the Legion on the flanks, and waited for the warlords.

As the Chinese advanced, the artillery tore holes in their ranks; the legionnaires fired into the solid mass, then charged. Negrier, his face as black with powder as a coolie's, was shouting himself hoarse and loosing off revolver shots at Chinese ensigns bearing black flags. He was about to order the charge when he heard that his aide-de-camp was lying wounded; he galloped across the line of Chinese troops, but suddenly slumped across the saddle. A bullet had ripped through his tunic above the heart; only the thick diary he carried in his breast pocket saved him. He would live, if evacuated to the base hospital. Grudgingly, he handed over to Colonel Herbinger, a hesitant and irresolute officer, who immediately suggested retreating. "No retreat," Negrier grunted from his stretcher. "Fall back on Lang Son and hold it."

Convinced that the Chinese would attack—they were, in fact, retreating—the nervous Herbinger ordered the destruction and evacuation of Lang Son. Legionnaires had a field day; they detonated the arsenals and heaved their cannons into the Son-ki-Kong River; they blew up blockhouses and buildings; they stared at Herbinger when he ordered them to heave 600,000 francs in silver piasters, just delivered by the paymaster, into the river. The Son-ki-Kong became a Klondike, but who cared? Only at the last instruction did they rebel. Not the barrels of Algerian *pinard* and French

rum! The legionnaires filled themselves, they filled their
water bottles, and left the teetotal Moslem troops to carry out
what was for them a distasteful duty.

The flight from Lang Son sent such a tremor through
Paris that Jules Ferry's government collapsed. Another
fortress was already causing the capital some anxious moments; any day the government expected to hear of a massacre at Tuyen Quang. From November, the square bamboo
fort on the Claire River had been garrisoned by 390 legionnaires and 200 colonial troops and a gunboat. Now a Chinese army of 15,000 men, equipped with cannon and led by
Liu-Vin-Phuoc, had encircled the fort and were threatening
to over-run it.

Tuyen Quang hardly appeared worth defending: four
bamboo walls with their backs to the river; in the middle, a
sugarloaf hill with 193 steps leading to a pagoda and ware-
house; outside, a ditch, several pagodas, and an Annamite
village. Beyond that, jungle. Tuyen Quang had to be held to
block the Yunnan army from swinging behind Negrier and
sandwiching him on the Chinese border. Could the quiet,
self-effacing commander, Colonel Edmond Dominé, hang
on? Fortunately he had with him the best sapper in the Legion, Sergeant Jules Bobillot. "Bobby," a former novelist
and journalist, cleared fields of fire into the jungle, built a
blockhouse west of the fort, and tunneled into the central
hummock to protect the officers and men from cannon fire.
Just after Christmas the first Chinese appeared—five hundred of them—and paraded within rifle shot. "What's this?
A dress rehearsal?" the legionnaires yelled. The next day
the Chinese paraded again, but this time they did not stop;
they got to the blockhouse before 350 rifles sent them
sprawling back into the jungle. Legionnaires would experience many such dress rehearsals in the next seventy years.

For three weeks the Chinese built up their forces before attacking the blockhouse. Eighteen Legion marksmen
held them off for three days before they were encircled and
had to sprint back into the post. Then the Chinese hoisted
their cannon on the hills overlooking the fort. Those 193
steps to Dominé's command post became a life-and-death
game for legionnaires as Black Flags tried to pick them off
with muskets. "My *pinard* ration if you make it up—my

rum ration if you make it both ways." A sinister sport, which helped, however, to break the tension and prevent the *coup de bambou*. "Going bamboo" was the Tonkin equivalent of the *cafard*; it struck more swiftly, impelling men to fight their way to the bamboo gates and dash crazily for the jungle or making them run wild with their rifles and bayonets inside the fort. Dominé ended the fatal game when two legionnaires did not live to drink their bets. In any case the Chinese had soon destroyed the winding steps.

General Liu had started digging; his army of Chinese and Annamites burrowed from the jungle toward the stockades. On February 13, at 2 A.M., an explosion set the fortress vibrating, the southwest salient disappeared, and with it five legionnaires. Black-clad figures swarmed into the gap. Sergeant Major Edward Husband led a section of legionnaires into the crater and fought hand-to-hand to seal the breach. Husband was an Englishman, though born in Paris of a French mother. At twenty-three he was the youngest sergeant major in the Legion, also one of the toughest. Around him and his section the crater filled with bodies, for the Chinese were attacking in waves; it took the whole Legion contigent four hours to beat off the suicide raid. In the darkness the Chinese stumbled and fell over their own dead, but gave up only when the sky lightened. In that attack they lost "Bobby," who lay in the crude ambulance hut dying from a shell fragment in his spine.

After six weeks of siege, most of the garrison had given up hope of being relieved or surviving. Only Dominé seemed unconcerned. His diary, read to French schoolchildren in the way that General Gordon's last days in Khartoum are recounted in British schools, makes Tuyen Quang sound like some tactical exercise without troops. "At present, the Chinese are making their way toward us through four subterranean galleries and I expect to see them blow up 150 meters of wall at once. . . . Our losses amount to thirteen dead." Like Gordon, no hint of danger, no appeal for aid.

On February 22, Captain Catelin heard the Chinese signaling. He pulled the guards off the western salient just before a mine lifted it and showered splintered bamboo and tons of earth on the fort. Captain Moulinay and a Legion company ran to plug the gap and took another, more formi-

dable blast in the face. Moulinay and twelve legionnaires
died instantly; another thirty wounded groped, blinded and
burned, from the shattered stockade. "Nothing could disturb
the men of the Legion," Dominé recorded. He omitted to
report that Catelin and his section were hit by a third mine
as they followed Moulinay's company. The Chinese were
wedging through the gap, firing their muskets and swinging
stubby swords. Catelin and the two sergeant majors, Camps
and Husband, flung themselves on the advance guard and
thrust them back with sheer rage at the deaths of their comrades. Husband, a bullet wound in his thigh, was bandaged
and returned to the fight.

Dominé went back to his bread-crate desk. "I must tell
you," he wrote, "that though the will is strong, we may
soon lack the energy and health to continue, and I feel it
would be in our best interest if as strong a column as possible could lift the siege of Tuyen Quang." That piece of euphemism was carried by an Annamite coolie who floated
forty miles down the Claire River to Vietri. The muted appeal had already been answered; a brigade of legionnaires
and native troops was marching from Lang Son.

Every night brought another explosion, a fresh attack;
during the day, shells fell in clusters in the compound. "*Les
salauds*—they've bust twelve barrels of *pinard*, and nobody
there to put his mouth to it." The wine spread like blood
over the rutted compound. The blackest day of the siege,
blacker even than February 26, came when six separate det-
onations scattered the guards and they had no more than
eighty good rifles to tamp the six holes against a flood of
Chinese. Two hundred Black Flags had cleaved through the
southwest wall. Only Sergeant Major Husband, still limping, stood between them and the command post. Gathering
his men, he dashed at the Chinese, falling from a bullet that
ripped through the bandage on his right thigh; his men ran
over his figure and drove the Chinese across the ditch. That
morning the Annamite coolie handed Dominé a piece of
sodden paper. "The relief column is on the way," it read.

The tattered garrison had something to fight for. Captain de Borelli's Legion company made a sortie to grab two
black flags from the Chinese, who desperately retaliated to
recover them. It was their last throw; they had to wheel

southeast to try to block the relief brigade and left only a few hundred troops before Tuyen Quang. On March 3, after the garrison had spotted the signal flares of the French force, Captain de Borelli took a patrol to reconnoiter the trenches. From an underground blockhouse came a burst of fire that wounded two natives and one legionnaire. Borelli made for the spot, revolver in hand. "No heroics, *mon capitaine*," called Sergeant Major Camps. As Borelli paused, his orderly, Thiebald Streibler, noticed a gun pointing at his captain; he flung himself in its line of fire to take the bullet in his chest. Streibler, a young Alsatian and son of a former Legion sapper, had just left a hospital after lying wounded throughout the siege. The last casualty of Tuyen Quang, he died that day, unaware that he had received a military medal for a previous action.

At Tuyen Quang fifty-six soldiers had died; twenty others would suffer all their lives from wounds; another 188 had less serious wounds. Dominé might have become a national hero, but, as unpretentious as his siege log, he died almost unnoticed in 1921. Borelli immortalized his legionnaires in a long poem, dedicated to Streibler. France treated the captain anything but generously; he remained a captain, with such bitter memories of his poor treatment that he decreed in his will that the two captured black flags, bequeathed to the Legion, should never be brought to France. For his part in the siege, Sergeant Major Edward Husband was promoted to second lieutenant. He quit the Legion as a captain in 1896, joined another regiment, and rose steadily in rank until he emerged from World War I as a brigadier general.

EIGHT

We've made our place among the wogs,
Together with mokes and mangy dogs
And old moukères.
In France they'd find us hard to suffer,
Its good folk'd panic at the cafard
Of the legionnaire.

The Legion seemed fair game for Catholic priests who infiltrated its ranks for much the same reason that the Salvation Army drops its tracts and newspapers in sleazy bars. Legionnaires offered an immense challenge. Not only had they strayed, but most of them were taking the wrong road to hell—the Protestant road. Priests found the Legion uphill work and many retreated with their egos dented. A few discovered to their consternation that the Legion was converting them: they began to admire the mute courage, the self-sacrifice and camaraderie of these damned souls. Such a man was Abbé Vathelet—Almoner to the French Marines. He gravitated toward the Legion battalion on the trooper *Mytho*, which was transporting them to Dahomey on West Africa's slave coast. Forty years old, a white Noah beard and black cassock floating over his paunch, the abbé cut a reverential figure. He was also a down-to-earth propagandist. From him legionnaires learned about the wicked Behanzin, the Shark King of Dahomey, and his bloodthirsty Amazon army. God, let alone the French, could not possibly allow an evil pagan like Behanzin to continue ruling in the style of his ancestors.

King Behanzin—Bec-en-Zinc (Zincbeak) to legionnaires—held fast to ancient traditions. He had a hundred
wives, five times as many concubines, and thousands of captured slaves. His father, Glélé, had toasted European visitors
like Sir Richard Burton, the explorer, with white rum brim-
ming from goblets fashioned from the skulls of rival chiefs.
Behanzin filled the skulls with English gin and gave each
chalice its former owner's name. Then, he was a more refined
man. Discarded goblets paved the fetish houses of Kana, his
holy city, or the palace courtyard of his hinterland capital,
Abomey. Paving materials never ran short, for Behanzin
scrupulously observed the ritual "grand and minor customs."
Privileged Europeans with strong stomachs were spectators at
these blood-chilling saturnalia. The "grand customs," marking a king's death, supplied the departed monarch with wives
and attendants as well as the latest news about the state of Dahomey. An act of filial piety, Behanzin claimed. A bloodbath,
his visitors whispered.

Last held when Behanzin mounted the throne in 1889,
the "grand customs" began with an orgy of feasting and
drinking, followed by frenzied and erotic dancing in which
the Amazons excelled. On came the victims, mostly prisoners of war, dressed in floppy white nightcaps and garish
gowns. Several hundred were slaughtered at the King's
grave; the others met a more original end. Hoisted in baskets
onto a high scaffold, accompanied by alligators, hawks, and
cats, they were paraded on the heads of Amazons while the
crowd below shrieked for their blood. The King read them a
final bulletin for his father; the baskets plummeted into the
screaming mob and their occupants perished under flashing
knives and drumming feet. To round off this ceremony, the
King and his chiefs then butchered several hundred of his
own palace staff and added their skulls to his floor and wall
collections. The day ended with another feast—on the hot,
roasted flesh of the sacrificial victims. However, still one
grisly pleasure fell to the King. Accompanied by his huge
harem, he proceeded to his father's grave and personally
sacrificed several dozen men and women. His Amazons lent
a hand. One French diplomat watched a young woman casually lop off a prisoner's head, then drink the blood on her

sword. He asserted that, during Behanzin's "grand customs" in 1889, some 3,000 people were sacrificed.

Compared with this hecatomb, the "minor customs," held twice a year, seemed merciful. Behanzin sent only a hundred spirit messengers to his ancestors. Sir Richard Burton dismissed the story that Dahomeyan kings floated their canoes in tanks of sacrificial blood; but no one could deny that Behanzin, with his gruesome orgies, was going too far in the last decade of the nineteenth century, even in Black Africa. His slave raiding angered the European powers. And, as the practical Abbé Vathelet pointed out, he had snubbed not only God but the Third Republic by enslaving and massacring French Christians. Behanzin had rejected French claims to the protectorate of Dahomey; he added, coolly, that France, after its defeat in 1870, had no terrors for a great king like himself. He and his 20,000 warriors would fight for a hundred years if necessary.

"The man is a devil worshiper," said the abbé.

"More sense than us," retorted a legionnaire.

"What do you mean?"

"God is good, isn't he?" The abbé nodded. "No point in buttering him up, then. It's the other fellow you've got to watch."

"Ah, these legionnaires," the abbé sighed.

"And these Amazons, padre? They're not going to ask us to fight against women?"

"It is your duty," the abbé explained. The Amazons were ogresses and witches, godless women trained to kill.

Introduced by Behanzin's grandfather, King Gezo, the Amazons formed the hard core of the Dahomeyan army. Brainwashed by witch doctors, a quarter of the country's women entered the army as girls. Behanzin selected the best for his harem; the others took a vow of celibacy and were executed if they lost their virginity. They were subjected to iron discipline, drilling with rifles, spears, and pangas. Burton and others watched them charge, unflinching, through walls of thorn bushes and trot for days in the clammy jungles of Dahomey. "No, they are evil women who deserve none of your pity," the abbé warned the legionnaires.

At Porto Novo, Colonel Alfred Dodds repeated the

warning. "No gallantry," he said. "The first man I find frat-
ting with these women will be shot." Dodds, a mulatto from
French Senegal, would need all his brilliance as a campaigner against Behanzin. He had no more than 4,000 men,
including eight hundred legionnaires. Between the coast and
the capital, about eighty miles inland, he would face at least
10,000 well-armed Fons and 2,000 Amazons. The Legion
commander, Major Paul Faurax, considered, too, that they
were cutting it fine.

Legionnaires, the most superstitious of soldiers, shared
these misgivings. Hadn't their train retreated at Tlemcen
when a sleeper cracked? And Faurax had come through
1870 without a scratch? Unlucky, going on a campaign
without one good wound. Then this "Holy Roller" padre
hanging around them instead of bandaging the souls of his
sailors! Old sweats shook their heads, unreconciled even by
extra rations and a daily half pint of tafia (white rum) to this
war against women.

Dodds had to move between the beginning of September and the end of November, the season of "little rains." On
September 1 the Legion began to march: eleven days cutting
through scrubby jungle and thick lianas at five miles a day
along the Ouémé River. At Dogba they had to sit for seven
days while the sappers bridged the river. They heard the
thud of war drums, but no one had seen a Fon warrior. They
would not attack such a natural defensive position, a clearing with its back to the river.

But at dawn on September 19 the jungle seemed to
quiver, then move toward the sleeping army. Tom-toms
throbbed. A black wall smothered the Marine outposts,
driving the guards into the camp. "In with the bayonet, legionnaires," Englishman Frederick Martyn heard Faurax
bellow. "Before the major had finished shouting we were on
the run toward the threatened side of the camp, and in a few
seconds were in the thick of them, ramming our bayonets
into their bodies up to the hilt, then throwing them off to
make room for another, like farm laborers forking hay, until
we had to clamber over the dead and dying men piled two or
three high to get at the living."

The Fons had prepared their ambush well: grabbing
lianas, snipers swung into the trees and began plunging fire

into the camp while the warriors charged with bayonets, spears, and pangas to the beat of their drums and chants of their witch doctors. One moment Major Faurax was urging his men into the attack—the next he was falling, his pith helmet rolling over his face. A bullet had struck him in the chest. "I've caught one all right," Martyn heard him utter. Captain Antoine Drude, his giant second in command, was running to lift the major when a second bullet hit him over the heart. "Leave me, Drude. I'm done for," he whispered.

In the morning light the legionnaires had their first sight of Behanzin's army. The lion and elephant hunters made frenzied charges, spears and rifles in one hand, a horse or goat tail in the other to ward off death. Throwing these fetish symbols at the legionnaires, they lunged after them, impaling their bodies on bayonets. For four hours Dodds' troops withstood these suicidal rushes. Only when the gunboat on the Ouémé opened up on the Fons did they filter back into the jungle, leaving three hundred of their dead in the clearing. Dodds had lost forty-five killed and sixty wounded.

Among the prisoners they saw their first Amazons, two proud women who refused to surrender their blunderbusses and spears. They were fine specimens: their bodies and bare breasts glistened with coconut oil and sweat; amulets of crocodile teeth adorned their arms, waists, and ankles; around their kilted waists hung cartridge pouches. With sullen dignity they stared at Dodds as he questioned them. "Shoot them dirty niggers, them savages, Colonel," called the Senegalese soldiers, who, if anything, were a shade blacker. Dodds did just that. The Amazons lined up with the other prisoners and gazed impassively at the firing squad.

"He should have spared the women," growled the legionnaires. Dodds, however, had seen what the Fons had left of one captured marine. "From now on, no quarter," he ordered.

Faurax died that day, and Drude took command as they hiked north to ford the river. A heavy, suety-faced man, he cursed and fumed as they slogged single-file through the bush and swamps. On October 4 they walked into more than 10,000 Fons, led by Behanzin himself, outside the village of Porguessa. Hundreds of Amazons tumbled out of the jungle at them, firing modern rifles from the hip and brandishing long knives. Maddened by their witch doctors and English gin, the warrior women rushed the Legion column whirling their rifles and knives and grappling with the men. "No chivalry," Drude cried. *"A la fourchette."* (With the fork.) It was inhuman work, sinking a bayonet into a woman's body; still more sickening to pull it out and watch her die. But it was kill or be killed. A legionnaire seized one crocodile woman by the waist; she turned and bit off his nose and would have finished him with her knife had not a lieutenant chopped her down with his saber. Besides leading the attack, the Amazons urged their men on with shrill screams, though they died quietly and stoically. Behanzin, with five times as many men as the French, should have won that battle. But his army turned and ran back toward Kana leaving two hundred male dead and thirty Amazons. The legionnaires looked with pity at the dead women in their blue skirts and red bonnets.

"They're good-looking women for niggers," muttered a wounded legionnaire. "But they don't fight fair. One of them gives me a come-on look and I'm doing just that when her big sister fetches me a back-hander with her cabbage cutter."

Abbé Vathelet was beaming. "I'm proud of you, boys," he said.

"Next time, let your water babies have a go," they replied.

They had won the abbé over; he even entrusted his precious crate of communion wine to Legionnaire Schmidt, an Alsatian veteran from Tonkin, which was perhaps asking too much of Providence.

Dodds forced them forward after the fleeing Dahomeyans, determined to end the campaign before the harmattan winds parched the hinterland. "Two days' march to Koto and you'll drink the purest water in the country," he promised. "Who wants water?" said the legionnaires. The Wells of Koto provided the only water for twenty miles around. But Behanzin realized that, if they fell, the road to Kana and Abomey lay open; his whole army lay waiting for Dodds. On October 9 the Fons attacked. Once more the

Amazons led the way, crashing in with spears and bayonets.
Behind them, rattling skulls and wearing Grand Guignol
masks, witch doctors were yelling, "Devour the rifles of the
enemy." A Legion lieutenant fell; the frantic women hacked
at him with long knives; they trapped Corporal Feldman
and Legionnaire Gosse and taunted them before butchering
them. This time they were winning. To save the column
Dodds ordered a retreat to a clearing where they could use
their artillery and rifles. He had reckoned on Koto Wells for
water and to rest his men before advancing on Kana and
Abomey. To attack would cost him several hundred men; to
turn back would demoralize his small force. They had four
days' water; they would let the Fons come to them. But Behanzin anticipated the trap. He, too, waited.

Koto they christened the Thirsty Camp. Eight days
they lay in the clearing; for four days they had no water to
make coffee, as vital as wine to legionnaires. They filtered
swamp water, boiled and drank it only to double up with
dysentery; they chewed grass and tree bark to keep their
tongues from swelling. "Last week at Adegon dead bodies
were floating in rain water," muttered a legionnaire. "Now,
they expect us to eat monkey and hardtack with our throats
full of sand." A Legion company tried a sortie to the wells;
in the camp they heard the ululations of the Amazons. Back
the men came with empty buckets. "What's up—a dry
wadi?" the others twitted them.

On the fifth day, not a drop of water. Drude turned to
the Abbé Vathelet. "Padre, we'll have to drink that crate of
communion wine." Opening it, they found nothing but
empty bottles. Drude rounded on Schmidt. "You nameless
swine, you've drunk the abbé's communion wine and committed sacrilege."

"I didn't know it was holy wine, *mon capitaine*," said
the Alsatian.

Dodds began to fear that his whole army might perish
from thirst and disease. Somehow, they must reach those
wells. The brave Captain Fitzjames volunteered to take his
company of spahis with 1,000 water bottles and fill them.
Dodds smelled a massacre, but said yes. That night the cavalry trotted off to return an hour later, the bottles overflow-

ing. For some reason the Fons had not attacked. As the men
tottered forward to taste their first water for two days, the
sky cracked above them; water deluged the camp and they
had to run to save their haversacks and tents, which were
floating away.

With too many sick and wounded, Dodds had to backtrack on October 16. His native porters did not have enough
strength left to carry the wounded; the legionnaires, with
two hundred of their own wounded to transport, volunteered
to bear stretchers with Algerian and Senegalese wounded.
"You'll get a double ration of tafia tonight," Dodds
promised. "For carrying our pals!" said a sergeant. "We
don't need tafia." Trudging with them, his black cassock
stiff with mud, Abbé Vathelet could find no words to praise
their unselfishness. Among the porters, he recognized
Schmidt, who had stolen his wine. "My son," the abbé whispered, "now that I come to think of it, I have a little of that
mass wine left. See me tonight and I'll open a bottle."

Two weeks later artillery carved through the Fons at
Koto and they seized the wells and the village. On those two
November days Behanzin lost 2,800 crack warriors and
Amazons; only the prisoners he had released and filled with
gin gave the French column any trouble. At Kana the same
story. A Legion charge broke the resistance of 1,000 elephant hunters and sent Behanzin fleeing north. So, this filthy
collection of thatched hovels stinking of sacrificial blood
was Kana, the holy city! The human skulls paving the fetish
houses and graveyards did look like cobblestones; as for the
famous House of Sacrifice, they had seen better in the
slaughterhouses at Sidi bel-Abbès. They drank the looted
stocks of French rum and English gin and lay down in the
red mud to sleep off their disillusionment.

Behanzin's chief minister, in floral ceremonial robes
and lion-mane headdress, arrived in Kana. "The illustrious
King Behanzin sends his greetings to his honored French
cousin, the Emperor Napoleon, and desires news of him,"
he announced to Dodds. Which Napoleon? Both were beyond greeting. Dodds listened. Behanzin would accede to
French demands for 7,000,000 francs indemnity and two
generals as hostages. More than a week later the envoy returned with two wretched slaves and 5,000 francs. Behanzin

had tricked them to gain time to flee north with his harem of wives and concubines, his witch doctors, ministers, and some of his warriors. As Dodds resumed his march, great columns of smoke spiraled in the coppery sky. The King had also set fire to his capital, Abomey. There the legionnaires celebrated the end of the campaign in style. They drank Behanzin's cellars dry and held their own "grand customs" in the King's palace before lying down to try to forget about Koto, the elephant hunters of Kana, and Amazon women dying with reproach in their eyes. "That suit you to sleep in a palace?" Drude asked the next morning. "One of those wogs must have had a head like iron," one of them replied.

Drude still had work for them—the needle-in-a-haystack hunt for Behanzin. They tracked him north and west into the mountains, then to the coast. Several times they missed him by minutes as he vanished into the rain forest. He had not dispensed with the "grand customs" for the fourth anniversary of his father's death. Now, however, he had to content himself with sending three luckless Portuguese-mulatto slaves into the world of King Glégé. For over a year Behanzin played hide-and-seek with the Legion company. Drude nearly caught him in the third week of January 1894 on the banks of the Couffe River. There the King had recovered some of his old poise; for the "minor customs," he murdered his principal wives, some ministers, his brother's children, and scores of prisoners from Ouidah, the coastal town. His last dispatch, by way of these spirit envoys, could hardly have overjoyed his ancestors. For Behanzin had decided to stop running; he surrendered at Yego, a village near Abomey, on January 26. Behanzin, the godless, heartless, lecherous, cruel despot turned out to be an impassively handsome, meek-faced man. The French conquest, his arrest, his impending exile—none of these roused a flicker of reaction in him. As the Legion escorted him to a cruiser at Porto Novo, he puffed a long, chased-silver pipe and strolled up the gangway without once turning to look at his remaining wives, who were wailing and tearing their hair and their garments.

"Haven't you brought back one of these nigger-women sergeant majors?" they asked at Sidi bel-Abbès when the

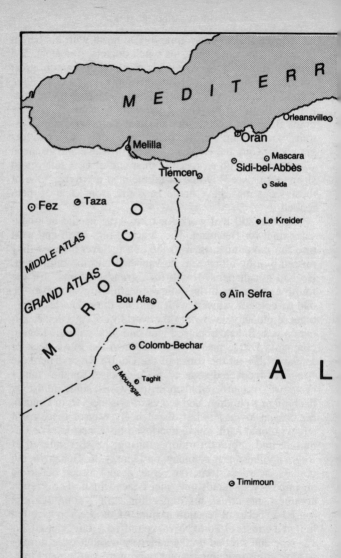

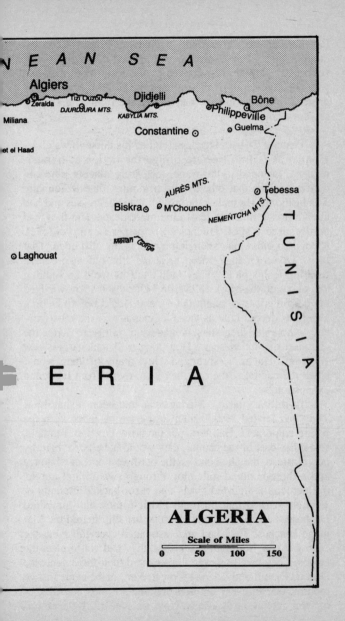

battalion returned. The young legionnaires listened to the incredible tales of the Amazons and learned that their vow of celibacy could only be removed by the King when they had won the equivalent of the military medal. "Most of them," grunted one legionnaire, "had earned the right to get themselves married."

General Charles Duchesne reined his horse to watch legionnaires felling trees to bridge the ravine at Beratsimanana. Stripped to the waist, men were placing pine and hardwood logs that others were trimming. One legionnaire was fashioning branches into rough wooden crosses and had already made nine. At least nine more deaths and they had hardly fired a shot! Duchesne, a former Legion colonel, spotted an older man swinging a pick at the cliff edge. That face? Tuyen Quang? *"Mon général,"* the old man called, pointing to his pick. "They didn't tell us we'd be fighting this one with the Mark 1895 rifle." Duchesne acknowledged the quip. Paris, too, might have mentioned it before landing him in as deep a hole as these legionnaires. Like most generals who value their stars, he had tried, vainly, to dodge the conquest of Madagascar. "How long to Antananarivo, *mon général?*" Duchesne shrugged. How many of them would reach the capital at the rate they were dying from fever and exhaustion?

In military terms, Madagascar had been a shambles. They had landed 20,000 men in the wrong place with the wrong equipment. Had they put the army down at Tamtave, 150 miles east of the capital, they would have been there by now. Instead, they had chosen the northwest port of Majunga and a three-hundred-mile slog through swamp and jungle, over crocodile-infested rivers and razor-backed mountains. Though warned that no roads existed, they had lumbered Duchesne with 5,000 metal chariots that still littered the Majunga beaches. They had underestimated everything but the enemy. Apart from two skirmishes, they had yet to meet the Hovas. They had, however, encountered their three generals: Hazou, Fazou, and Tazou—Forest, Fire, and Fever. In two months, one in every ten of Duchesne's troops had died of malaria, typhus, or dysentery. Now, on June 12, 1895, he had ordered the Legion to construct a road from Beratsimanana to the capital, more than two hundred miles away.

The conquest of Madagascar had begun in April 1895 when the Malgasy Government rejected the French claims to a protectorate, saying it could survive without French civilization. The ruling Hova race were anything but savages; the capital had its own newspaper; courts dispensed justice and the government collected taxes to develop agriculture and fishing. The English had helped. The London Missionary Society had opened schools throughout the island and (this irked the Catholic French) had converted Queen Ranavalona III and her prime minister to Protestantism. A remarkable man, Premier Rainilaiarivony. Nearing seventy, he had, as tradition dictated, married each of his queens—the present young and beautiful ruler, her mother, and her great-aunt. None had complained about his ability as a politician or lover. To resist the French invasion, the premier had conscripted 30,000 farmers and villagers, and had imported cannons and rifles and an English colonel, Shervington. He agreed with the premier's seers and witch doctors on strategy: let Hazou, Fazou, and Tazou soften up the French.

"Each stroke of pick and shovel in this country means fever," wrote a French captain. Still, Colonel Barre and his eight hundred legionnaires toiled on from dawn to sunset. With primitive saws, sledgehammers, crowbars, and iron wedges, they felled trees, broke rocks, and pushed the road forward a few hundred yards a day. Ticks and red ants swarmed on them as they slept in the bush; the quinine they consumed by pints merely seemed to feed the malaria parasite. They defied Duchesne's injunction about drinking the brackish, polluted water and came down with typhoid and dysentery; they would have ignored his other instruction about sexual diseases, but who had seen a Hova woman?

Soon, the road they were making had become a funeral route; the famous Lefevre chariots now served as hearses to transport piles of dead to the cemetery at Superbieville. Yet the Legion suffered less than the others. "French troops go into hospital for repatriation, natives to be cured, legionnaires to die," said an officer. The Legion also kept cheerful. With them was Lieutenant Pierre Langlois, still

carrying his Saint-Cyr textbooks. These men amazed him as
they laughed and sang and joked, constructing what they
called the Graveyard Trail. They even found time to look
after this young officer.

"They come to us with white knees, lieutenant, and we
make them generals like old Duchesne, or marshals like the
one that's just died, MacMahon," a legionnaire said, grinning at Langlois.

A padre shared his mess, and his views on legionnaires. Father Danjoy had lost his orderly and altar boy in
the Beoni swamps and replaced him with Langlois' most
wayward legionnaire. The incredulous lieutenant noted a
complete transformation in the man: at funerals and mass,
his face glowed with beatitude and grace. Father Danjoy
whispered, "I've never had a better altar boy. The very soul
of honesty and devotion. What fervor when he prays! What
exaltation! Why, he makes me reproach myself for my lack
of faith." The day came though when a disenchanted priest
found his stock of mass wine gone and a drunken, babbling
altar boy wrecking his tent. Langlois had lacked the heart to
confess that the man was an atheist. Worse still, a baptized
Protestant.

Duchesne realized that the graveyard road would finish
his army unless he acted. He picked 4,000 men, equipped
them with 3,000 mules, twelve light guns, and twenty-two
days' rations; he was gambling to take Antananarivo in
three weeks or lose the campaign.

If the road had all but broken their spirit, that trek all
but finished the four hundred remaining legionnaires who
made up the advance guard. *"Marche ou créve,"* the sweats
muttered. The March or Croak column. Those who dropped
out died. But who could tell fever from the old-soldier act?
Langlois pushed an old Breton who was lagging; he tottered,
fell, and died without a murmur. "Don't worry about it," said
Dr. Dantin. "Fever takes these old soaks like that."

At Tsynainondry, the Hovas stood and fought from
trenches gouged in the mountainside; their guns laid down a
thick barrage, though happily they had not fused the shells.
"Don't salute [duck]," shouted a veteran as he slogged up
the hill. With some trepidation, Langlois kept his head up.
The courage and tenacity of these exhausted men astounded

him. Their humor, too. Duchesne, cock-hatted, galloped on his black charger to where most of the Hova shells were landing.

"What does he want—a blighty wound to take him out of it back to Paris?" called a legionnaire.

"For one of the "brass' he's a chic type. He doesn't duck."

"Why should he, *mon vieux*? He's one of us—an old legionnaire. We all have it in the blood in our army."

They walked over the Hova trenches, stumbling on with time and their rations running out. They lacked even the strength to bury their dead; they covered them with brushwood and limped on—over Mount Lavohitra, its white shrubs bursting like exploding shells. Down into another ravine and up the sugar-loaf hill of Sabotsy. Again the Legion plowed through Hova and French artillery fire, in perfect marching order! In the Hova trenches it was slaughter, until a herd of pigs ran out of a village and attacked the legionnaires; they butted and bit until the Legion had to turn on them with their bayonets. "These swine fight better than those swine," a big German roared.

At last they climbed the crest and saw the capital. *"Tananarive, Tananarive,"* they shouted. For the first time the legionnaires looked on the lovely Malgasy women, with their violet eyes and malicious smiles. They seemed to taunt the weary men, laughing at their scarecrow appearance. Antananarivo, with its rococo wooden palace, its mission churches, and sprawl of government buildings, was prepared to resist. The Queen's guard put up a fight until Duchesne's cannon set the tindery buildings ablaze. One shell finished the city and ended the campaign; it dropped on the palace and threatened to detonate the powder kegs in the vault. A white flag fluttered; the Queen's emissary, in white-plumed hat, bore a surrender document.

On September 30, Duchesne entered the capital, accompanied by the two Legion companies that had survived the campaign. Malgasy women showered them with flowers and put up even less resistance than the Hova troops. All Duchesne's strictures on hygiene went overboard; the local rum that he had outlawed tasted like nectar after the brackish water they had drunk.

Duchesne, the bluff soldier, was having too much trouble in the palace to worry about the morals of the Legion. Queen Ranavalona broke down and wept when the general ruled out as premier her prime minister and husband. Duchesne consoled her by promising to pick another premier. "You know the custom," she said. Duchesne had no choice but to replace the handsome, dignified Rainilaiarivony. Paris selected the former home secretary, Rainisimbazafy. Duchesne shuddered on seeing him. Wispy white hair, sagging dewlaps, a potbelly. And so old that his feet never left the floor as he huffed and shuffled forward. Apprehensively, the general announced the choice to the Queen. She looked at Duchesne with a horrified glance that seemed to say, "But you've picked the ugliest one of all." Duchesne apologized. Through her tears, the Queen said, "Will this man enjoy all the functions attached to the post?"

Duchesne hesitated. "Madam," he said, "we have decided that, henceforth, the prime minister need not sleep in your palace." The old man fumbled into the royal presence. "I name you prime minister," said the Queen. He bowed. "But we have decided that you shall not sleep in the palace." He bowed even lower, then scuffed out backward.

So ended the conquest of Madagascar. Its figures tell the story. Twenty dead in combat, just over one hundred wounded. Deaths from other causes: 5,736.

NINE

We're the damned from every land,
From every war we carry a sore;
Not one among us will forget
Our ill luck, shame, or that fillette.
In our veins runs good, warm blood
Even if we have cafard *in the head.*
To give or take hard knocks, sacré nom
We blithely step out for La Légion.

Admiral Prince Waldemar of Denmark came to greet the tall young man wearing a khaki uniform with a seven-flamed Foreign Legion grenade in each tunic lapel. For several minutes they chatted in the garden of the manor house outside Copenhagen before the prince asked the lieutenant, "Have you brought it?" The officer produced a lead soldier from his pocket. The kepi with its white neckcloth, the blue tunic and red trousers, the crimson epaulets stamped it as the replica of a legionnaire. The lieutenant, Christian Wilhelm Selchauhansen, was home on leave from Algeria in July 1901. Seven years before, he had joined the Legion on detachment from the Danish army. Slim and blond, with a monocle over one of his green eyes, he was a great hero among legionnaires, having fought in Tonkin and Madagascar; now he was with an elite mounted company on the Morocco frontier. Protégé of Prince Waldemar and his wife, Princess Marie d'Orléans, he had been invited to lunch, with specific orders to bring the toy soldier. Soon, he knew why.

The admiral's young son ran over when he spotted the

Legion officer; for two hours, while they strolled, then had
lunch in the garden, he bombarded Selchauhansen with questions—about the Arabs, about Tonkin and Madagascar, and
especially about legionnaires. He confessed that he had a
lead soldier from every French regiment except one: the Foreign Legion. Not even his mother had been able to get him
one, and she was the granddaughter of Louis Philippe, king
of the French and creator of the Foreign Legion! Patiently,
Selchauhansen told the boy about Berbers and Tuareg,
mountains and desert, about his men who marched and
fought and died standing on their feet. And, as he left the
young prince dreaming, he slipped the toy legionnaire into
his pocket. (Twenty years later, the boy's reverie would become reality and he would join the Legion to figure as one of
its most famous officers.) From Algeria the Danish lieutenant sent postcards to Prince Aage. In the summer of 1903
the postcards stopped; the young prince and the rest of Europe read about the massacre of El Moungar.

   In the parched country south of Aïn Sefra, each week
brought another attack on French supply convoys by Bou-
Amama's cavalry, operating from Morocco; for these ambushes the Berber leader chose the open spaces and drifting
dunes between Legion forts. Figuig, Zenaga, Taghit—these
areas of sand-blasted rock became a cemetery for hundreds
of legionnaires. At Taghit they had just lost thirty-nine
killed and fifty-seven wounded when a battalion of the Second Foreign Legion Regiment received orders to escort a
vast camel convoy to supply French forts and outposts. The
3,000 camels and supplies for 3,000 men offered such bait
to the Arabs that the battalion divided it into three separate
columns to cross the flinty El Moungar Plain, notorious for
ambushes. On September 2, 1903, the second echelon,
under Captain Vauchez and Lieutenant Selchauhansen,
started its night march. At nine in the morning, Vauchez
halted. Minutes later the vanguard of 5,000 Berber and
Shamba warriors rode out of the dunes. Panic seized the animals; the six hundred camels and fifty mounted-company
mules stampeded; the Legion column splintered into three
sections, all fighting for their existence. Wounded men were
crawling away from the maddened hooves and out of the
rifle fire from the high dunes.

Caught in the open with his company, Selchauhansen gathered the men into a square; but against armed tribesmen holding the high ground they faced extinction. The Dane decided to charge. He and twenty men covered only fifty yards before half of them fell. Two bullets hit Selchauhansen, in the chest and arm, sending him sprawling into the sand. Several legionnaires doubled over to pick him up but he waved them away. "Into a square and keep firing," he commanded. "But lieutenant . . ." his sergeant stammered. "It's an order," said Selchauhansen. He had fought at Zenaga that May and remembered how many men they had lost recovering their wounded. From behind a mound of sand, lying on his back, he directed the fire of his legionnaires. Two men disobeyed his order and crawled to rescue him, only to die by his side. Sergeant Tisserand had rallied the rest of Selchauhansen's company and beat off a fierce Arab charge; he carried the wounded Captain Vauchez onto a dune, where he dug himself in.

"Captain Bennelet and Lieutenant Selchauhansen?" Vauchez asked.

"The captain's dead, sir. The lieutenant's badly wounded but won't let them pick him up."

"C'est un brave," muttered Vauchez. Over the sergeant's pointing finger he could see the blond hair and the twisted figure of the Danish lieutenant in the hollow between the dunes; bullets spurted around him as the tribesmen tried to finish him off. "I don't fear death," he remembered Selchauhansen once saying. "That's my fate. But I fear dying in the memory of these brave friends and comrades in the Legion."

For six hours, in the vibrating heat, Selchauhansen lay there. An eternal calvary. Between long silences his voice encouraged his men, though it was growing weaker. Screams from tortured legionnaires drowned it. In an attempt to clear the sand crests, Tisserand mounted a counterattack but this petered out, leaving three more dead men on the plain. In the late afternoon a dust cloud appeared; the third column had heard the fire and was coming to their aid. The Arabs made one final attack before dissolving into the dunes. When the legionnaires ran to pick up Selchauhansen, they saw that a third bullet had struck him in the head during the last charge. Despite his ordeal, life still flickered. He and Vauchez reached the sick bay at Taghit, to die the next day. Selchauhansen had his wish; he became a hero in the Legion. As a memorial, two Danish officers are detached to serve with the French unit, even today.

The El Moungar massacre, in which 113 legionnaires died, so shocked Governor General Jonnart that he cabled the War Ministry to ask for Colonel Lyautey as head of operations on the Algerian-Moroccan frontier. Colonel Louis Hubert Lyautey had impressed Jonnart with his advanced ideas on colonization, though French chiefs of staff did not share his views. They had enough trouble: anti-militarists and Jewish muckrakers stirring up the Dreyfus Case; Catholics and intellectuals trying to put the army in its place, like this Lyautey fellow, whom they had put out to pasture at forty-nine with a regiment in eastern France. General Gallieni might have spoken well of him in Tonkin, but Gallieni/Lyautey was a dangerous humbug. Hadn't he written that article advocating that the army should wet-nurse conquered natives by setting up schools, hospitals, and churches? What did one expect from a moneyed, Catholic socialist? They bowed to Jonnart, however. Summoned to Paris, Lyautey was convinced that the generals intended to reprimand him for attending a service in honor of the late Pope; instead, they offered him command of the Oran Division, with full powers to stop catastrophes like El Moungar. In North Africa, Lyautey had finally found his life's work; in the Legion, the men to realize his ideas.

It was something of a miracle that Lyautey was alive. At two, his nurse had dropped him from a second-story window as they watched a parade on the Place Stanislas at Nancy. A hussar's shoulder had cushioned his fall, but he still spent two years in bed, and only at twelve did they let him try his injured spine without a steel brace. He coasted through Saint-Cyr and the staff college, seemingly destined for the highest rank, until that article in 1894 about the social role of the army. General Boisdeffre, the chief of staff, dressed him down and shipped him to Tonkin. There Colonel Joseph Gallieni was practicing what the young captain had outlined in his article. Gallieni threw away Lyautey's staff-college textbooks and sent him into the jungle to learn how to handle men the hard way. In a Haiphong hospital he met legionnaires, lying wounded in dark, airless cells. "What a tonic before a legionnaire plunges into the jungle," he wrote home. Paris ladies would do better to send money for a new hospital than cigars and liqueurs, he added.

In the tangled mountains of Upper Tonkin he came to know the Legion spirit. Trapped near Hoang-man, with a small force, Lyautey released carrier pigeons with an SOS. Fifty legionnaires, led by Captain Bérenger, cut their way through ten times as many Chinese to bring Lyautey and their nineteen dead down the hill. Two years later he marched with a column of legionnaires and Tonkinese against a Chinese fortification; when they had seized the peak, the legionnaires gathered bouquets of wild roses and solemnly presented these to Lyautey, who never forgot the moment. Between the scholarly and devout captain and these social rejects and roughnecks grew a strange bond.

Lyautey applied Gallieni's doctrine of pacification. He would destroy unruly tribes, but once they had submitted he would build modern towns and villages to replace their tented camps and link them with roads and railways. Such pacified areas would spread their boundaries, like an oil stain, as Gallieni said. He accepted nothing, questioned everything. What is a heavy column if legionnaires wear steel-tipped boots and carry haversacks for a six-month campaign? Why leave men decaying in outposts that have no tactical meaning? The oil stain began to ooze from Lyautey's headquarters at Aïn Sefra, a nomad halt between the mountains and dunes, to the defense line he had traced on the Algerian-Moroccan frontier. But the oil slick worried Paris. Britain and Germany had expressly forbidden encroachment on Moroccan territory. His chiefs warned Lyautey not to touch the Moroccan forts of Tagda and Ras el-Ain. But who in Paris could read a map, or knew what lay outside Algiers and Oran? The new colonel made his own map, inventing towns beyond the boundary set by Paris, London, and Berlin. War Ministry officials searched in vain for Berguent and Colomb-Bechar, which the Legion had occupied. Lyautey had begun the occupation of Morocco by default.

A curious amalgam of thinker and man of action, Lyautey lived in Aïn Sefra like some medieval squire, dining off silver plates and letting native sheiks kiss his hand; he loved the desert and the Legion, which had adapted to it like jerboas in their sand holes. On a thoroughbred Arab, with tiger-skin saddle and silver stirrups, he would ride with mounted columns, then doff his embroidered burnoose to squat on an ammunition box and sample Legion stew, which he rated the best in the world. When he had washed it down with *pinard* and a cup of scalding coffee, he would hand the cook a hundred francs—enough to feed the battalion—and take himself around the lines to chat with Tonkin veterans. The Legion liked to see his gray, cropped head and flowing Kaiser Wilhelm mustache and was flattered when he traced in the sand the next day's fighting or the new road he wanted them to construct.

One evening in the summer of 1905 he returned to his tent to find an anonymous letter. Was this what the Legion really thought of him? Lord High-and-Mighty, the hard-of-hearing pro-consul who dispensed feudal benevolence to the African vassals, whose vision imagined the desert where peace reigned and flowers bloomed? He ran his eye over it again. Yes, a caricature maybe, unflattering perhaps, but just. And written in a style that would have done his own letters proud. According to the officers he quizzed, only one man could have written such a parody: Lieutenant Albert Jaegle. The young legionnaire lieutenant came to Lyautey's tent fearing the worst. "So you think I'm a benevolent despot," Lyautey growled. *"Oui, mon général—* but your despotism is tempered with generosity and justice and your benevolence is shown only to those who can return it."

This impromptu retort delighted Lyautey, who offered the young officer whiskey and cigars and kept him talking all night. In Jaegle he seemed to rediscover some part of his own youth and the spirit that had offended his chiefs. They had much in common. Lyautey from Lorraine and Jaegle from Alsace belonged to that bit of France still occupied by the Germans. They spent their nights writing: Lyautey composed long, erudite letters, chiefly to his mentor, Gallieni; Jaegle wrote about his mounted column of legionnaires. "And my men, the legionnaires of the mounted company, whose old mules dream philosophically of the repose they will never enjoy. . . . Under the thin canvas of their six-men tents lie the tough warrior-convicts, my legionnaires, great-hearted men of defeated vanity and hope. . . . For too long I have followed the rough grumble and the swaying packs, the thin plaint of the fifes and the jarring bugles that keep step with the Legion along the African tracks." Lyautey came to look on Jaegle as his son and predicted a great future for the soldier-poet.

Mounted columns like Jaegle's seemed to challenge dissident tribesmen. In February 1908 more than 2,000 of Bou-Amama's cavalry bore down on two companies of legionnaires in the Mellah Gorge; the two hundred legionnaires fixed bayonets and tried to break the charge. Only a handful of them left that battlefield. New recruits often bypassed Sidi-bel-Abbès and Saida to come straight to the Colomb-Bechar area to replace the dead and wounded. On April 13, as Jaegle's column prepared to depart, the company sergeant major harangued a bunch of these rookies. "You're going to have your baptism of fire tomorrow. Show yourselves worthy of those who have already fallen." At dawn the next day the mounted company and another Legion infantry company came under attack from 5,000 Moroccans near the deserted village of Menabha. When the Moroccans broke off, 120 legionnaires were dead or gravely wounded. Legionnaire Forster, a young Swiss from Geneva, died the next day at Colomb-Bechar. To the priest, he whispered, "People grow old quickly here. Yesterday, they were baptizing us—today they're giving us the last rites." Two officers had been killed and three others wounded. Jaegle now commanded the mounted company, and seemed determined to avenge the dead of Menabha.

On May 13 cavalry scouts signaled a strong Moroccan force in the palm groves of Beni-Ouzien, west of Menabha. Were these the men who had ambushed them? A deep wadi separated Jaegle's company from the dead-quiet palm grove. When the lieutenant spurred his horse into this gully it vibrated with fire from every palm tree. Pinned in this ravine, they waited for artillery to bombard the grove. How many thousand Moroccans lay there? Jaegle knew the advantage lay with the enemy, but his small company would have to blunder in and take its chance. The tribesmen waited until the guns had stopped and the legionnaire captain and his first men had reached the edge of the grove before opening up. Jaegle got through to find himself fighting hand-to-hand with his saber; in the palm fronds, snipers picked his men off. Legionnaires Meyer and Francq saw their captain fall and died trying to save him; other hands grabbed him as the Moroccans pounced. Jaegle's company might have sacrificed itself in that grove had not a young lieutenant rallied the men and fought back to the ravine to wait for reinforcements to attack again. Paul Rollet, a lithe monkey of a man who could march as far in rope-soled shoes as his mules, survived this and one hundred such encounters to become the symbol of the Legion.

When they carried Jaegle to the first-aid post the doctor shrugged. The captain died the next day. He sent for his toilet kit, combed his dark hair and shaved so that "I can meet death with dignity." To a general who commiserated, he said, "Don't pity me—just say that you're pleased with me. You see, I'm dying as I wanted to die—like a good Alsatian and a good Frenchman."

Lyautey had been touring his district and did not hear of Jaegle's death until he returned to Aïn Sefra. For weeks he grieved about the loss of this brilliant young man. At Colomb-Bechar he erected a magnificent memorial to Albert Jaegle and his friend Maurice Coste.

Early in 1907 some Frenchmen employed in Casablanca port were murdered. At last Lyautey had found his pretext for invading Morocco. General Antoine Drude, with a battalion of legionnaires and native troops, occupied the port without firing a shot. The Legion moved in to occupy towns and forts, and to build. Lyautey noted in his diary in 1908: "In Morocco, in three and a half months, despite the snow and the icy winds of the Atlas and the incessant incursions of murderous and keen enemy, the Third Battalion of the Second Foreign Regiment has opened one hundred kilometers of excellent autocyclable roads, thus saving the state 5,000,000 francs and bringing civilization to tribes that had known up to now nothing but misery, poverty, and sickness. A superb unit that knows how to build as well as fight."

While France wrangled with Germany over Morocco, Lyautey went home to command an army corps at Rennes. But, in April 1911, the Moroccan capital of Fez errupted in riots. Sixty-eight Europeans were massacred; the others, trapped in their houses, beseeched French aid. Lyautey returned as resident general. Immediately he set up his headquarters in the center of Fez, deciding that if this city fell he had lost everything. In the last weeks of May it seemed the rebels had won. From his terrace the new resident general could observe the legionnaire companies—one led by Captain Rollet—retreating from the Merenides, the position that dominated the town. If the Legion were finished . . . Lyautey went to bed that night convinced that France had lost Morocco. But the Legion had held out long enough for French artillery to break up the rebel attacks. The next morning Lyautey was at his desk, planning new roads and railways to link the country's chief cities.

It did not worry him that the German gunboat *Panther* had anchored in Agadir harbor to protect German interests; he shrugged off the Franco-German crisis and growled when an unknown Austrian archduke was murdered at Sarajevo: "Balkan stories . . . I've seen so many in the last twenty years. To work." But Sarajevo was the final crisis. Lyautey had to wave good-bye to his beloved legionnaires trooping to Algerian and Moroccan ports, bound for France and another conflict with Germany. To create the impression that France could still master Morocco by force, he issued every French resident a legionnaire uniform. Old and middle-aged men wore the white kepi and the blue cummerbund and exhibited their rifles and bayonets on office desks and shop counters. "I've taken the meat out of the lobster, but I've kept the shell," Lyautey would say and grin. His Legion—"my most cherished troop"—would soon be back, he told himself.

TEN

Here by devoted comrades laid away,
Along our lines they slumber where they fell,
Beside the Crater at the Ferme d'Alger
And up the bloody slopes of La Pompelle.

Alan Seegar: Champagne, 1915

The old-timers who arrived in France from Africa in the autumn of 1914 had never witnessed anything quite like it. The thunderous slanging match between thousands of heavy guns, the lethal dialogue between machine guns, and bloody collisions between armies of half a million men stunned these desert warriors, trained to marching and skirmishing over hundreds of miles of vacant space. What shocked them more was the motley crew of recruits pouring through the Legion depots in Paris. Poets and painters, students and playboys, a baron and a boxer, Greeks, Poles, Czechs, and Americans. This war would get the Legion a bad name. None felt it more than old Corporal Weidemann, sixteen years in the Legion. His daily catechism to the Americans, who formed his section, mingled defeatism and despair. "Neffer," he muttered, "neffer vill you make goot soldiers. Germany vill vin the var, but I haff giffen my vord to France and I vill keep it." Weidemann did. He was brutally killed by his own countrymen in the first days of 1915 at Cateau.

Altogether, just over 44,000 foreigners from fifty-one countries swelled the Legion ranks between 1914 and 1918.

By the winter of 1914 the new legionnaires had learned to handle a rifle and bayonet and were drafted into the trenches along the Somme and around Artois to shake down with the African sweats. The enlisted men had no proper uniforms. General Castelnau's plethoric face went livid when they paraded before him. "They told me they were sending the Legion. What are these—naval artillery?" The men were wearing Paris firemen's trousers and blue, marine tunics.

They had a rookie corporal called Zinovi Pechkoff, who had defied his father and jumped on the Rome-Paris train after the declaration of war. His father was Maxim Gorki, the illustrious Russian writer, friend of Lenin and Stalin. In another company, Frederic Sauter-Hall had just become a corporal, wearing a fireman's tunic and a curate's trousers. Of mixed Swiss-Scots stock and better known by his pen name, Blaise Cendrars, this poet and novelist would write some of his most emotive prose about the Legion he had joined. Sticking to Cendrars like the mud on his puttees was a chit of a Cockney called Arthur Griffith, who had spent most of his adult life in the Legion. Louis II of Monaco was serving under the name of Colonel Grimaldi. Among the Americans was Bob Scanlon, the Negro boxer, and Hendrik van Loon, the distinguished historian. They met characters like Legionnaire Koniakoff, a Russian painter and priest who had done twenty years in Tonkin and Algeria. This orthodox priest had seduced a girl in his congregation; when she left him, he joined the Legion. He puzzled even Legion officers who had pliant ideas on discipline. If they barked at him, Koniakoff would look wounded and reply, "How can you talk like that to a man who has the power to make God descend into the Host! I am clothed with a divine character and I am also a victim of love."

In May they moved up the line to a point north of Arras. Ahead of them lay a low crest and they heard their officers mention Hill 132 and Hill 140 and Vimy Ridge, though the names and places meant nothing. A brass hat with a walrus mustache and a chest full of kitchen equipment reviewed them. General Henri Philippe Pétain, they said.

For weeks the French barrage had kicked up sprays of chalk on the white fortification lines. Suddenly, at ten o'clock on May 9, the guns ceased along the thirteen-mile front. The men could almost believe it was Sunday. The Legion officers, in their best uniforms, wearing fresh white gloves and carrying swagger sticks, mounted the parapets. *"En avant,"* they shouted. In the sharp sunlight, the men began to jog over no man's land. Despite the artillery fire, the barbed wire lay intact. As they reached it, machine guns opened up. "The coffee grinders," someone said. Men began to fall as if butting up against a plate-glass wall, but the line did not wilt. The first German dugouts and machine-gun nests were cleared with the bayonet.

"Cuántos están aquí?" Valdes, the Spanish grenadier, shouted into a dugout. *"Cinco."* He tossed five grenades into the hole. A minute later a bullet twisted him around and a grenade detonated in his hand. Koniakoff, the priest-painter, sprawled across the second string of barbed wire, dead. And with him, scores more. Still they trotted on, sweating under heavy packs, making for the long white scar on Vimy Ridge. Corporal Pechkoff had gone down, his arm smashed near the shoulder by a bullet; he waved his section on, rolled into a trench to wait for the stretcher-bearers. That night they amputated his arm; for most it would have spelled the end of soldiering. Not for Pechkoff.

The legionnaires had gained three miles and had, in fact, overrun Hill 140 and were on Vimy Ridge. On that bare crest shells began to burst among them. But they came from behind. Their own gunners had mistaken them for retreating Germans, refusing to believe they could have reached the ridge so soon. Hundreds perished under that barrage. Legionnaire Reybaz contended that the error stemmed from the fact that the men had not pinned the huge, blue identity squares on their backs before the battle.

That day at Artois only the lucky lived. Their colonel, fifty officers, and 1,889 men had died, and their nine divisions had no reinforcements to hold the ground they had won. As Bugeaud had said of them seventy-five years before, "Had they been less brave they would have lost fewer men." Somehow, Cendrars had survived, and his shadow, the titchy Legionnaire Griffith. "Wha'd I say, Corp. You're lucky," the little man told Cendrars.

The next Sunday the regiment was pitched into the same front, as if Hill 140 had merely served as a gruesome rehearsal. Again the church bells tolled for mass; the white earthworks ahead seemed copies of those on Hill 140; machine-gun fire skittled the ranks, which, however, appeared less solid after May 9. Only the names changed: Souchez, Carency, Givenchy, and Cabaret Rouge. Blaise Cendrars brought his platoon off Vimy minus Legionnaire Garnero, whom they left for dead, though Cendrars would run into him in Paris ten years later. Those battles of Artois had cost them seventy-one officers and 2,513 men; but somehow Cendrars, Griffith, and the others had walked through this hell untouched. "Wha'd I say, Corp. You have the *baraka*."

An incongruous pair, Corporal Cendrars and Legionnaire Griffith: the poet and intellectual fighting for his personal ideals, and the illiterate, irreverent, time-serving Londoner. Then that crazy mixture, the Third Regiment, was like their evening *soupe*, a bit of everything. Cendrars' small section, entrenched in the mud of the Somme Canal that nightmare December of 1914, boasted another poet, a circus strong man, a liftman, and a painter; he had two quaint American surgeons, Legionnaire Bywater, aged seventy-two, and Wilson, aged sixty-nine, who belonged to the Seventh-Day Adventists and refused to fire their rifles. "We didn't join for France or against Germany," they said. Why, then? "For the mud baths. The trenches are very healthy." Few lived long enough to prove the American thesis. Bywater died at Vimy and Wilson at Souchez cemetery.

Nothing about the Legion surprised Cendrars, an extravagant character himself. Until Griffith arrived. In late December he ambled up the line to drop, dead-beat, into Cendrars' trench. Well beyond active-service age, he had a pinched face, with sickness showing through the African tan; a deep, hacking cough racked his thin body. Cendrars moved over to offer him a dry place beside the fire. *"Merde,"* Griffith swore, dumped his kit, and flopped down under a blanket in a dark, muddy corner. Cendrars guarded the only trench in that sector within rifle range of the Germans; on the canal he had rigged a battery of seventeen Lebel rifles, their triggers linked to fire salvos and fool the enemy. There he placed Griffith on guard the night after his arrival. Toward midnight, Cendrars wandered around to ensure that Griffith was surviving the bitter cold. The little Cockney was standing, naked, a bayonet in his hand. As Cendrars watched, he plunged into the slimy water, stayed down for more than a minute, then surfaced. He spotted Cendrars. "Hey, Corp, it's no great shakes but I bet there's eels in the bottom." And down he went again, like an otter. How it did not kill him Cendrars never understood, for Griffith had transplanted poorly from the African sands to the Somme mud. He was a loner. *"Fiche-moi la paix,"* one of his few fluent French phrases, burst from him if anyone disturbed him while he smoked his black tobacco and spat phlegm. Sometimes, when the *cafard* took him, he would loose off his rifle and let fly with unintelligible Cockney oaths. "Goddamn them—I should have made them pay," he would shout.

Cendrars noticed, however, that Griffith never groused on patrol, nor missed a guard or fatigue, nor reported sick. He had all the legionnaire's superstitions, believing that Cendrars' *baraka* would pull them through the worst machine-gun fire or bombardment. So, he shadowed the corporal—into the blazing shell hole of Notre Dame de Lorette, through the Ouvrages Blancs and across Vimy Ridge, down to Souchez cemetery and on to Carency. "Don't think I can savvy any more of them," he would gasp after each ordeal. But somehow he coughed and spat and stumbled after the platoon until they withdrew the shreds of the Legion from Artois to rest and regroup in the manor park at Tilloloy.

Spending a glowing June among the ornamental trees neither softened Griffith's black moods nor cured his TB; he kept to

Lebel Rifle

himself, puffing his pipe and doubling up with coughing paroxysms. In the last week of June he crawled into the *gourbi* Cendrars had built himself under a copper beech. "I'll take your place, Corp. I'm done in." Realizing that Griffith was dying, Cendrars offered to fetch the medical officer. "*Sanferryan*, Corp. I've had my lot. I just want to be left alone. No *toubibs. Compris?*" Cendrars lounged in the sun and read and watched the little man. Nobody could ask a legionnaire about his kin, but finally, as Griffith weakened, he began to gasp the secret he had kept for twenty-five years. A state secret. "I'll only tell you 'cos I'm a goner, see?"

In 1890 jobs weren't easy to come by in London. You took what you got. He'd jumped at what they offered him. Steady work, though the pay wasn't anything to write home about. Not what you'd call a clean job. At twenty Griffith became a London sewerman. As a new boy they'd handed him the dirtiest beat in London. Some men always catch it. Not only the most stinking sewers, along the Thames side, but a maze of black, twisting passages and dead ends where a man could lose himself for good. "A rough ol' number, I tell you, Corp." Nevertheless, the London sewers gained some weird hold on Arthur Griffith. Sunday, his day off, he would spend exploring the inkiest corners of his beat with a lantern, imprinting each section of the labyrinth on his mind. One Sunday, in 1895, he happened on a hole he had never seen, nor anybody else for that matter. Why, that hole must have been there for a couple of centuries. . . . He groped along it, then noted its position in his mind. Still it took three weeks for Griffith to rediscover the entrance.

The guards at the colonnaded façade of the Bank of England chased the shabby little man who presented himself with a demand to see the guv'nor. For months he haunted the front door of the bank with the same request; they laughed when he told them it was a matter of national importance. Finally, to rid themselves of this nuisance, officials ushered him into the governor's office. The man in morning coat and sponge-bag trousers regarded the ill-dressed workman. "They tell me you are a sewerman, Mr. . . . Griffith."

" 'Sright, guv'nor. We're both civil servants, like."

"Yes. . . . Now what is this matter of national importance that's bothering you?"

"It's like this, guv'nor. You've a lot of sugar and honey in your Jack and Jill—money in your till." The governor, still puzzled, nodded. "Well, I'll bet a pound to a Thomas Tilling that I can get past all your rozzers and your flunkeys and your iron bars and your iron doors and lift as much as I need."

"That's impossible," said the governor.

Griffith fished a pound from his pocket and laid it on the table. "At midday tomorrow I'll collect your shilling where you keep all them gold bars," he said.

As Griffith told Cendrars, the governor was no Charlie. He accepted the bet. At noon the following day the procession of senior security staff proceeded through each grille and iron door of the bank to the vaults beneath. They opened the great steel door, and there, on a pile of ingots, squatted Arthur Griffith.

"But how . . .?" the governor stuttered.

"That's a long story, guv'nor."

They quizzed and they threatened; they wheedled and they coaxed. The canny Griffith told neither the governor nor his guards how he had penetrated the vaults. "All I'd say, guv, is that if I can do it, so can others." The head of the bank finally caught the hint.

"Exactly what do you want, Mr. Griffith?"

"Give me £1,000 and I'll keep out of England for good," said Griffith. "You have my word as a sewerman."

That day—as he whispered to Cendrars—he signed a pledge to tell no one of his discovery and to stay out of England. Soon he had gone through his money and joined the Legion. He had kept his word. And that secret would die with him. "Not even will I tell you, Corp," he gasped. At the end of June he turned over in the *gourbi* and died.

Three months later Cendrars went with the Legion to Souain, just above Chalons-sur-Marne, to take part in the Champagne offensive. They now numbered no more than 1,600 men as they lay before the German fortifications on the crests. Despite their losses, morale remained high, and the Legion still had some of the old "Africans," who made

the best of this or any other war. Where, for instance, did
Sergeant van Lees get his wine from? Rare Burgundies and
clarets jostled with vintage champagne in his dugout. Pétain
and Castelnau, the army commanders, had no better cellar
than the gangling Dutchman. Van Lees ran his section like
some private army. A black flag fluttered over his trench in
no man's land and he picked and rejected recruits like a feudal lord. The best Legion cook, the best wines, the best cigarettes. What more did he want? Cendrars was convinced that
the sergeant wanted either to opt out or to fight his own war.
Like so many legionnaires, he overstepped the mark and
was broken. He and his great rival, Sergeant Popoff, played
poker for food, wine, cigarettes, their equipment, other people's equipment. Came the day when they threw their machine guns into the kitty. Van Lees won. Popoff accused
him of cheating. Knives flashed. Both the scarred sergeants
started again as legionnaires, second-class.

The Legion sat out the start of the great advance. From
September 22 the guns—each battery sited by Pétain—
thudded at the fifteen-mile front. Three days later nearly
200,000 men slogged through the downpour and spent
themselves on the German blockhouses. Two miles north of
the Legion lines lay the Navarin Farm, which had resisted
every onslaught. The order came for the Legion to attack
it—a blind, sacrificial assault in which everyone else had
failed. At four in the afternoon the legionnaires rose out of
their waterlogged trenches. Cendrars heard the crashing
notes of the *Boudin*. (That would be Corporal Boulloux,
standing in no man's land.) He and his section plodded parallel with the road until they hit the barbed wire around the
farm. Machine guns began to racket; the wire clogged with
bodies; and, as at Artois, the French gunners were not making too fine a distinction between their own men and the
Germans.

Legionnaire van Lees was striding ahead of Cendrars
one moment—the next, he had vanished. A shell burst on
top of him and he literally volatilized. Cendrars witnessed
the macabre sight of his empty trousers floating down into
the mud. That, and an eerie, empty scream in the air were
all that remained of van Lees. A few minutes later Cendrars
himself was hit by a bullet that smashed his hand and wrist.

Though weakened by loss of blood, he led his section until he and it had bogged down without reaching the charnel house of a farm, the sinister Kultur Redoubt, and the other German blockhouses. Not one of them, the eight hundred who died and the eight hundred who teetered off the battlefield, had reached the Navarin Farm. Cendrars was sent down the line, then to Paris. Had he lived to see him, Griffith would have cried, "Wh'd I say, Corp. Dead lucky. That's a real blighty one you've copped." They amputated most of Cendrars's right forearm. For him, no more war. Later he would write: "It was well worth risking death to meet such legionnaires." Some of his best writing he devoted to people like Griffith and van Lees—and the derelict Navarin Farm, which destroyed or altered so many men. One of these was Legionnaire John Ford Elkington.

They had marched a long way that morning, the legionnaires who were moving into the lines. Beyond Rheims they halted by a stream to quench their thirst. A staff car flying a British pennant edged through them. The brigadier in the front seat spotted a face he recognized among the legionnaires. Leaning out, he shouted, "Hallo, Elkington. How are you?" One of the legionnaires quickly turned his face away, then lost himself among the men. "Did you know that brass hat?" someone asked him. Elkington shrugged his shoulders. Minutes later they resumed their march, Elkington keeping to the middle of his platoon with his friend David Wheeler. That had been a near one, the first time in almost a year that a face had appeared out of his past.

Elkington had joined the Legion in October 1914. In Paris they had asked no questions and he had told no lies. His name, John Ford Elkington, and his age, forty-nine, were real; the rest he was prepared to forget, if he could. No one in his company ever knew more than his name, his humble rank as second-class legionnaire, and his number, 29274. Except that his fellow soldiers realized that Elkington could have taught their NCOs and some of their fresh-faced officers how to handle their men; his instinct for command, and obedience, struck the more senior officers. They noted, too, that he hid very badly the fact that he had something to hide; some thought that he was an English gentleman down on his luck.

With the new recruits, Elkington had trained in a Rhône Valley camp; from there they marched through France for the Battle of Artois. At Lyons, where they bivouacked, the men had an evening pass. Tired of the Legion *soupe*, Elkington wandered into the Grand Hotel and ordered a meal. Across the dining room he caught sight of a legionnaire from his own company sitting over the biggest dinner he had seen in months. Their gaze crossed; the man approached and said, "Why don't you join me?" He introduced himself as David Wheeler, then said, grinning, "You know, I took you for a tramp."

"I thought exactly the same about you," said Elkington.

In the Legion men paired off to share everything. So it was with Elkington and Wheeler, though they neither knew nor questioned each other's past. Not until many months later did the Englishman realize that Dr. David Wheeler had been a well-known American surgeon from Buffalo who had volunteered to work in a French Red Cross hospital. His wife followed him as a nurse. Wheeler, an outdoor type, began to reproach himself for sitting in the comparative safety of a front-line hospital; the human wreckage filling his operating theater depressed him. At forty-two he joined the Legion. French surgeons pleaded vainly that he would further the war effort more as a surgeon than a *poilu*, but Wheeler enlisted just the same. He and Elkington shared a bivouac, marched and ate together, swapped cigarettes, newspapers, and books; they talked about everything—except themselves.

Elkington said that the surgeon had no trace of fear in him; Wheeler thought the same about his comrade. On the Artois crest, when everything was crumbling around them, Elkington rallied a section and led it forward to salvage the men from French shells falling at their backs. At Souchez cemetery, a week later, he stopped a platoon from charging to oblivion until he had cleaned out a German machine-gun position. Even African veterans respected this quiet man who seemed to find his voice only in combat.

At Souain they teamed up with the rest of the Legion. They had no illusions about the coming battle; to break through the German defenses would, the legionnaires knew, cost 100,000 lives. "The Legion will take the hard knocks as usual," the men muttered. With the rest of the Legion, they watched the first attacks fail; walking wounded filtered back through their lines with numb faces and frightened eyes. On September 28 their turn arrived. For Elkington's battalion they had picked the choice morsel—the Horseshoe Wood and the Navarin Farm. Surely no one thought they could crack that! Just before the bugle sounded the charge, Captain Junod, a Legion veteran, mounted the parapet in full-dress uniform. *"Mes enfants,"* he shouted, "we are going to certain death, but we are going to try to die like brave men." Mud sucked their feet down as they plodded forward. Edmond Genêt, American descendant of a French Revolution minister who had deserted the U.S. Navy to join the Legion, described what happened. "We had started out to advance in solid columns of four, each section a unit. It was wonderful, that slow advance. Not a waver, not a break. Through the storm of shell, the Legion marched forward. One lost his personal feelings. He simply became a unit, a machine."

Legionnaires Elkington and Wheeler had stuck together. They wormed past the first two lines of wire and slithered across the empty trenches into Horseshoe Wood. Around them the trees splintered under the impact of shells and bullets; they moved slowly, stopping to clean out trenches with grenades, trying to pinpoint the machine-gun nests. Another line of trenches, then only one more between them and the left-hand edge of the wood and the baleful Navarin Farm. Elkington had run ahead of his section. With grenades, he sent a handful of Germans fleeing; he was waving the men forward when a hidden machine gun opened up on them.

Elkington pitched, wounded, into a trench. Wheeler reached him at the very moment that he, too, was hit. The surgeon's calf lay open, but he saw that Elkington's wound was much worse; several bullets had smashed his right leg. "Old fellow, I'm afraid they'll have to take that off," he said. He bandaged the leg, gave Elkington a shot of the morphine he carried; he had just finished attending to his own wound when he fainted on top of the Englishman. For several hours they lay in the rain-filled trench, until long after nightfall when the remnant of the Legion had left the field and the stretcher-bearers crept into the trenches.

For nearly a year Elkington lay in a Paris hospital recovering from his wound. They managed to save his leg, though he would limp for the rest of his days. It was in the hospital, in the summer of 1916, that they brought the French Official Journal to him. He read the citation: "The Military Medal and the Croix de Guerre are conferred upon John Ford Elkington, Legionnaire in Company B 3 of the First Foreign Regiment. Although fifty years old, he has given proof during the campaign of remarkable courage and ardor, setting everyone the best example. He was gravely wounded on September 28, 1915, rushing forward to assault enemy trenches. He has lost the use of his right leg."

What could he do but accept the decorations, the highest that the French army can bestow? Strangely, he refused to pin the two ribbons on his uniform. "I don't wear medals," he grunted when asked why. Those medals, however, had given him away; the secret he had guarded for nearly two years came out at last. Among those who read the French citation was King George V. A few weeks later, at his behest, another notice about Elkington appeared, this time in the London *Gazette*. "The King," it said, "has been graciously pleased to approve the reinstatement of John Ford Elkington in the rank of Lieutenant-Colonel of the Royal Warwickshire Regiment with his previous seniority, in consequence of his gallant conduct while serving in the ranks of the Foreign Legion of the French Army." The King also awarded Elkington the DSO.

Elkington had been cashiered from the British army under the stigma of cowardice. The first part of his story was well known in Britain. In the middle of August 1914, he had landed with the advance units of the British expeditionary force in France. He had a distinguished record. A professional soldier, he had joined the Royal Warwickshire Regiment at twenty, serving with it in India. In the Boer War he had several times shown great courage, winning the Queen's Medal with four clasps "for conspicuous service." He arrived in French commanding the First Battalion of the Warwickshires. At Mons, on a front already buckling, the battalion made a fighting retreat, with the rest of the British army, to Le Cateau. There, on August 26, it stood and fought from dawn till noon against the full weight of the German thrust. In that battle and the retreat southwest, Elkington's battalion lost heavily; the remaining men and their colonel were exhausted. At Saint-Quentin, Elkington begged the mayor for food and permission to rest his troops. The mayor, fearing a German bombardment and a battle that would destroy his town, refused—unless Elkington signed an agreement to surrender if the Germans advanced. At the end of his strength and out of consideration for his men, Elkington signed. The Germans did not advance; they had to swing west to deal with a brilliant counterstroke devised by Gallieni. Saint-Quentin was thus spared. Not Elkington. That paper damned him. Ordered back to England, he was brought before a court-martial. He admitted his error and made no excuses. They broke him just the same, dismissing him from the service for conduct that "rendered him unfit and incapable of serving his Sovereign in the future in any military capacity."

On October 14 the whole country learned of Elkington's moment of shame. A War Office announcement in the London *Gazette* read: "Royal Warwickshire Regiment—Lt-Colonel John F. Elkington is cashiered by sentence of a General Court-Martial. Dated September 4, 1914." The first officer of the war to suffer court-martial and cashiering. Elkington had served 30 years in the army; he knew nothing but soldiering. A senior officer who visited him at his home near Pangbourne when the announcement appeared asked what his plans were. "I am going to join the Foreign Legion," he declared. He said good-bye to his wife and two children and sailed for France. All they had was the occasional letter, explaining where he was and saying that he liked the Legion.

Elkington returned to England in September 1916. He could once more wear the scarlet tunic he had been forced to discard for the Legion khaki; he never wore his medals, British or French. All he would ever say was, "I did nothing of particular note. I was with the others in the trenches." His tunic still hangs in the regimental museum.

Dr. David Wheeler, who Elkington claimed saved his life, fought with the Legion until 1917 when he joined an

American regiment. Four months before the war ended, he was killed.

In August 1914 about seventy Americans queued at the Foreign Legion recruiting center; the French major looked at them and snorted that they would be fighting the next war by the time they made soldiers. The Americans insisted. Kiffin and Paul Rockwell, from Atlanta, signed among the first. Kiffin was wounded on May 9 at Artois, recovered to join the American Lafayette Squadron and shot down the first enemy aircraft in Alsace. Jules Bach, an engineer, and Siegfried Narvitz, a philosophy professor, came in with two Negroes, Robert Percy, a barber, and Bob Scanlon. Ivan Nock, a mining engineer, had thrown up his job in Peru to get into the war and became a hero. Harry Collins, a Boston sailor, had jumped ship at Marseilles. There was a Yale man, William Thaw, and four Harvard men, including Alan Seeger, who had arrived in Paris two years before and had just published his first book of poems, *Juvenilia*.

Seeger came to mean to Americans in 1914 what Apollinaire did to the French and Wildred Owen and Rupert Brooke to the English. His lyrics, written in the trenches, spoke of love and life, though they were shot through with the presentiment of death; they breathed the joy and promise of the earth, tempered with the horror and fatalism that the poet and his comrades experienced in the front lines. Seeger is the English poet of the Legion. "I have joined up," he confided to his diary, "in order that France, and especially Paris, which I love, should never cease to be the glory and beauty which they are."

Seeger's idealism did not impress old legionnaires like Corporal Weidemann. Where did Legionnaire Seeger learn to mishandle a rifle like that? In the Mexican army, the poet lied. "Not eefen the Mexican army is zo clumsy," the old corporal said. However, he licked the American contingent into some order by the end of the year. Some saw action at Artois, but most spent 1915 in the Somme trenches on endless patrols. At the Château de Craonelle, Weidemann rallied them to beat off a German attack. Seeger and Kiffin Rockwell saw Weidemann die, then the Germans batter his body when they discovered he was a legionnaire. A captured German, taken on patrol, told them, "The Germans know that you are going to attack and have sworn to exterminate you. They will shoot any Legion prisoners." The German was an ex-legionnaire himself. The Legion had its own way of answering the threat. One of their Greek patrols would venture into no man's land armed with nothing but knives, and return with trophies to show how many Germans they had killed.

Other Legion units had bled so freely at Artois and the Navarin Farm that the two regiments fused into the Regiment de Marche, which fought under that name for the rest of the war. Though it had spent its strength twice over, the

08/15 Spandau. German H.M.G.

Legion had already made its mark; when they butted against strong resistance, French generals now called on the Legion. The beginning of 1916 found them again in the Somme, preparing for the great summer offensive to crack the German defenses around Amiens. The trenches had changed hands several times; they stank of death and chloride of lime, of cordite and mustard gas. Sitting in the mud, the le-

gionnaires heard of the great battles around Verdun. Seeger
was among those who volunteered to help stem the German
advance. The French, he said, would be divided into two
camps: those who fought at Verdun and those who didn't.

In April a new commandant took over the battalion in
which most Americans served. With him they had no need
to speak French—he was a New Zealander. Colonel James
Waddell had won a scholarship to study in England but had
left his university to fight with the British army in the Khy-
ber Pass. In 1900, at age twenty-seven, he joined the Legion
and campaigned in Tonkin and with Lyautey's mounted
columns around Colomb-Bechar. He had just recovered
from several serious wounds received while fighting with
the Legion battalion in the Dardanelles; he had won the Legion of Honor and the Croix de Guerre with seven palms.
Seeger and his friends reckoned themselves fortunate to
have Waddell, a resolute soldier who was considered
among the best tactical commanders produced by the Legion during the war. In his quiet way Waddell made this
hodgepodge of legionnaires feel they were the best battalion in France. He had some outstanding men. His tall, gangling adjutant chief, Max Emanuel Mader, was the ace
NCO of the Legion; on parade he looked more like a general than a battalion sergeant major with his chestful of
medals from Algeria, Tonkin, Morocco, and the battles of
Artois and Champagne. A German, he had an old score to
settle with the Fatherland. Two Argentinian brothers,
Cristóbal and Fernando de Quiros, not out of their teens,
had gained two Croix de Guerre and eleven citations since
the beginning of the war. The younger sons of the Marquis
Antonio Bernaldo de Quiros, a direct descendant of
Christopher Columbus, had forced their way into the Legion. At eighteen Cristóbal took a boat from Buenos Aires;
he first joined the British army, since his father objected to
his serving with a French regiment. He maneuvered his
transfer to the Legion. Fernando, his younger brother, was
studying in Madrid. Hearing about Cristóbal, he sold his
schoolbooks to pay his train fare and fight by his side. The
Spanish authorities, although alerted by his parents, failed
to stop him at the frontier. No one had undertaken more
hazardous patrols than these two brothers; no one had

walked closer to death at Artois and the Navarin Farm. *"La muerte no nos quiere,"* they would say. (Perhaps death didn't want them.)

At the end of June they moved up the line. The Americans scrapped their project for spending the Fourth of July in Paris. Seeger wrote home on June 28, "We go up to the attack tomorrow. This will probably be the biggest thing yet. We are to have the honor of marching in the first wave. . . . I am glad to be going in the first wave. If you are in this thing at all, it is best to be in to the limit. And this is the supreme experience."

Not until American Independence Day did they learn their objective: Belloy-en-Santerre, a splintered village that the Germans had turned into a defense bastion. Ringed by machine guns, it sat isolated by 1,000 yards of steep slope. The hardest oyster to open again, the legionnaires grumbled. The Americans clinked mess tins full of champagne to celebrate the Fourth of July and gazed solemnly at the fractured silhouette of Belloy in the bucketing rain that filled the shell-torn ground. Just before five o'clock a cluster of green Very lights glowed above them, haloed by rain. *"En avant, La Légion."*

Waddell's first company cut half-right across the rise; immediately German machine guns opened up, knocking the men over like a reaper. Waiting with the reserve company, Fernando de Quiros saw Cristóbal stagger over a shell pit; he must have primed a grenade, for it exploded in his hand; one by one the string of grenades around his neck detonated and he vanished. Fernando had no time to look for him as he, too, moved across the murderous slope.

In the second group, Legionnaire Alan Seeger was striding up the slope. His closest friend, Rif Baer, an Egyptian, was following. "I caught sight of Seeger and called to him, making a sign with my hand. He answered with a smile. His tall silhouette stood out against the green of a cornfield. . . . His head erect and pride in his eye, I saw him running forward with bayonet fixed. Soon he disappeared and that was the last time I saw my friend." Seeger had trotted through the worst of the barrage and had almost reached the first group when a bullet hit him; he rolled into a trench. Near him, George Delpeuch, an American friend, heard

Seeger cry, "Oh, my stomach." Wounded himself, not daring to lift his head—none of the wounded who survived that day raised their heads—Delpeuch heard Seeger call several times for water. He called for his mother. After that, silence.

But Waddell's men had entered the village. Taking cover in a ditch three hundred yards west of Belloy, they rose and dashed through the storm of bullets into the first houses. Now they had to contest each house, each inch of ground. Already half the battalion had vanished; of the eleventh company only a corporal remained with a handful of men. The wounded in their shell holes could observe Waddell's men gain the garden walls, could hear the clarion notes of the charge, then the sound of exploding grenades. The charge again—now from beyond the village. They stirred in their holes; the stutter of the German machine guns had stopped. Forgetting his pain, each called to the next man, "Belloy has fallen." *(Ils ont pris Belloy.)* They shook the dead lying beside them to announce the miracle. To confirm the fact, balloons bearing the Legion banner soared in the rain over the derelict town.

On the other side of Belloy, Waddell was rallying his battalion to stand off counterattacks. German shells turned the village into a quivering, blazing inferno while fresh shock troops unloaded from German trucks on the crest. Even the first-aid teams had to ignore the wounded and stand to on the fringes of Belloy to beat back assault after assault. On the second counterattack, Wilfred Michaud, an American who had enlisted with the Rockwells, fell mortally wounded. He cried, "I die happy because I have killed three Germans." Ten times that night they resisted new waves of Germans. No one counted the German dead, but the Legion had taken 730 prisoners, including fifteen officers. A German major muttered to Waddell, *"Sie sind nicht Männer, sie sind Wildtiere."* (They're not men, they're wild beasts.) As the daylight leaked over the sodden ground the men did look like savage animals; no one brewed morning "juice" that day; they needed something stronger—rum, brandy, and *pinard* went along the lines. They had taken Belloy, the invulnerable redoubt. But at what cost?

A fatigue party started out to pick up the wounded and

dead. Fernando de Quiros had risen some hours before and
was turning over corpses near the spot where he had last
sighted Cristóbal. *"Pas de chance, petit?"* a corporal called.
He shook his head. Until nightfall he searched in vain, but
the next morning he discovered his brother, whom he could
identify only by the metal disc around his neck. He bore the
body back to the French lines, measured a grave with his
own body, and buried Cristóbal.

The burial party made for a white handkerchief hanging limply from the butt of a rifle stuck by its bayonet in the
mud. Beside it a body lay naked, contorted. A long face,
prominent ears, thin mustache. The number—195522—
proved it. Alan Seeger's presentiment had caught up with
him. For the poet and idealist who had sought glory in life
or death, his end seemed futile and inglorious. They buried
him, as they did everyone else, where he lay. He had already
written his epitaph:

> *I have a rendez-vous with Death*
> *At some disputed barricade,*
> *When Spring comes back with rustling shade*
> *And apple blossoms fill the air—*
>
> *I have a rendez-vous with Death*
> *When Spring brings back blue days and fair . . .*
>
> *And I to my pledged word am true,*
> *I shall not fail that rendez-vous.*

Seeger's picture has an honored place in the Legion
museum, beside that of Cendrars; his poems, the more
poignant for his early death, still remind us of the tragic
hope, the horror of days like Belloy. There they know
Seeger's story. After the war his father searched unsuccess-
fully for his son's body. He ordered a bell for the recon-
structed church at Belloy so that when it tolled the angelus
each evening it would remind people of Alan and the others
who died. The others were many. Of the 2,000 legionnaires
who started across the slope, no more than eight hundred
survived.

*   *   *

A different general, a different river. General Robert
Nivelle had replaced Joffre after the Somme fiasco. He
would try the Marne. The same nauseating trenches, the
same rolling land steaming in the rain. Another village,
hedged around with artillery and machine guns. Auberive,
if the name mattered. Another million men, including the
Legion. But, by April 1917, legionnaires had taken the hint
from Vimy, Navarin, and Belloy. No more shell-fire parades; now they attacked in sections of a dozen men; they
crawled, crept, ran instead of marching in phalanx. The brutal task of seizing the key Bethmann-Hollweg trench fell to
the company commanded by Captain Fernand Maire,
whose father had propped up the dying Colonel Chabrière
before Magenta.

Maire ate, slept, and especially drank the Legion, the
beau idéal of the men. As a boy in Brittany he had run into
an old legionnaire, drunk and singing on the Quiberon
quayside:

> *Quand on a bouffé son pognon*
> *Ou gâché par un coup de cochon*
> *Toute sa carrière*
> *On prend ses godasses sur son dos*
> *Et l'on file au fond d'un paquebot*
> *Aux Légionnaires.**

That, and his father's stories, had hooked him. From
military school, he joined the Legion. He could drink
"earthquakes" (raw white wine spiked with absinthe) until
his senior NCOs sank under the table; when he ran out of
imperatives he cursed the men in a mixture of French and
pidgin Arabic. Where he led, they followed. At dawn, on
April 17, he barged into the great gallery that split the German lines; the Germans clung to every dugout, every blockhouse; the bayonet was king. Finally, Maire and his

---

*When you've blue'd your last tosser
 On the brothel and boozer,
 And you're out on your ear.
 You hump your bundle to the quay,
 Pick up a ship and stow away
 To be a legionnaire.

company stood wallowing in mud and blood, masters of the trench, but facing both ways to hold it against German counterpressure.

With Maire holding the key trench, Colonel James Waddell's battalion leapfrogged toward Auberive. Three days and two nights it took to reach the objective; the men ate their monkey and drank the *pinard* from their water bottles as they marched. With grenade and bayonet, they had to scour each trench. By evening on April 20, Waddell's battalion had entered Auberive and was rounding up hundreds of dazed Germans. In those three days half the regiment and most of its officers had gone.

At dawn on April 21, Adjutant Chief Max Mader and a handful of his men were snatching a few hours rest from what was one of the bloodiest battles of the war. Nothing seemed to stir among the shell holes and the trees, riven by the great barrage that had preceded the attack. Yet when Legionnaire Bengertner peered again he noticed something moving across the valley—a bluish smudge. *"Mon adjutant, kommen Sie vite,"* he called in his legionnaire mixture of French and German. *"Was gibt es?"* Mader hurried from his niche and followed the pointing finger. Two French infantry sections were marching to take over trenches they thought cleared of the enemy. Bengertner swung his arm to something else: a German machine-gun position. Both legionnaires could pick out the gun muzzle swiveling and the NCO indicating the point where the French troops would cross the German line of fire. "They'll wipe them out," Bengertner said.

"Maybe not," Mader grunted.

Legionnaire Bengertner and Adjutant Chief Mader were both Germans who had killed more of their countrymen than most. Bengertner, still a German citizen, had every chance of being shot if captured; Mader would suffer the same fate, though he had become a naturalized Frenchman four years before the war. These men had no qualms about killing Germans. Had they not given their word to the Legion and wasn't that enough? Mader reckoned the German army owed him something.

Twenty years before, Max Emanuel Mader, then eighteen, had been conscripted into a German pioneer corps at

Stuttgart. Awkward and heavy-footed, he became the butt of his NCOs and one drill sergeant in particular. Late one night in 1898 Mader was returning to barracks through a deserted district of Stuttgart. "Ah, Mader, you *Schweinhund*. Why aren't you in barracks?" It was his sergeant. "I'll have your guts for garters tomorrow." The NCO saw the tall private close with him. "Mader, what are you . . .?" Mader had his hands around the sergeant's throat. "It was just too much," he said later. "I got his throat in my grip and . . . well . . . it didn't stand up to the pressure." Mader then made a mistake. He deserted and, at the beginning of 1899, signed on with the Legion. Had he killed the sergeant? Mader believed so, though he never proved it. At any rate the German army had left him with bitter thoughts; now he had a French wife and a small son.

Ten minutes more and the *poilus* would stride into that German trap. Mader surveyed the problem. He could not call on Maire or Waddell; he formed a plan. Back in the trench he detailed fourteen legionnaires to arm themselves with grenades; they slithered along the gallery, which hid them so far; they then doubled across the dead ground on the French side of the machine-gun post and arrived just as the sergeant was siting the French troop. *"Achtung,"* Mader shouted; as the Germans turned, fourteen grenades exploded among them. The French arrived to witness a German adjutant chief interrogating the surviving German in his own language and the style of Stuttgart barracks. The man broke. "There's a 105 battery camouflaged in that quarry two hundred meters away," he babbled.

Mader did not tarry to receive the thanks of the officer whose troops he had saved; he and his legionnaires were soon gazing down on seven heavy guns served by nearly a hundred men. Posting his men at the quarry mouth, he knocked out the guards with grenades. The astonished German gunners heard a bull voice addressing them in their own tongue. "You are prisoners. Thrown down your arms and come out, one by one." Seven guns and nearly a hundred prisoners! Mader had to sew yet another ribbon on his tunic, the coveted symbol of Chevalier of the Legion of Honor. By the end of the year he had been promoted to second lieutenant.

Mader's luck did not hold for the rest of the war. He fought at Verdun and was then thrown into the line to stem the last great German push on Paris. At Amblény Brook, between Compiègne and Villers-Cotteret, a shell burst smashed his right arm and shoulder. He came to in a hospital at Villers-Cotteret to find a Protestant pastor praying over him. "I am Gadolik," he said. A priest confessed him and stood by to give the last rites. But Mader recovered and emerged from the war the most decorated legionnaire ever. Some of the millions of visitors to Versailles might have seen a tall distinguished figure with his right sleeve hanging. Mader finished his days as head guardian of Versailles and kept "open house" for Legion veterans who called to reminisce with him. He lived to see the Germans again invade his adopted country; he never said much after the 1940 Armistice. When senior German officers wished to tour Versailles, the head guardian was always engaged somewhere else. Several times he escaped detection by losing himself in the more remote wings and secret *caches* of Versailles. He died just before the end of the war, in his bed.

On Bastille Day, 1917, a detachment headed by Captain Maire marched past in the military review. President Raymond Poincaré pinned the Military Medal on the Legion banner, the sixth that it bore as the most honored flag in the French army.

"Rope-soles is back," the word ran in the trenches at the beginning of June 1917. Paul Rollet had returned to the regiment he had entered from Saint-Cyr in 1899, the same year as Mader. Reluctant to sit out the war in Morocco, he had transferred to a line regiment in which he served three years. No one who commanded as Rollet did could escape wounds. Within weeks of arriving in France a bad face wound laid him up; he dodged his hospital attendants and on September 6 went back into the front, where he received a second wound in the head. "The bandage is already there," he barked at the ambulance men and stayed at his post. But he hankered for the Legion and became head of the marching regiment. In many ways this scar-faced little man personified the Legion. "Abnegation is the spirit of the legionnaire," he exclaimed. He practiced it himself, in his quaint way, for he liked a drink and the company of women. In everything else, however, he had a Jesuitical approach, believing that the bond between legionnaires was almost monastic.

Rollet might have dropped into the Verdun trenches straight from a Saharan mounted column; he wore its light twill jacket and trousers, and every African legionnaire knew that he had no shirt under his desert tunic; his celluloid cuffs and collar were looped together with elastic—one reason that legionnaires never failed to salute him. They wanted to see what would happen. Usually, when his hand shot up, well beyond his kepi, the left cuff disappeared and his collar climbed up his Adam's apple. His only concession to trench warfare was sometimes to discard his *espadrilles* for shoes. A little monkey of a man, he spring-heeled along the galleries, quizzing men about their welfare and snarling at those who looked sloppy in their turnout. Many a general's eyes popped at Rollet's own bizarre appearance. He spurned the steel helmet, wearing a battered kepi; he carried neither revolver nor cane, but, of all things, a pink parasol. No higher in stature than the top lip of the parapets, the colonel brandished his parasol to rally the legionnaires. A queer fellow, the generals muttered as he paraded before them in rope-soled shoes, blackened by his batman, to receive another step up in the Legion of Honor.

No one questioned his ability or his leadership. In August 1917, Pétain claimed the Legion to help break through at Verdun. Pétain and General John Pershing, commander of the American forces, watched Rollet's men attack on August 20. In the morning twilight Waddell's battalion bounded into the German trench network east of Cumières Wood; the generals heard the legionnaires singing *"La Madelon"* as they turned to strike at the bristling Forges trench and the Ouvrages Blancs. Though both generals had allotted all day to seize those positions, here was the Legion in possession before ten o'clock. "We can't hang around here," Rollet grunted. That night he gained another two miles; the next morning Waddell's battalion had taken Regneville, believed impregnable, and were heading for Forges town. Up came a dispatch rider from divisional headquar-

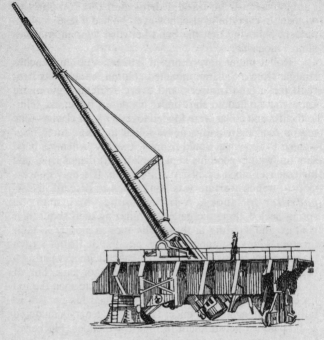

The Paris Gun

ters. "Where are you exactly? Why have you moved beyond your objectives?" Rollet scribbled his reply. "You have given the Legion too limited an objective. It has assigned itself others." Maybe this was why Rollet, born into a military family, had remained a junior officer until the war.

At the end of March 1918 the Germans had cracked the French and British armies on the Somme. From Saint-Gobain plateau, the Kaiser Wilhelm Geschutz, a fantastic 21 cm. gun, mounted on a railway carriage, was shelling Paris, some seventy miles away. Back came the Legion to its nightmare area of Belloy, though this time to staunch the German thrust through Hangard Wood. The Germans had annihilated several thousand men by bombarding the wood with mustard gas, which still dripped from the spring leaves.

On April 25 the Legion attacked with no artillery preparation but the first tanks from a British unit, crude iron monsters that lumbered along at Legion pace. Men and armor felt their way into the wood at dawn. As the acrid, oily odor of the gas hit them, the whole forest shook with flame and fire. Within minutes one battalion had shrunk to a handful of groping men. Rollet came running. Two more battalions tussled hand-to-hand with the Germans. The tanks formed a bloc, keeping the enemy at bay with machine-gun fire while the legionnaires crashed in with the bayonet. By the end of the day eighteen officers and 833 men were killed and wounded. But they had cleared Hangard Wood. Like Belloy, that battle stank a long time in their nostrils. Among the casualties they transported a slight figure with an angular face, Fernando de Quiros.

Before it had made up its losses, the Legion was rushed to Villers-Cotteret, behind Soissons, which had fallen to the Germans. Again Paris was menaced. In that combat the great Mader got his final wound. There, too, Corporal Bottone, of Bologna, achieved something that ranked higher with the Legion than the citations they had received for Hangard and Soissons. Near Amblény, under one of the most terrifying bombardments of the war, Bottone and his section crept into an old mill to take cover.

"I smell flour," Bottone said to his mate.

"Bottone, you've been smelling flour all your life. Why shouldn't you if you're a baker?"

Bottone followed his nose. Twelve sacks of flour lay under the twisted rafters. He and his section ignored the shells landing all around them and temporarily opted out of the war. Humping the sacks to the cellar, Bottone got busy constructing a makeshift oven out of stone blocks and metal sheeting. Within an hour he was singing at the top of his voice, kneading dough in an old zinc washtub. That night, from the mill, hundreds of sticks of warm bread passed from hand to hand along the Legion lines; legionnaires raised their aluminum mess tins to toast Corporal Giovanni Bottone in *pinard*. "That Bottone is worth the Croix at least," one man observed. So they wrote their own citation, awarding the corporal the Croix de la Légion de'Honneur for conspicuous gallantry under enemy fire at the mill of Saint-Baudry.

They had one more ordeal—to drive a wedge through the Hindenburg Line in the Councy and Saint-Gobian forests north of Soissons. On September 2, Major Maire took Terny-Sorny, capturing five hundred prisoners and beating off several counterblows. For thirteen more days they had to keep fighting against Germans who now threw everything at them—shells, bullets, and poison gas. Neuville, Sorny Ravine, Laffaux Plateau, Vauxaillon Tunnel. They were resting, exhausted, when General Mangin sent down the order to take the tunnel. Rollet, who had lived on bread and water for nearly two weeks, grabbed a drummer and several buglers and marched ahead of them as they played the *Boudin*. Red-eyed and barely able to stand, the legionnaires fell in behind Rollet and followed his tripping rope soles. Vauxaillon Tunnel formed one of the keys to the Hindenburg Line. The men stumbled along the cutting, walking through their own and a German barrage to get at the battalion entrenched inside the pitch-black tunnel. Tracer bullets from both sides ricocheted from the tunnel walls and even collided with each other when not stopped by a legionnaire or a German; the air stank of mustard and poison gas, burned powder, and the sickly smell of blood. Few of the battalion that entered the tunnel emerged from the other side. Those who did had cracked their part of the Hindenburg Line.

Vauxaillon was their last battle of the Great War. Of the 44,000 legionnaires who served in those four years, just under 31,000 were killed or reported missing, presumed dead. Of the 8,000 who had formed the hard core of the regiment at the outset, perhaps fewer than fifty survived until November 11. At Château-Salins, Rollet led the Legion in a French army victory parade. Paul Ayres Rockwell, who had enlisted with Seeger, watched them breast the hill and march, with their long desert stride, past the castle and into the Lorraine village. Ayers said, "Colonel Rollet, his breast covered with medals, his sword drawn, rode at the head of the legionnaires. Behind him came the Legion band and the Legion battle flag, which was decorated with the Cross of the Legion of Honor and the War Cross with nine palms and three stars, representing twelve citations in the order of the day—more citations than ever had been won before by any fighting corps . . ."

They were earned then—in blood and guts.

ELEVEN

We have to show the others how,
Even let the Top Brass know
That we're the best
On parade or march-past.
That other bunch, of matelots,
Of riflemen or zouzous!
Everyone's a clot
Beside our lot.

In the last month of the war General Charles Mangin was reviewing Legion units at the front. Stopping before a twisted, wiry captain with a scarred face, he asked, "What were you doing before the war?" The captain answered, "Fighting, *mon général*." Mangin paused. "And what are you counting on doing after the war?" he queried. "Fighting, *mon général*." With what remained of the Legion, Captain Leon Lafitte returned to Morocco to make good the four-year interruption. Arabs, Berbers, Riffians—the Legion now dubbed them all *chleuhs*. Lafitte's private army, which he formed into a guerrilla army, sowed such terror among the *chleuhs* that when they wanted to frighten their children they threatened them with Sidi Lafitte. Berber poets extolled or vilified him. When they eventually killed Captain Lafitte they could not believe it. Major Maire had him buried twice as deep and booby-trapped his coffin with grenades to prevent the *chleuhs* from snatching and destroying his body.

The Legion was back home. Sidi bel-Abbès and Saida

began to fill with new faces. Many were German storm troopers who had fought against the Legion during the war; others were attracted by the growing legend; these included the usual leavening of misfits down on their luck. The legionnaire, bronze face framed in white kepi and loose neckcloth, the desert reflecting in his blue eyes, was becoming the Beau Geste hero. This vogue, which brought novelists like P. C. Wren, and later film makers, to Legion headquarters and outposts, did not much appeal to Colonel Rollet. Invited to see the film *Morocco*, which portrayed legionnaires making love to beautiful women, notably Marlene Dietrich, who then followed them into the desert to help them fight the latest sheik, Rollet grumbled into his fan-shaped beard, "The truth about the Legion is perhaps too simple for the cinema."

No. Morocco was nothing like that. Morocco was a cruel fanatic, Abdel Krim, and a Legion renegade called Klems, the suicidal martyrdom at Mediouna, and the storming of Djebel Badou. Morocco was the poignant story of Legionnaire Geleach and the insouciant heroism of veteran Legionnaire Goulet. Morocco was not Marlene Dietrich, but a military brothel with three native women, which served the hated zouaves and spahis as well. "A one-eyed pro, a bald one, and a lame one—take your pick." But Rollet might equally have contended that the Legion could outdo even the Hollywood scriptwriter. What would he have made of the day Rollet was inspecting a bunch of new recruits at Saida?

"Nationality?"

"Russian, *mon colonel*."

"Profession?"

"Lieutenant, *mon colonel*."

To the next man: "Nationality?"

"Russian."

"Profession?"

"Major, *mon colonel*."

Rollet glared and turned to the next man. "Nationality, you twister?"

"Russian, *mon colonel*."

"And what were you, scoundrel?"

"General, *mon colonel*."

"Eh! *Non!*" roared Rollet.

"*Oui, mon colonel,*" said the legionnaire. "And these men—they were my general staff." No one had told Rollet that General Wrangel's Cossacks had arrived after the defeat of the White Army by the Red Army. These men formed a squadron of cavalry that outshone the Arabs in horsemanship and played a major part in the pacification of Morocco.

Four years after the war, perhaps the most romantic legionnaire of them all arrived at Sidi bel-Abbès. Prince Christian Aage had spent two years in France with an infantry regiment, but still dreamed of the Legion and avenging the death of Lieutenant Selchauhansen. In 1922 the bank that handled his fortune crashed. "The dirtiest joke that can happen to a man—his bank going bankrupt," he said. Aage admitted, though, that it was a providential act, which firmed his resolve to join the Legion. He packed his wife and seven-year-old son off to Italy and went to see André Maginot, the French war minister. "I'd like to join the Legion," he said. "We shall consider it an honor, Your Highness," said Maginot.

His first night out to sea, between Marseilles and Casablanca, Aage found himself sitting opposite a captain at the dining table. He noted the seven-flamed Legion grenade on the man's lapels, the empty left sleeve pinned to his tunic. The captain ignored the big man in civilian clothing; his whole being was engrossed in snorting, worrying, and guzzling at a piece of mullet that he dissected with great sweeps of his fork and shoveled into his scarred mouth. Suddenly his face suffused, his shoulders convulsed, a hand clutched at his throat. Aage sprang to thump his back, putting his full weight behind the blows. The offending mullet bone ejected like a spent shell. "*Assez, assez,*" cried the captain. "*Que voulez-vous faire—me tuer?*" Grudgingly, he accepted a drink from Aage. "Who are you?" he asked when they reached the bar.

"Prince Aage of Denmark."

"I don't give a damn about titles."

"But I'm going to join your regiment at Meknes."

"Go to hell as far as I'm concerned."

"But I'd like to see you in the Legion."

"Why? I'm no friend of yours." And he stumped off, puce-faced and growling about what they were letting into the Legion these days. In Casablanca harbor he approached the Dane. "Now I can tell you who *I* am." A raucous whisper reached Aage's ear. "I'm the son of a well-known man."

"Ah!"

"I'm a Russian."

"Ah!"

The captain whispered his name. "Maxim Gorki." He muttered a good-bye and disappeared. It was Pechkoff, who had rejoined after the war and was one of the Legion heroes. No one noticed his empty sleeve; it made no difference to the Legion or to his ability; when mounting a horse, he gripped the reins between his teeth and vaulted into the saddle. He could handle a rifle, revolver, or sword as well as anyone.

Aage went on to Meknes. He and the Legion suited each other like champagne and caviar. Legionnaires fascinated him. Monks of the great adventure, he christened them. He considered their courage as something mythical that these men constructed around their strange personalities. Only one thing terrified them—the past they had fled to take refuge in the Legion. "An officer knows inside a week if he clicks or doesn't click in the Legion," Major Maire once said. Aage clicked. Tall, blond, blue-eyed, he was the most handsome officer in the Legion. The men felt proud to have a pure blue blood commanding them; someone with innumerable cousins among European royalty, including King George V of England; someone whom princes and film stars visited in his spartan rooms at Bel-Abbés, but who treated them as equals. He could drink champagne or *pinard* like a camel, then sit in as a drummer in the Café de France band at Ksar es-Souk. One night a Legion patrol arrived at this restaurant to find the prince, shirt-sleeved, fighting a bearded colossus of a sapper from a mounted company. The MPs wanted to pursue the legionnaire who had vanished. "No, it was a fair fight," Aage said. His legend grew.

Aage moved out of Rabat with the columns that were subduing the Berbers of the Middle Atlas. Lyautey's "lobster-shell" occupation force had not only kept Morocco quiet but had extended French territory. Tribes in four sectors had, however, risen during the war. Armed, financed, and advised by the Germans, the Riff and Djebaba tribes raided first across the Spanish border, then spread their insurrection to Marrakesh and other parts of French Morocco. Aage went as liaison officer with the Second Regiment.

On June 24, 1923, Berbers trapped Aage's battalion in the El Mers gorges. Pinned all day in a fiery ravine, the battalion lost eighteen officers and 250 legionnaires before help arrived. Aage had to identify the dead and inform their next of kin. He noticed two bodies: a young Legion subaltern lying on top of an old veteran who had been carrying him to safety when struck down. As he sifted through their personal papers that night he discerned a strong resemblance in the photographs both men had. The same woman, though twenty-five years older in the subaltern's photo. He studied the snapshots through a magnifying glass. Incredible! From the papers both men came from Brussels. The older man, Jean Vandenbrock, had enlisted twenty-five years before the officer. Aage pieced the story together. Vandenbrock had been engaged to the young officer's mother, Marie Mollenbeck; they quarreled and he joined the Legion, unaware that Marie was bearing his child. Knowing nothing of Vandenbrock, his son also enlisted in the Legion. Fate brought them together in the same company; the old man had tried to rescue his son from the El Mers ambush. It read like a bad film script, Aage felt when he had confirmed the details. They'd never lend it a moment's credence in Hollywood.

The next month, on the same campaign at Bou Afa, Aage witnessed a demonstration of the sort of courage he maintained legionnaires invented for themselves. They brought a gray-haired old campaigner into the crude field ambulance with a smashed leg that had to be amputated. The proud old legionnaire refused an anesthetic and lay without a word or a wince while they cut off his leg. Watching this, Aage nearly passed out. "Anything you'd like?" he asked the old man. "I'd like a quart of *pinard, mon capitaine*." Aage poured him two quarts and was pouring a third when the old die-hard fell back, dead.

By the end of 1923, Lyautey had pacified most of Morocco. Across the border the Riffian chief, Abdel Krim, had defeated the Spaniards but had not yet dared attack the French side. The Legion built and garrisoned outposts; its mule columns patrolled between these and escorted camel trains to those not linked by roads. In those forts in the bare mountains of Morocco and Algeria the toughest of men wilted. The drugging heat alternating with intense cold, the monotony and futility of barrack life, the isolation, the lack of books and newspapers, the absence of even the military brothel with its native whores—all this provided ideal breeding conditions for the *cafard*.

The tiny cockroach would insinuate itself into the brain and begin its fatal monologue. "You ran away from life to this? You wanted to be a gladiator, a romantic hero knocking over sheiks and women. What are you? A prisoner in a white jail of your own making, a galley slave breaking rocks for half a pint of *pinard* a day!" The *cafard* has a literature as long as the common cold and baldness, and almost as illuminating. George d'Esparbès, the nineteenth-century French author, listed it as the fourth Legion killer. The three others? Drink, malaria, and syphilis. Bullets ranked a poor fifth. *Pinard* and *cafard* were boon companions, according to d'Esparbès. "When it's on him [*cafard*] the legionnaire will sell his cummerbund, his bayonet, his rifle. Before he's marched off to the cells, he grumbles, 'I could have got fifteen francs instead of ten sous.'" Studying such legionnaires, psychiatrists divided into two camps. Dr. Albert Maire, who ran an asylum for court-martial offenders, reckoned that men joined because they were alienated; the Legion did nothing to alienate them. Italian psychiatrists contended that the legionnaire was a throwback to primitive man, for whom fighting came as naturally as eating and sleeping. "The brutalities of a continual and merciless war suits them and is even so essential that the well-being of barrack life in peacetime is unbearable," an Italian psychiatrist wrote. Though this medical verdict may be difficult to sustantiate, the *cafard* does seem a peacetime bug, and treatment consists of giving a man a rifle and the occasion to use it.

A Legion commander, Colonel George de Villebois-Mareuil, summed up the typical legionnaire: "The legionnaire lives in a dream. What sort of dream? He would find it hard to explain that even to himself. But it is to this obsessional dream that he attributes his misfortunes. He calls his dream *le cafard*. If he is asked the reason for some outburst he will give no other reply. It is always *le cafard*. The word means a great deal. It is not surprising that hazy memories of the past that may have been in sharp contrast with his present circumstances should sometimes overcome his better judgment. His life is abnormal, and by that token he does not willingly accept the monotony and commonplace routine of the present for what it is. His instinct is to dramatize everything, to weave legends around his life. He atones for the dullness of his surrounding conditions by indulging his imagination—so much so that, in the end, he comes to believe in his own fantasies."

Erwin Carle, a German legionnaire who spent long months in Saharan outposts, describes his own *coup de cafard*: "The Foreign Legion *cafard*, a near relative of tropical madness, is a collective name for all the inconceivable stupidities, excesses, and crimes that tortured nerves can commit. The English language has no word for this condition. In *cafard* murder hides, and suicide and mutiny; it means self mutilation and planless flight out into the desert; it is the height of madness and the depth of despair. I, myself, lived in a continual state of irritation. The least trifle put me in such a rage that I can hardly credit it today. My vexation, my irritation, my brooding was the madness of the Legion. No legionnaire escapes from it." Carle watched legionnaires spilling blood over the half pint of wine allotted to them each day; over crusts of bread; over bits of boot polish; over the fatigues they had to do. "It was really strange how many legionnaires had a screw loose, often only harmless peculiarities, but which could increase to madness. . . . The *cafard* is at its worst in the hot season when the sun burns down relentlessly from the cloudless, deep blue sky, with the strange greenish coloring peculiar to the horizon. Then the Foreign Legion barrack yard lies deserted. It is so hot that stones on the yellow, clayey soil seem to move in the glimmering, overheated air. Then, in the infernal heat, the *cafard* has often been the cause of great disaster. . . ."

The tiny bug can whisper, "Why go on breaking your

back? In this mob you die sooner or later. Why not sooner? You have a rifle, a bayonet, a length of cord." The Legion makes no play with its suicide figures, but they are high among young recruits and old-timers. The homesick young German hears his comrades singing "Anne Marie," he goes to the barrack room, takes his rifle . . . Soon after he joined, Second Lieutenant Pierre Sergent had a suicide in his company. A young legionnaire had hanged himself from a hook on the wall. Sergent raged when the men refused to reveal what they had done with the rope. Finally, an old sweat whispered, "*Mon lieutenant,* it is useless to go on searching. The legionnaires have cut it into small pieces and shared it. The rope which a man used to hang himself . . . that's lucky."

The *cafard* never ran short of ideas, some of them ingenious. No Legion doctor could ever accept a physical symptom at its face value. A yellow face might mean jaundice or that a legionnaire had eaten pomegranate skin marinated in milk or coffee. Conjunctivitis? A castor-oil bean fragment placed under the eyelid could provoke it. Fever? The trick was to soak tobacco in quinine and smoke it. Abscess? Dental tartar rubbed into a cut or a hair drawn through the skin with a needle. Major Maire took two weeks to detect perhaps the most diabolical dodge. A man reported sick with a vicious dog bite in the leg. Rabies? queried the doctor, and sent him to the new Pasteur Institute in Algiers. In the next fortnight the MO referred half a dozen men to Algiers with similar bites. Maire grew suspicious. He discovered that the first legionnaire had picked up the head of a dead dog, equipped it with a strong spring, and "bitten" himself. Now he had gone into business, "biting" any legionnaire for the price of four liters of *pinard* so that they could enjoy a week in Algiers.

An infective parasite, too, the *cafard.* Sometimes striking a whole battalion. In the early 1920s, Maire had 106 men desert in a body to Spanish Morocco. He devised a rough-and-ready solution. Summoning friendly Berber chieftains, he addressed them before his battalion. "For every deserter you bring back to me, twenty francs for you. If you bring me his head—a hundred francs." It stopped the epidemic.

For its three capital offenses—treason, desertion before the enemy, and murder—the Legion has rarely exacted the death penalty. Indeed, it expects desertions in the first six months of service, the make-or-break period. A legionnaire signs his contract and, from that moment, starts from scratch. In some ways his treatment resembles shock therapy. He marches out of Fort Saint-Nicolas, the grim fortress reception center in Marseilles, clad in ill-fitting fatigue clothes, a denim cap, and somebody else's old boots. Even tramps look better before they join. The men are packed into the ship's hold like animals, then into cattle trucks from Oran to Bel-Abbès. At the depot an endless round of fatigues and a heavy-fisted German NCO complete their humiliation. Only when they have reached rock bottom can they expect to become legionnaires, with the dubious privilege of marching up to forty miles a day humping an eighty-pound pack. At this stage, when a man is recovering his self-esteem and discipline has toughened his body and mind, he is tempted to desert. Invariably caught and brought back, he fears the worst and is astounded when the colonel hands him a month in the cells. Officers bend the rules to give recruits the benefit of the doubt. But if they try again . . .

Adolphe Cooper, an Englishman, knew what a second, unsuccessful desertion and Legion discipline meant. Cooper did two stints with the Legion, wrote two books about his adventures, and left with a colorful service sheet. He enlisted as a boy of fifteen, giving a false age, and fought in the dreaded Kereviz Dere ravine in Gallipoli in May 1915. Just after that combat, in which he won the Croix de Guerre, he had his first experience of Legion methods. On May 3, Lieutenant Falcon paraded the company. "Slowly he came to where I was standing with an Algerian Arab called Mahmoud on my right. When he reached Mahmoud, I saw that the lieutenant was holding a revolver behind his back. With ice-cold deliberation, he pointed the gun at Mahmoud's forehead and shot him dead." He said that Mahmoud had hidden during that day's action; anyone who did likewise would be executed.

Reclaimed by his family as too young for service, Cooper returned after the war for a second spell with a

mounted company; he began to learn the ways of legionnaires. "In the Legion it is up to his comrades to cure a man
of any tendency to fear. If, when he is first under fire or
sees a man die beside him, he shows signs of breaking up,
instead of sympathy he gets a hiding and has such a bad
time that he realizes death is better than the life of a coward
in the Legion. Then he develops the courage of desperation.
Most legionnaires have nothing to lose and life itself is not
held very dear. Then, too, there is the tradition which is so
strong that a man cannot be for long in the Foreign Legion
without wanting, like his comrades, to do better than the
soldiers of any other regiment."

Cooper says that he saw more than one legionnaire
shot in the back by so-called comrades, usually to resolve a
homosexual squabble. Legionnaires normally preferred
women, but since even the military brothels did not visit remote outposts, many resorted to homosexuality. "The
warped relationship started innocently enough—a man
sharing his cigarettes, water, or food with the most effemi-
nate legionnaire he could find. Gradually the friendship became something different and the man looked on the victim
as his own property." Another legionnaire, Walter Kanitz,
claimed that homosexual practice was widespread. "It is
easy to see that the Legion makes an ideal breeding ground
for abnormal sex behavior. The environment of a legionnaire, the circumstances surrounding him, are such that a
normal man's resistance to homosexual activity is easily
broken down. The fact that for years he has to live in close
proximity to scores of men of low moral standards only fa-
cilitates and speeds up the process." On the other hand,
Bennet J. Doty, an American who fought the Druses in
Syria in the 1920s, found nothing strange in the camaraderie of his company. Barrackroom rascals and ruffians
were transformed into patient and devoted fighting men
when a battle began. After the combat of Rezzas, in which
he won the military medal, Doty was finishing his evening
soupe. "Sylvestre Budney, the young Pole who was a *bleu*
[rookie] in my squad, came to me. Brixey, who had been
killed that day, had been his *copain*, his buddy. 'Will you
be my *copain* now?' he asked like a schoolboy, and I said I
would be his *copain*. This is a serious relation in the Le-

gion; with your *copain* you share your cigarettes, the contents of your *bidon* [water bottle], or your *musette* [knapsack], everything you have; you stay side-by-side in the fight; you give up your life if it is needed to help him; he is your brother."

The Legion treated Cooper's first desertion attempt with its usual tolerance; but after his second bid he rode his mule, Aisha, to Colomb-Béchar and the penal battalion, where the more truculent types were "reformed." A tented penitentiary, its only walls were hundreds of miles of shimmering desert or savage mountains where Arab bounty hunters knew the latest value of a head. They had Arab guards who shot when in doubt; when they had no reason to shoot, they and the Legion NCOs used the whip and rifle butt. Desperate prisoners often broke and ran to invite the bullet that would end their torture. A man did four months at Colomb-Béchar, but many untameables had endured years in the brickworks and quarries because prison terms for offenses committed in the penal battalion did not count.

On arrival the legionnaire received a set of filthy denims and old boots without laces. Until the denims had been scrubbed white, he got no food. Within the camp boundaries he double-marched bare-footed across blistering sand, carrying his boots in the left hand and raising his right arm in a perpetual salute. A whistle governed their day; before dawn it blew reveille; it shrilled their half hour of physical training; it summoned them at nine o'clock to the brick factory and quarry; it ended this purgatory at 7:30 P.M. In heat rising to 130° F. in the shade, they had to mold 1,000 bricks a day—three times normal output—or quarry stone with sledgehammer and chisel. Those who made 999 bricks went without food that night. These slaves, with shaven skulls and sun-blackened bodies, must learn humility before being accorded the honor of rejoining their units. Crude military psychology demanded that they atone by sheer physical effort as a monk might purge his soul by fasting and prayer. "The Legion is a moral paradise but a physical hell," one colonel asserted. At Colomb-Béchar they had refined the tortures of hell to teach men that they mattered less than the bricks they fashioned, the stones they quarried. The rebel would gouge a huge hole in the sand for days until his NCO deemed it deep enough to fill in. The man's muscle and sweat and being were less than that sand. Others carried and stacked hundred-pound boulders for weeks, then shouldered them back to their original spot. It tamed most men, though one performed his duty, then spat in a guard's face and kept on spitting. Why? "If they ever release me from here, I'll kill the first NCO I meet," he snarled. Prisoners released from the penal battalion had changed. Improved or broken? The Legion contends they came back better soldiers.

Cooper agrees with them and he experienced more than his share of trouble. One day, returning from the brick-work, Cooper spotted a sergeant who had dropped a ciga-rette on the ground. He was stooping to retrieve it when the whip lashed out; as a reflex, Cooper clenched his fist. With-out having struck the guard, he got fifteen days' imprison-ment. "At that time there were no cells in Colomb-Béchar and, when a man was ordered to prison, a hole like a grave was dug in the ground and in this he had to lie on his back, with a small piece of canvas stretched over him, and the man in charge generally arranged the canvas so that his head was unprotected from the blazing sun."

The first day he had bread and water; the second, noth-ing. "The third day I was starving and parched with thirst. A man told me that he would get me something really nice to eat so that I thought he was taking my part and was really going to do me a good turn. He brought me a mess tin of *soupe*. I could see the grease on top and pieces of meat floating in it; it looked good and I sat up in my 'grave' and seized it ravenously while he smiled benignly. I took a great gulp and nearly choked; it was pure brine, so salted that I could hardly swallow it, but I was too hungry not to eat it all. Then began the torment of an intolerable thirst. I begged the sentry for some water. The man came and said the pipes had burst and I should have to wait." Thirst-maddened, Cooper struck the guard, who knocked him unconscious with his rifle butt. When he came to, Cooper found his hands were bound behind his back and tied to his ankles. The *crapaudine*. Men trussed and left lying in the sun like a toad (after whom the torture was nicknamed) suffered agony; their joints locked, their muscles went into spasms, and many were gagged to stifle their screams. Some lost their reason. Cooper survived those hours in the sun, though racked with pain and his mind wobbling.

His punishment ended, he appeared before the commanding officer of the penal battalion, Captain Edouard Salomon. This officer had done two years in Tonkin as an NCO before being commissioned at the start of the Great War. Cooper knew him for a hard man who lived like an ascetic and never accepted even a day's leave. It was this man who "converted" Cooper. "He really talked to me as a father might to a son. The whole change in my later service came from that conversation with him." Cooper never returned to Colomb-Béchar, though many of the more incorrigible characters did. The Legion never despaired of reforming them and never seems to have thought of discharging the most hardened offenders. As one legionnaire remarked, "Getting bounced from the Legion? They don't bounce people from hell."

Paul Rollet had an instinctive psychological insight into the legionnaire mentality. In 1925, when he arrived from Morocco to take over Sidi bel-Abbès, he quick-marched his battalion commanders around the great barracks. He looked askance at the numerous office staff. "Any of these legionnaires been in Morocco?" he asked. He broke his tripping step at the new cinema, then the library, where several men sat reading. "Morocco?" he queried again. He put the same question to gardeners, musicians, veterans, everyone he met. He finally halted at the canteen, where they were serving coffee, hot chocolate, tea, and had a counterful of sweets. Rollet's blue eyes glared their disbelief. "Legionnaires spending their pay on chocolates and tea," he growled. Within a week the scribes and the gardeners, the library staff, and the musicians had formed another Legion battalion in the Morocco campaign.

Rollet realized that extraordinary men demanded extraordinary methods. His mercenaries fought neither for country nor causes nor the scanty pay; they considered themselves a race apart. And he noticed that, the moment a legionnaire lost the feeling of living on the outer fringes of society, he seemed also to lose his strength, his human value, and his borrowed identity. A Legion like every other

French army unit would no longer believe in its own myth. More than any other, Rollet fostered that myth. Every legionnaire should have Camerone engraved on his heart and mind; under Rollet that ceremony became something between a saint's day and a drunken revel. He built up the museum, which every legionnaire had to visit and study. The music, too. He transformed the Legion *clique* into one of the finest regimental bands in any army. The *Boudin* would be the Legion hymn and only to the *Boudin* would the Legion march in review—out of step with the rest of the French army. If Rollet disliked books like *Beau Geste* and *The Legion of the Damned*, he detested the horror tales that the press, especially in Germany, printed about his Legion. "We're not choir boys—neither are we criminals," he said. To those who reproached his men for drunkenness, he replied, "Maybe this halt is their last. If they go a bit far, who's to blame them for it?" This colonel never imprisoned a man for being drunk, but if he failed to perform his duties the next day he went to the cells with his pay docked. Rollet often personally escorted drunken legionnaires back to Bel-Abbès barracks and saw them past the guardroom. But they had to appear—fit—at reveille the next morning.

He would go to unusual lengths to keep his men out of trouble. In October 1924 an elderly Danish woman journalist appeared at Rabat to do a legion-of-the-damned report. "I wish to see Prince Awghie," she said, giving the Danish pronunciation. "Doesn't live here, ma'am," said the guard commander. "She means Aahzh," somebody said. On her way she spotted a makeshift jail with several Danes among the prisoners. Aage decided to let Rollet handle her.

"Aren't you ashamed of keeping people in such a cage?" she demanded.

"We have some headstrong types here, madam, and they have to see reason," Rollet replied.

"Listen to me—they are Danes and the Danes are honest people."

"I know some that are scoundrels," said the colonel.

To prove Rollet wrong she invited thirty Danish legionnaires to dinner in a luxury hotel. From the bar Prince Aage observed developments. The dinner began quietly; when the row filtered through to the bar, Aage did nothing;

when mirrors shattered and chairs and tables splintered, Aage still did not budge. Then he heard the scream of the Danish woman. When he ran to rescue her the honest Danes had stretched her on the table and were ripping off her dress, shoes, and stockings. She was pop-eyed with fear and was screaming weakly in Danish. "You see," said Aage, blandly. "Colonel Rollet did warn you. Have these scoundrels done you any harm?"

"No, Your Highness, not yet, not yet." Back she fled to Denmark. Who would dare have suggested that Rollet planned the operation and handed its execution to his battalion commander, Aage?

TWELVE

The city sleeps beneath an orange moon;
I have a rendezvous with my loved one.
But the Legion's on the way,
Yes, on the way,
To the fray, the fray.
No need to fear, Jeannine,
We shall surely meet again.

Legionnaires in their outposts on the Spanish Morocco border knew that sooner or later Abdel Krim would attack. In 1921 they had opened their gates to the few thousand soldiers who had escaped torture and massacre when the Riffians smashed the Spanish army. They heard at firsthand how the tubby, black-bearded messiah and his Beni-Ouriaghel tribesmen had descended on Anual and slaughtered the garrison; how the Spanish commander, General Sylvestre, had committed suicide. Of his army of 19,000, only 3,000 survived. Three years later the Spaniards had to fall back on Tetuan, leaving thousands more dead and almost the whole country to the Riffians. Lyautey's stealthy occupation of the northern fringes of French Morocco was already rousing tribes who had sworn allegiance to Abdel Krim. In the spring of 1925 the Riffians invaded French Morocco, bursting into the Taza Corridor, held by the Legion. By June, Abdel Krim was threatening Fez and French rule in Morocco. The Legion mobilized most of its 25,000 men to repel the invasion.

At this moment, while his battalion was preparing to

meet the menace of Abdel Krim, Legionnaire Goulet inherited a fortune.

Goulet's battalion had halted in the small township of Le Kreider; in no time the battalion and the town buzzed with the news. When it reached his ears, the company commander, Zinovi Pechkoff, smelled trouble. He knew Goulet. One of the oldest legionnaires, his service sheet stretched on, recording the promotions, demotions, and punishments—all because of his thirst. He had been a sergeant under Captain Rollet at Fez in 1911, and corporal a dozen times over. Goulet sober was worth half a dozen men. A sick bugler and Goulet blew reveille and lights-out; a dead mason and Goulet could build a plumb wall; a cook or mule driver shot, why, Goulet could make the *soupe* or handle a mule. Goulet drunk was a scourge. When his latest binge had landed him in trouble, he would appear before Pechkoff with a penitent face and the invariable excuse. "It's like this, *mon capitaine*. My old man was a soak and the old lady hit the bottle, too. So, what chance do you think I had?" Somehow, with Goulet, those phrases always touched the heart.

Now he was rich, they said. In fact Goulet had inherited 4,000 francs from a parent who had died. Not a vast sum, but more than a legionnaire, second-class, could translate into *pinard* or absinthe. It set Goulet's head spinning. Flashing his solicitor's letter, he "touched" barrack mates and brothel owners, Arab, Jew, and Gentile, on the strength of his fortune. After he and his comrades had been drunk for a week, the creditors demanded their money. "You're having us on, Goulet . . . there's no inheritance," they said. What did Goulet care? He was enjoying himself. He kept his own doubts quiet and promised them interest—on the next loan.

Goulet's bequest had become a hollow joke when at last the money arrived, the night before the battalion had to depart for Morocco. With the 4,000 francs on his desk, Pechkoff summoned the old legionnaire. "If I give you this money I don't want every legionnaire in the company drunk on the march tomorrow," Pechkoff said. "There'll be no trouble, *mon capitaine*," Goulet promised. A dubious Pechkoff handed over the wad of notes. Goulet's hands trembled so violently that he let them scatter all over the floor.

That evening the company sergeant major brought sixty passes for Pechkoff to sign. "What's this? There's no cinema show touring the town," said Pechkoff. "It's *Monsieur* Goulet," the sergeant major said sarcastically. "He's giving a banquet."

"Where?" asked Pechkoff, wondering how anybody could hold a banquet in Le Kreider.

"Chez Madame Jeannot—the widow who keeps a small restaurant." This lady had won the tussle with the canteen girls for the honor of preparing Goulet's fete and abstracting some or all of his riches. "I wouldn't sign those passes, *mon capitaine*." Pechkoff signed. Had not Goulet given his word? Just the same, he detailed a sergeant, two corporals, and twenty legionnaires to make sure that Goulet remembered his promise.

That night a huge charabanc, decorated with streamers, rattled along the Morocco road. "The Battle Wagon of the Real Legionnaires," proclaimed one banner. "The True Sons of France," read another. Such a banquet no legionnaire could ever remember or hope to enjoy again. Champagne by the case, *pinard*, brandy, absinthe—every kind of liquor flowed for five hours. The hungry ones had food, too. But Goulet held to his bargain. At midnight everything was calm. The next morning he presented himself to Pechkoff with the residue of his estate—1,000 francs—and an address to which it should be sent if anything happened to him in Morocco.

They joined the long Legion columns trekking into Morocco. In his book *In Morocco with the Legion*, journalist G. Ward Price describes how they looked. "Some of the companies of the Legion that I passed on the march in the valleys of the Grand Atlas looked like a procession of souls in purgatory. Under a sun that was registering 105 degrees Fahrenheit in the shade, they were plowing along through sand six inches deep, their feet sinking into it at every step. Passing motor lorries and mule convoys kept them smothered in a permanent cloud of fine dust, the kind that inflames the eyes, parches the throat, shrivels the tongue, and cracks the lips. . . . With haggard faces they plodded on, the streaming sweat clogging the dust on their cheeks into a mask of mud, an eighty-pound pack on their backs, containing blanket, tent section, food and entrenching tool, with rifle, bayonet, sixty rounds of ammunition, water bottle, and sometimes a haversack full of bombs as well." For all the change eighty years had wrought in the Legion, it could have been Constantine or Miliana, Abd el-Kader instead of Abdel Krim. Legionnaires still had the same acquisitive hand, picking desert villages locust-clean, the same unkempt beards hiding the same type of face, the same harsh discipline that meant roping stragglers to a mule.

This time, however, they were fighting a modern army. Abdel Krim had mustered an estimated 100,000 Riffians. He had captured heavy guns, rifles, ammunition, and supplies from the Spaniards, and he had European advisers. The Riffian leader had observed that torture had sown panic among the Spaniards; he and his tribesmen had no compunction about inflicting atrocities on the infidels before butchering them. A favorite trick was to flay prisoners alive, or burn off their skin with lighted torches.

In the Taza Corridor, east of Fez, the Riffians had destroyed or seized most of the sixty-six Legion blockhouses. Lyautey had to recover Taza, a vital link between Algeria and the main Moroccan cities. The Legion was determined to win back its forts and avenge comrades who had died under torture. Against well-armed cavalry its mission was not easy. Pechkoff's battalion ran into several thousand Riffians at Moulnay ain-Djenane and only just levered itself free of the ambush.

At Astar, a bare peak straddled by a Legion fortress, the Riffians had massacred the garrison. They had to reconquer it to protect the mobile group in the valley. For two hours Pechkoff's company slogged upward under fire. Lieutenant Jean Guyon dashed forward, driving the tribesmen out of the fort. Hundreds more were swarming out of the hills, but they had to hold on. Legionnaire Goulet (How had that old man made the climb?) sat at a loophole, pipe in mouth, blasting away at every brown burnoose. Pechkoff's battalion runner had been killed. Who to replace him? Goulet, of course. For thirty hours the veteran marched through the Riffian fusillade. Not content with carrying messages, he staggered up the hill with boxes of ammunition. Finally, Pechkoff could pull his men back. Among the last came Goulet, still battling. In the face of such nonchalance what could Pechkoff do but propose the old soak for a medal?

In the second week of June, Pechkoff's battalion lay before Mediouna, at the foot of the triangular Djebel Khail. From Gar-Mezziat they could pick out the white oblong shape of the fort; from time to time a heliograph flickered. "We cannot hold out much longer." For weeks a French lieutenant and twenty Senegalese riflemen had resisted a Riffian army that had seized half the fort and was besieging the other half. Twice Pechkoff's battalion had attempted to punch a hole through to the defenders, but had had to retire with heavy casualties. The tribesmen had dug two trench lines, one facing the fort, the other to ward off relief forces. "No water left," the flashing mirror spelled out. "We blow up ourselves and the post tomorrow." Lieutenant Jean Guyon approached the battalion commander. "Give me forty volunteers," he said. "I'll get them out." Guyon had come up from the ranks, winning six citations in France and two in Morocco. A week before, he had displayed great courage at Astar. Reluctantly the battalion commander said yes.

A message dropped from a plane told the garrison of the operation. Guyon issued his orders. Each man would take a rifle, grenades, and dynamite to blow up the post when they had saved the garrison. They would creep through the Riffian lines at eleven o'clock that night; the battalion would cross the Ouergha ford to decoy the enemy. The suicide mission was secret, but soon the whole battalion was discussing it; within an hour they had double the number of volunteers. First came Guyon's friend Lieutenant Jean-Baptiste Fain, a Saint-Cyrian who had joined the Legion four months before. "Why him and not me?" legionnaires complained to their officers. A young private handed Pechkoff his pay. "I'm a drunk—I'll be useless if I buy wine. . . . I know you'll need me tonight and I don't want to be able to drink."

Just before Guyon left, two more officers slipped into the detachment—lieutenants Wable and Beulaygue. The

moment the men had disappeared the battalion crossed the
ford and waited in the darkness. At midnight they saw pin-
pricks of light like fireflies and heard the muffled bang of
grenades; at eight kilometers they could not guess what was
happening; they stayed on alert all that night. At sunup they
peered at the fort. Nothing appeared to have changed.
Someone shouted, *"Il y en a trois qui reviennent."* Sure
enough, three men were picking their way through the
ravine. Only the NCO, Sergeant Victorowski, had any co-
herent idea of what had befallen the four officers and thirty-
seven men the previous night.

Guyon's group had stalked and killed several sentries.
Two trenches still separated them from the fort. They had to
grenade them, but those explosions brought the whole
mountain down on them. "As we approached the post, hundreds of burnoosed warriors opened fire on us," said the
sergeant. "Tossing grenades, firing and bayoneting, we tried
to smash through and into the post. . . . Ten of us managed
to get in. . . . I saw the lieutenant who commanded the post.
He said, 'I've mined the post and it will go up in several
minutes. There's nothing for it but to get out.' I saw one
lieutenant heaving grenades furiously right and left. Another
was fighting with the bayonet against twenty men who
wanted to take him alive. Several of us had fired our last
shots and were using the bayonet. I noticed eight or ten men
tussling with knives against a terrible crowd. We were fighting on the edge of a ravine. I couldn't see the ground and
fell into the ravine. I waited there several seconds and fled."

A spahi squad galloped down to the fort, but came
back shaking their heads. More than 150 Riffians were lying
dead. Of Guyon and his sacrifice mission, nothing.

Guyon's aged parents wrote to Colonel Rollet. His father said, "I know the pious custom, honored in the Legion,
to glorify the memory of heroes fallen for France. My son
was among the bravest, and the six citations he received on
the French front during the war exalted his courage, his
bravery, and his audacity. We are two old people who no
longer have a son and we weep for him, but we are proud of
him."

On June 12, a few days after Mediouna, Marshal
Lyautey arrived to share the Legion's grief. With him came

the French premier, Paul Painlevé, who decorated the pennant of the Sixth Battalion with the Croix de Guerre and palm. He then strode over to Legionnaire Goulet to pin the military medal on his chest for gallantry at Astar. Limping after him, leaning on his stick, Lyautey solemnly took off his right glove and shook Goulet by the hand.

"*Mon vieux*, how long have you been serving?"

"Nineteen years, *Monsieur le Maréchal*."

"Nineteen! And are you going on?"

"Of course, *Monsieur le Maréchal*. Right to the end. To the death."

"Fine. Now you'll come and see me presently."

Goulet duly presented himself at Lyautey's tent to rub shoulders with the prime minister and half a dozen generals. Lyautey sat him down, poured him a cup of coffee with his own hand, then clinked to his continuing health.

But it was more than an old legionnaire could stand inside several weeks. Inheriting a fortune, then having Papa Lyautey himself pouring his "juice." Goulet swallowed great draughts of *pinard*, brandy, and native gin offered by comrades who urged him to recount his meeting with the marshal and the prime minister. By the end of the evening he was so drunk that he could not carry Pechkoff's orders or remember much of his greatest day. Within a week Goulet had reverted to type. ("*Mon capitaine*, I'm a soak, like the old man and the old lady. Can you blame me?") Finally they had to ship him into a hospital to be dried out.

That day was Lyautey's private farewell to the Legion. A few weeks later the marshal, who had made Morocco the showplace of North Africa, left for France. He had witnessed the arrival of Marshal Pétain, the hero of Verdun, with an army of 160,000. France and Pétain held contrary ideas to the marshal's about pacifying Morocco; Lyautey saw many of his concepts spurned, and resigned. Only the British saluted the old man as his ship passed through the Straits of Gibraltar; the French prepared no official welcome in Marseilles. The man whose motto was Shelley's— "The soul's joy lies in doing"—lived out the last nine years of his life in Lorraine as a recluse.

*   *   *

No one gave Abdel Krim much chance against Pétain's big battalions. But the Riffian leader proved an enterprising general and French officers noted with amazement how well he was using captured Spanish artillery. Legionnaires might have enlightened them. Serving as one of Abdel Krim's chiefs of staff was their most famous deserter—Sergeant Joseph Klems. This renegade, they knew, was a brilliant gunner who had learned his trade during the Great War and later as a reserve officer in the German army. A romantic legend had grown up around Klems. He had the legionnaire penchant for romanticizing his life, but the main facts are known. He arrived in Bel-Abbès in May 1921. The model German soldier, his courage, intelligence, and sense of discipline took him quickly to sergeant in a mounted company of the Third Foreign Regiment. But new recruits soon learned to give Sergeant Klems the widest of berths; those cold blue eyes bored through them, and nobody ever put up his barrack-room kit or ironed a crease to satisfy him; the bitter mouth opened only to bark orders or dole out punishment. "A touch of wind round the heart," a canteen wag muttered when someone remarked that Klems had actually smiled. More often he brooded, especially when he overheard his countrymen singing nostalgic or patriotic songs in the bistros.*"Lieb' Vaterland, mag'st ruhig sein, Fast steht und treu, Die Wacht, die Wacht am Rhein."* This and other songs would send him to the pile of perfumed letters that arrived each week from his home town of Düsseldorf in pastel envelopes. The next parade would erase such sentimentality.

His mounted company went to the Taza Pocket, the trouble center of Morocco. Fragrant billets-doux in bright envelopes began to reach him less frequently. Fifteen days. Then twenty. Klems raged, sulked, and finally began to drink more than he could hold. In the summer of 1922 he received a letter that troubled him profoundly. "Bad news, Klems?" a fellow NCO asked. Klems shrugged. Applying for a few days' leave, he went to Fez and began a wild round of the bars. One night he staggered, drunk, into the Hôtel du Maroc, where a Legion officer recognized and cautioned him. Klems felled him with a blow. Brought back to his unit, he was broken to private and listed for court-martial. It was too much for Klems' pride. On the night of August 24, 1922, he escaped from the cells, grabbed a light machine gun, and struck north across the Spanish Morocco frontier. The weapon gained him safe-conduct from the Riffians, who, however, treated him as a slave for several months. In Abdel Krim's mountain fortress Klems spotted the captured guns from Anual and Melilla, lying idle. He sought out Abdel Krim, persuading him that he should instruct his tribesmen to use such guns. To convince the Riffian chief of his loyalty he changed his faith and name, assuming the Arab name Hadj Alemàn (German Pilgrim). Soon he had drilled several artillery batteries. Legionnaires who deserted and joined Klems found that he had lost none of his bite; many of them deserted again when the former sergeant threatened to shoot them if they did not fight well enough.

When Abdel Krim attacked French Morocco, Klems had become his chief of staff. Riff minstrels wrote poems and songs extolling this tall blond warrior who seemed inspired by Allah to lead them, who walked through infidel shells and bullets as though the Prophet himself shielded him. The American writer Vincent Sheean encountered Klems in a Riff fortress during the campaign. "By any legal or conventional standard the Hadj Alemàn was, I suppose, a liar, a thief, and a murderer," Sheean said. "Yet, I could not help thinking him, on the whole, rather a good man. His influence in Riff councils was always exercised on the side of mercy and moderation."

But not even Klems could halt the slow, grinding machine that Pétain had constructed to crush the Riffians. One by one the village fortresses crumbled under heavy artillery and air raids. On April 23, 1926, the Riffian chief made his last stand at Targuist. Three days later he rode into the French lines to make his *targuiba*, or submission ceremony, in a pomponed burnoose under a huge sunshade and with his own band. Pétain did not trust the legionnaires within rifle-shot of him; they remembered the Riff War as one of the most cruel ever fought, and might have made him pay for the battalions he had massacred, for the hundreds of their comrades he had subjected to the water-drip and the ant-hill tortures. The corpulent, short-legged messiah took the road to exile in the Indian Ocean and the war was over.

Joseph Klems had refused to make his *targuiba*. Sick,

and suffering from a wound received at Targuist, he disappeared into the Riff Mountains with two of his four wives to hide out for six months. For the second time in his life a woman betrayed him—the youngest of his wives. To Messaoud, in the heart of the Riff, she came to whisper to a Legion captain that El Hadj Alemàn was lying ill in a cave. A section surrounded the cave; a lieutenant called on Klems to surrender. From the darkness stumbled a figure leaning on a stick. Under the tousled blond beard and the Arab headdress, the lieutenant recognized Klems. "You fought a good fight, Klems. The Legion respects you," said the lieutenant. The German, shivering with fever, was carried back on a stretcher. In February 1927, still on a stretcher, Klems appeared before a court-martial at Meknes. He pleaded that he had joined the Riffs when they were fighting the Spaniards. "I am not a traitor. I am a naturalized Arab who has fought for the freedom of his country and his people against the brutal yoke of a foreign power, as any true believer would do." The court sentenced him to death for desertion and treason. But his trial had stirred world opinion. Even in France, Klems appeared more hero than villain, while in America, newspaper dispatches had transformed him into a figure of desert romance. The German Foreign Ministry, supported by French communist deputies, petitioned for his life. Klems went to Devil's Island to serve a life sentence. When he had done seven years, the French finally acceded to German demands for his release; by then his name had been immortalized in Sigmund Romberg's *The Desert Song*, which drew on his experiences for its hero. In 1934, Klems returned to Germany. He might have made a fortune out of his memoirs, but he considered his heroic days behind him. Just before the war Klems was arrested on suspicion of a minor crime. When the Berlin police entered his cell the next morning Klems was lying dead. He had slashed his wrists.

On August 24, 1933, the last act of the pacification of Morocco was played out when the Berbers of the Grand Atlas made their ceremonial *targuiba* at the foot of the Djebel Badou, besieged for nearly a month. "Walk the track but make the road," Lyautey had counseled. The Legion took up picks and shovels to build roads in the conquered mountains. They constructed the highway of Taguerrount; they turned 150 miles of goat track into a broad road between Marrakesh and Ouarzazate; with sledgehammer, chisel, and crowbar, they gouged the tunnel of Foum Zabel out of hard rock. At the entrance to the tunnel—seventy yards long, ten feet high, and twenty-five feet across—a legionnaire engraved this inscription: *The mountain barred this road. The order nevertheless came to pass through it. The Legion executed the order.* And, at the exit, he chiseled: *The energy of their muscles and their indomitable will were their only means.* To create those hundreds of miles of roads, bridges, tunnels, the Legion had plenty of cheap labor. Even without the background of the Riff and Berber revolts, the lure of the desert, battalions of new recruits filled Bel-Abbès and Saida. To *bleus* and young Saint-Cyrians, it was the Foreign Legion as it had always existed; the older hands noticed the changes.

For one thing the more colorful officers, such as Zinovi Pechkoff, had gone. He had left to reorganize the Peruvian army, but would end his career as an ambassador and a general. General Paul Rollet, the soul of the Legion, had retired in 1936 after the French army had instituted the new post of Inspector General of the Legion to allow him to remain at Bel-Abbès. The title did nothing to alter him, though age had mellowed him and sharpened the famous eccentricities. The Legion reflected his quaint personality. A thing apart, with its own rules, its wild, lilting tunes and songs, its own stride, its own motto—*Legio Patria Nostra.* Rollet designed a massive Monument aux Morts and had the legionnaires quarry and polish the granite to erect it at Bel-Abbès.

Rollet married late. His young wife, Nenette, a former nightclub hostess in Morocco, inspired much the same emotion in legionnaires as Madame Bernelle. All would rather have cleaned Bel-Abbès parade ground with a toothbrush than report for fatigues at Madame Nenette's house. Dust on her index finger or a minor breakage meant fifteen days without pay. Rollet lived for six years after quitting the Legion, though he was still regarded as France's First Legionnaire. He died in a Paris occupied and governed by the

Germans. In his small cortege walked the commandant of greater Paris, General von Stülpnagel, who had requested permission to attend the funeral "as a great personal honor."

Before her husband died, Nenette had the sculptor from the Musée Grévin in Paris model the general in wax. The young wife of one Legion officer took years to get over the shock she received when Madame Rollet ushered her into the Legion chief's study in Bel-Abbès. "And this is my husband, General Rollet," she said. Rollet was seated at his desk in full uniform, as though handing out the day's punishments. So lifelike was the effigy that many an old legionnaire quaked on entering the study to find Rollet's blue eyes staring at him. One of them could not clean the office in the presence of his old general. Forgetting—or perhaps only too aware of—the effects of the African sun on wax, he placed the dummy outside. Rollet finished as a rainbow puddle on his doorstep. Legion archives do not record what happened to the legionnaire, but Madame Rollet commissioned another dummy, which still sits in the museum. Rollet had left the Legion its ideals and its traditions. But would they survive?

Political disorder had forced the creation of the Legion; social and political upheavals in the nineteenth century had helped fill its ranks with the dispossessed and disaffected. Refugees, revolutionaries, petty criminals—this human cross-section mirrored European society and politics. In the thirties Germany was the troubled country; into the Legion came thousands of Jews and anti-Nazis to escape repression. But why, with so many vituperative attacks on the Legion in the German press, did the recruitment of the younger Germans mount instead of decline? Bel-Abbès intelligence officers soon provided the answer: they were Nazis, ordered to infiltrate the Legion, to spy, to staff its NCO grades, and to sabotage its effort in the event of war. This Fifth Column of Nazis led to distrust between officers, NCOs, and men.

When war did break out, the Legion screened its ranks ruthlessly for Nazis, who were sent to Colomb-Béchar to patrol and build roads. Still the French High Command felt that the Legion contained too many Germans to play the part it had in 1914. In France three foreign regiments were formed hurriedly from volunteers; some officers and NCOs came from Bel-Abbès to train them before they moved into the Maginot Line.

But what to do with the legionnaires in Bel-Abbès and Saida? For six months the general staff dithered, but in February 1940 the rumor circulated: Finland! The North Pole! One battalion of volunteers mustered at Fez, the other at Bel-Abbès. The 2,000 men had a new colonel, a veteran who should have died several times over in the Flanders trenches—and whom many legionnaires had wished dead since. A firebrand of a man, Colonel Magrin-Verneret suffered no one, officer or legionnaire, gladly. He would lead the new formation, which he called the 13th Demi-Brigade of the Foreign Legion to Finland.

The men's chagrin grew when they heard that Prince Aage would not take his battalion to Finland. Many had hoped—Aage among them, it was said—that he would command the demi-brigade. The official reason for keeping him in Africa: his Nordic origins might prove embarrassing in Scandinavia. His own battalion guessed the real reason when it paraded before the legionnaire prince. Aage was ill. He greeted each man, or shook him by the hand. His kepi, as always, was slightly askew, his bearing erect; but the men noted the flushed face and the weary blue eyes, which misted as the men presented arms and the *Boudin* sounded.

"The Thirteenth—why pick that number?" asked one old sweat as they waited in Taza station the morning of their departure. "A bad omen," another observed. As though to confirm their superstition, a bugle note sounded the fanfare of Aage's battalion. Stupefied, the legionnaires heard the bugler blow taps. Along the train and on the platform, men came to attention as they whispered the news to each other: *"Le Prince Aage est mort."* The men emptied the *pinard* in their water bottles to the legendary Aage. Despair, some muttered. No, a heart attack, said others. Aage had in fact died a legionnaire's death—his liver had given out. To the men embarking for the Arctic Circle, still clad in their tropical gear, it seemed that the Legion had already changed, that the heroic days, the romantic era of the Beau Geste, had passed away with Prince Aage.

THIRTEEN

And when will you French begin to understand
That war is tooth for tooth and eye for eye,
And these dead heroes from another land
Spare you a mourning when they die?

At eight o'clock on May 1, 1940, the adjutant made an entry in the war diary: "The colonel is still hiccuping, but the sea is calm." The officers speculated whether Colonel Magrin-Verneret had caught hiccups from the pretty English girl he had escorted around Liverpool, or if he had a bout of nerves over the coming Narvik action. The colonel scanned the diary that night and growled truculently to the adjutant, "Another entry—hic—like that and you'll—hic—be in prison." He meant it. His hiccups were no joke. They normally lasted nine and a half days, during which he could swallow nothing but ice cream, milk, or fruit juice.

In the French or any other army, Magrin-Verneret would have been invalided out with 100 percent disability pension. But this colonel lived for the Legion, then the army, then France. His origin was a mystery. Some said he was the natural son of a Hungarian prince, and no one ever heard him speak of his father. From childhood he had to fend for his mother and an aunt who wanted to set him up in a shop. The boy rebelled. At eight he disappeared and was found twenty miles from home, en route for the Boer War to fight the British. Finally his mother relented, and he went to Saint-Cyr to emerge in time for the Great War. He was badly wounded seventeen times. His three head wounds meant deep and crude trepanning operations that did nothing to improve his temper and helped to cause his hiccups. Bullet, shrapnel, and surgical scars covered his puny frame and he trailed his right leg, which surgeons had to shorten because the bone was smashed. If most officers and men secretly dubbed him paranoiac, his senior staff knew he had earned the right.

In April the colonel had received new orders. The Finns had signed a treaty with the Russian aggressors, but the Germans had marched into Norway and were now menacing British and French shipping from the northern fjords. Churchill had planned an Anglo-French landing at Narvik to establish a bridgehead and deny the Germans iron ore. The Legion sailed to Liverpool, then Greenock to join the Narvik convoy. For the only time in their lives, legionnaires were traveling first class. On the *Monarch of Bermuda* they stared, wide-eyed, at their cabins, each with its white-coated steward. The first morning out, a gong sent them running for their life jackets. It was breakfast. And what breakfasts! They jettisoned the tins of monkey and biscuits on which they had lived for weeks and ate through the five-course menu from porridge to marmalade. Did these British know there was a war on? No, thank God, somebody said.

The British had already fought two naval battles that had gained them mastery of the maze of fjords around Narvik and had enabled them to put ashore British and Polish units that would operate with the Legion. The Germans, however, had air supremacy; when the convoy touched Norway on May 5, the legionnaires had their first taste of aerial bombardment: Messerschmitts and Stukas bombed and strafed the warships and transports bunched in the narrow seas.

Before mounting the attack on Narvik, General Béthouart, the French commander, and Magrin-Verneret decided they must clear the Germans out of Bjervik, a hamlet of wooden chalets at the north point of the fjord. They had tough opponents, General Edouard Dietl and several divisions of crack mountain troops. Dietl fumed when he learned that the Legion had arrived. "The Alpine Chasseurs, that's fine. But the Foreign Legion, those international thugs. The British should be ashamed to use them against us." It would have irritated him even more had he known that Germans were opposing him too. The French had changed their papers, giving each a Breton name, birthplace, and family history in case he was captured. Thus legionnaires Müller, Klen, and Wetzel became Le Moal, Brannelec, and Trémeur.

The midnight sun, the pitching of HMS *Vindictive*, and his hiccups had kept Colonel Magrin-Verneret awake for more than a week. In clipped phrases he got out his orders: the British would put them ashore in landing craft at midnight on May 13; they would drill straight through the German mountain division. At zero hour he was limping about the deck with the *Vindictive* and every other warship in the fjord blasting at Bjervik, crying, "What good's a—hic—colonel? What would I do if everything was a—hic—sham-

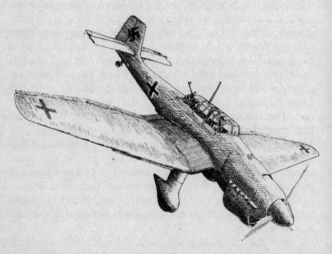

Ju 87 "Stuka"

bles?" From his vantage point it looked bad. The landing craft had run into a fierce barrage of shell and machine-gun fire from the town and the hills behind. Bullets spun off the steel sides of the craft in which the legionnaires crouched.

First to ground and crawl forward under fire was Lieutenant Jacques Renard, a German! He had joined as a legionnaire in 1920 and fought against the Riffians before changing his name and nationality. On the left, Captain Dmitri Amilakvari had run into trouble; his supporting troops had failed their rendezvous in front of the vital Hill 98, key to the bridgehead. Amilakvari, a Georgian prince who had done sixteen years in the Legion, rallied his machine-gun company. Bullets ripped through his white cape and one grazed his throat while he issued his orders. With half his company he charged the hill as though it were a Moroccan djebel and drove off the Germans. For good measure he pressed on to seize Elvegard.

Colonel Magrin-Verneret waded ashore, to run into a low-level strafing and bombing attack from German planes. A drunken legionnaire lurched across his path. "Where do you think you are—heading for a Marrakesh brothel on July 14?" he bawled and pushed him onward. His hiccups had finally stopped. He handed another rocket to Sergeant Volent, who arrived in the middle of the raid with his half-tracked vehicles. "Why aren't these trucks camouflaged?" he snapped. "We couldn't find any paint, *mon colonel*," said Volent, who had driven from their first disembarkation site.

"How long have you taken to get here?"

"Three days."

"Three days!"

"I had to make the road and fell trees to bridge the rivers and ravines, *mon colonel*."

Magrin-Verneret glowered at him. "Good," he said, grudgingly. "You're a legionnaire."

Bjervik, the quiet little Christmas-card village, had fallen. It had quivered under the bombardment; now it smoked and blazed.

The attack on Narvik had been fixed for May 28. But four days prior to this, admirals Cork and Orrery, commanding the British fleet, received a telegram from London. "His Majesty's Government has decided that your troops must evacuate northern Norway as rapidly as possible. The reason is that the troops, the ships, the guns, and other war matériel are imperiously required for the defense of the United Kingdom. . . . The Norwegian Government has not yet been informed." When they learned of this decision on May 26, Béthouart and Magrin-Verneret argued against abandoning the Norwegians; the taking of Narvik would at least give them a chance to regroup. Admiral Cork saw little point in seizing the port merely to cede it, but agreed to give the French, Norwegian, and Polish troops air and naval support. The legionnaires, who guessed what was happening, lifted their issue of British rum and drank to General Béthouart. "May he get his third star." Honor and loyalty to the Norwegians! What a joke! This one was in Béthouart's honor.

Narvik looked like Gibraltar covered in ice and snow. Every form of armament protruded from the promontory blockhouses and Hill 457, dominating the port. They would also have to strike east along the railway line to Dietl's headquarters near the Swedish frontier. The Legion would take the shortest route, while the Alpine Chasseurs, the Norwegians, and Poles worked in from the rear and flanks.

At midnight on May 27 the British cruisers *Cairo* and *Southampton* and the destroyer *Fame* opened up; the sun lay on the frozen crests, its long rays flickering on the wake of a hundred "puffers" and landing craft; tracer bullets swept the narrow beach and Messerschmitts seemed to graze the hilltops as they sprayed men and ships with fire. Caught between Hill 457 and Orneset spur, the Legion and the Norwegians were pinned for several hours, until Colonel Magrin-Verneret arrived. As he limped forward he realized the situation could end in disaster; behind him the British warships were zigzagging in the fjord to dodge the dive bombers, several small ships already blazed, and a huge smoke pall hung over the *Cairo*, which had received a direct hit. Dietl's Bavarian troops could well thrust them into the sea. A situation to gladden Magrin-Verneret's heart. An instructor for many years as Saida, he grabbed a submachine gun from a rookie legionnaire and emptied its magazine at several Germans on the slopes a hundred yards away. "That's how it's done, *mon enfant*," he shouted. "Now, forward." The Legion First Battalion scrambled behind him and did not halt until it had cleared the hill and the first railway tunnel.

A legionnaire passed him at the salute; the colonel observed the man's bloody face, the makeshift sling around his arm, the left leg dragging. "Who are you?"

"Legionnaire Samarsam, *mon colonel*."

"But there are stretcher-bearers."

"They told me, 'You can march.' "

The colonel waved him on. "He's been marching for two hours," he muttered. "You know what kept him going—that order that's drummed into them when they join the Legion—if hell falls on him, the legionnaire keeps marching."

Suddenly the Hurricanes appeared overhead; the sky cleared of German aircraft; the two cruisers began battering the German positions; the Legion took another tunnel, another ice-bound slope. Narvik now lay behind them, abandoned by the Germans, who had begun to bomb the lost port. The Legion had played the major part in the first French victory and the first large-scale combined operation of the war.

Hurricane

* * *

After Bjervik and Narvik, Captain Gélat had given Legionnaire Charles Favrel a choice: Croix de Guerre or promotion to corporal. To duck fatigues, Favrel, a former Breton sailor and journalist, chose the two stripes and found himself detailed for the worst job in the army: an execution. Two Luxembourg brothers, André and Henri R——had slipped away while their company was resting in a tunnel to pick up two girls at Orneset, five miles behind the forward positions. An MP patrol, searching for looters, had roused them hours later. "As an example, they will be shot before their company," Colonel Magrin-Verneret ordered. Now Favrel and four men were trudging in snowshoes, with the two Luxembourgers tied together, toward a firing party. André, the tall blond brother, remained quiet, but Henri, dark and loquacious, explained to Favrel what had happened. Any one of them might be facing a firing squad for such an offense, Favrel thought. Execution? It's murder.

When they halted for a breather, he turned to Henri. "Listen, chum, you've noticed I'm a corporal without stripes. Fine! I've been thinking about your case and here's what I've decided. You pretend to make a run for it. In open country. The escort will fire on you—that'll be your chance! If you're wounded, the Old Man might pardon you. If you're killed, you won't have the ceremony to go through."

Henri stared at him. "Corporal! You've no right to do that!" As Favrel recovered from his shock, the little man went on, "I appreciate it, believe me. Only, don't you see, to escape would be to own that we're guilty. . . . We're not guilty. So, weighing everything up, we'd prefer to be shot! I'll try to die like a man. . . ." Henri hesitated, then said, "It may be stupid to ask you this, corporal, but I'd like it if you were in the firing squad."

"But why would you want . . . ?"

"For me, it'll be better to be shot by a friend. . . . You mightn't like it at the time, but after you'll feel happier that you've done me a good turn." The astonished Favrel found himself shaking hands on this death pact. Captain Gélat gave Favrel a knowing look when he volunteered for the firing party. Sergeant Major Blanc, a veteran who had witnessed the executions at the Chemin des Dames in 1917, when they shot men by drawing lots after the French army mutiny, picked the men. The two brothers walked to their graves, two dark bruises in the snow; they would not have their eyes bandaged.

"Load!" the sergeant major said. It was almost a whisper.

"Aim!"

Favrel had the smaller brother in his sights. "And then his right arm, stiff as an artificial arm, jerks slowly until level with his heart. . . . I am trembling. . . . Oh, God, help me! This heart, the heart of a man who, for that moment, has wished to be my friend, I have it in the sight of my rifle."

"Fire!"

"The little one made a curious bound. . . . Like a rabbit shot point-blank. . . . Yes, like a rabbit, a poor little rabbit. . . . And I turn my head away to stop myself from crying. . . . The bang of two shots fired at an interval: Sergeant Major Blanc's two mercy shots."

For six days the Legion chased the Germans over the mountains, marching, fighting, and camping in blizzards that drove the temperatures to 60° below zero Fahrenheit. Ten miles from the Swedish border, Béthouart ordered them to turn about and make for Narvik. The legionnaires grumbled at having to retreat; they could have thrust the Germans into Sweden and internment. Instead they had the bizarre task of making dummies to fool the enemy as they filtered back.

On June 8 they embarked. Narvik was now filled with Norwegians waving a bewildered good-bye, wondering what reprisals the Germans would exact. . . . Narvik was Captain Amilakvari shouting high-voiced protests at having to dump his machine guns in the sea to make room for men on the ships. . . . Narvik was Spanish legionnaires crying on the necks of the mules they had led throughout Morocco and would now make German sausage meat. . . . Narvik, finally, was General Béthouart's third star and another oak leaf on General Dietl's Iron Cross.

But life on the *Duchess of York*, a floating palace apparently unsullied by war, tempered their despondency. The liner had a ravaged look when the last white kepi strode down its gangway at Brest on June 14. Colonel Magrin-Verneret had no sooner set foot ashore than the port officer announced, "The Germans entered Paris this morning." The Wehrmacht had smashed the French army and driven the British onto the Dunkirk beaches. "We shall fight on," said Magrin-Verneret. As he settled his demi-brigade near Brest, a young French lieutenant from an infantry regiment came up to him: "You'll only cause trouble for us if you don't lay down your arms," he said. There and then, in their mess tent, the Legion colonel drew his revolver and shot the man dead.

With a handful of senior and junior officers, he drove to army headquarters at Rennes to wake up the peppery General Jean Guitry at 4 A.M. "What is my mission, *mon général?*"

"How many anti-tank guns have you?"

"Two."

"Ah, you're rich," growled Guitry. "Now, here's your mission. Stop the Panzer Division. Recover elements of the French Tenth Division behind them and block the German advance. Hold on to the death." At this, Magrin-Verneret bridled. "I can't stop the whole German army with half a brigade. Men don't fight well when they know they're going to die and I'm not sacrificing my legionnaires. Give me a mission to hold so many days and so much ground."

"I'll leave it to you." Guitry shrugged.

"I won't waste any more of your time—*mon général,*" Magrin-Verneret said. With Major Pierre Koenig, Amilak-vari, lieutenants Lamaze, Knorré, and Arnault, he pushed on to reconnoiter the Liffré Forest, near Rennes. They had to take to the woods when a German Panzer Division rattled past them. The rest of that morning and the next day they hid in a farmhouse behind the German lines. In two com-mandeered taxis—one driven by Koenig, the other by an or-derly—they regained the Brest area to find that the regiment had disappeared. The colonel believed it had fallen into Ger-man hands. "Only one thing to do—get to England some-how," he grunted as they bedded down in a wheat field that night. But every boat seemed to have been commandeered by fleeing troops. A sailing dinghy took them to an island off Dinan, where they lay until Lamaze sighted a launch sailing into the harbor. Yes, the skipper was making for England and would take them—for all the money they had with them. The following night they sailed. "It'll be—hic—tough on us—hic—starting as second-class privates in the British army," Magrin-Verneret confided to Arnault. At midday on June 21 they landed at Southampton. As Arnault walked to the bank to draw money for the officers the next day, he spotted a white kepi outside the station. "The whole regiment is here," the legionnaire told him. It had crossed on the Twickenham Ferry from Brest the day before and was now bound for Trentham Park camp, near Stoke-on-Trent.

Vichy radio had announced that the 13th Demi-Brigade of the Foreign Legion had ceased to exist, with other units that had taken refuge in England. "Right! We're now the 14th Demi-Brigade," said the colonel. He changed his name to avoid reprisals against his family. He was now Monclar. He first called at Saint Stephen's House on the Victoria Embankment to see an obscure brigadier, Charles de Gaulle, who had just broadcast a rallying call to Frenchmen to fight on. "My men have just won the first French victory on land. We still have some ammunition and we're at your disposal." On June 30, de Gaulle reviewed the Legion at Trentham Park. The men had a choice, he said. Fight on with Britain or return to Morocco. About 1,000 legionnaires left for Africa; the others signed a six-month contract to fight with the Free French. "Why six months and not the duration of the war?" Arnault asked Monclar later. "I didn't trust the Churchill–de Gaulle agreement. I knew I had enough in the pay-chest to keep the men going for six months," Monclar replied.

At Aldershot two new officers joined the Legion. Lieutenant Jean Simon and Second Lieutenant Pierre Messmer had heard Pétain's armistice announcement near Clermont-Ferrand and had immediately struck south, seeking an aircraft to take them to England. At Marseilles they decided it would have to be a ship, so for weeks they worked on the docks, loading cargo vessels and sounding out French captains. Captain Veillemin listened to their plan, which fell in with his own ideas. Simon and Messmer signed on as deck hands on his ship, the *Capo di Olmo*, captured from the Italians and interned. They put out with a French convoy for Oran, but in mid-crossing the captain and the two officers staged a breakdown. To the French destroyer that hove to and offered help the captain replied that he could repair the fault and catch up. When the convoy was over the horizon he set course for Gibraltar and handed over the ship to the British. Simon and Messmer landed at Liverpool with the next convoy from Gibraltar. Simon would later reach the highest rank in the French army, and Messmer would become war minister and later prime minister.

From the few legionnaires who escaped from France the demi-brigade heard something of the tragedy that befell the three regiments formed to defend the Maginot Line. The Eleventh came off worst. Composed of African veterans and five hundred French conscripts, it had no conception of modern warfare, no anti-tank guns, and the lightest of equipment. In its blocking position between the Chiers and Meuse rivers, at Inor Wood, the 3,000 men stood like a stake driven into the earth while the Germans threw everything at them—mortar bombs, heavy artillery, waves of Stuka dive bombers, and machine-gun fire. Everything buckled around them; retreating French regiments clogged the roads. But the Eleventh stood firm until its ranks thinned under the avalanche of steel and fire and it had to retreat. Legionnaire Karel Hora picked up the wounded Sergeant Verhuewen, a Dutchman, and placed him on a half-track. All around them lay the Germans; two machine guns blocked the road ahead. His officer, Lieutenant Roux, with only a revolver in his hand, said to Hora, "We'll make them pay for our pelts." At that moment Hora noticed a Dutch legionnaire stumbling over the dead strewing the road. Lifting a submachine gun from one body, he slipped a magazine into it. "*Mon lieutenant*, you will get through," he shouted. Down the track he walked as casually as he might through a tulip field, spraying both machine-gun positions with bullets. He clumped back to Roux. "You will pass now, *mon lieutenant*," he gasped, and fell dead beside the vehicle.

"Why fight?" whispered the French soldiers as the men

Half-track

regrouped after Inor. "Why get yourselves killed before the armistice?"

"The Legion dies on its feet," a Belgian shouted back.

Indeed, the men scarcely knew why they were fighting, but for ten days they contested every acre of ground. When the German attacks slackened, the legionnaires counterattacked; the men ate and slept with bayonets fixed, prepared to die rather than surrender. Finally they had to withdraw to Saint-Germain, where a German army had completely encircled them. Major Henri Alegron, of Polish extraction, volunteered to try to break through and cover the rest of the regiment. "I won't be back," he told another officer to whom he handed his papers, with instructions to send them to his wife. On June 17 he led a hopeless charge with the Second Battalion against a German armored division; Alegron died in the first minutes; nine other officers were killed and nine out of every ten enlisted men. At the most it gave the other two battalions half a day's respite. "Go home with your wounded," said a German colonel to the MO who was gathering the wounded from Alegron's battalion in the pouring rain. "We shall look after the dead and do them the honor due to men of their quality."

Colonel Jean-Baptiste Robert could no longer stand and fight. He had one last task—the regimental standard must not fall into German hands. On June 20, at Blenod-les-Toul, he soaked it in petrol and ordered a legionnaire to set it alight, then sign with him the declaration that it had been burned. The tassel he buried in a cookie box by the church wall. Later a woman ambulance driver dug it up and smuggled it through the German lines to hand it back to the Legion. Of the Eleventh's 3,000 men fewer than eight hundred remained. But 450 of those could still march. Somehow they kept ahead of the German advance and by the end of October—four months later—they had returned to their depots in France to be shipped back to Morocco.

They found a transformed Legion in Algeria and Morocco. With their long-standing hatred of the Foreign Legion, the Germans were now demanding that Vichy disband it. Hitler had already repatriated the Nazis planted in North Africa before the war. Now they were claiming the Jews and other political refugees from Germany. For the Legion it was a sad hour. The Nazis jeered openly at their officers and NCOs as they goose-stepped toward their ships at Oran, their arms raised in Nazi salutes. But at Bel-Abbès, Saida, and the Moroccan depots, the Legion defied Vichy and Hitler by refusing to give up the Jews, the Czechs, and the Poles who had fled the Nazi regime. Those men in the ranks who had not assumed a false name now got one, complete with identity disc and service record. Some men, of whom the Germans had photographs, could not be disguised and, from time to time, the German Armistice Commission would swoop down on Legion units. However, the "Arab Telephone" and the "pavement radio" gave officers at least twelve hours' warning, enough time to post a man to In Salah, Reganne, or Timimoun.

From the summer of 1940 the 13th Demi-Brigade had to sustain the honor of the Legion and of Free France. No one realized this better than Colonel Monclar as the brigade stepped ashore at Port Sudan after sailing around the Cape of Good Hope. The British put out no flags for this strange mercenary army; for one thing, the sticky hands of legionnaires battened on their equipment if they turned their backs, appropriating trucks and motorcycles; for another, the Sudan and Eritrea were a British show. At Kassala the Legion was relegated with the supply trucks; at Keren, however, they helped to sweep the Italians aside like so much dust and the British forgave them their intrusion and their scrounging ways. "We must go on and take Massawa," Monclar urged the British command. Finally Monclar got his way. On April 7 legionnaires assaulted the forts of Montecullo and Umberto, then swarmed after the fleeing Italians into Massawa.

This was Monclar's last battle as a legionnaire. De Gaulle drafted the demi-brigade, which had reverted to its old title, into Syria, held by 80,000 Vichy French under General Henri Dentz. Monclar bluntly told de Gaulle that he would never fight against Frenchmen, regardless of their politics. Koenig took over. The Vichy troops have agreed to join us, the demi-brigade was told. However, beyond Deir Ali, in front of Damascus, legionnaires of the 13th Demi-Brigade and the Sixth Foreign Regiment faced each other. An outpost of the Sixth presented arms to their fellow legionnaires; but when the patrol commander ventured forward, the Vichy legionnaires made him and his men prisoners. From one battalion of the Sixth a bugler blew a sardonic version of the *Boudin;* the *clique* of the 13th replied as though to mock them. The battle was on. It looked like Barbastro all over again, with the two legions annihilating each other. Through the gardens of Damascus the battle swayed; the Australian division pushed in behind the Free French legionnaires and finally the Vichy regiment surrendered.

The Legion joined the Eighth Army units in North Africa. They left Monclar behind. At fifty he had not, however, finished as a soldier. When the Korean War broke out he had Rollet's old job, Inspector General of the Legion. Without a qualm he ripped off his three stars, donned his old combat uniform as a colonel, and, at fifty-eight, led the French contingent with the United Nations troops in Korea.

Bir-Hakeim, the Chief's Well. Marked as a caravan crossroads on the edge of the Libyan Desert. The demi-brigade discovered neither well nor track when, with four Colonial and Marine battalions, they took over from the Guards and the British 150th Brigade on February 14, 1942. General Pierre Koenig and the First Free French Brigade had been allotted the southernmost tip of the Gazala Line,

which the Eighth Army had constructed to defend Tobruk
and strike at General Erwin Rommel's Afrika Korps, one
hundred miles west. In February, no hint of trouble. "That'll
soon change," muttered the legionnaires. "We're the men
whose bootprints fill with shells." The perimeter of the six-
sided box measured nine miles. Along the forty-mile Gazala
Line the Eighth Army had already planted 500,000 antitank
mines; Koenig extended the frontiers of his box to twelve
miles with mines and ordered his 3,300 men to dig; within a
month they had no fewer than 1,200 slit trenches, gun pits,
and command posts, and even their trucks lay cabin-deep in
sand. The African hands felt their blood re-warm; they had
one swim a week in the Mediterranean and ample food and
water. No *pinard*, though. The thoughtful British had
bought up the whole stock of Palestinian wine for the legionnaires; when it arrived, in steel containers sizzling in
the sun, they could not even use it as vinegar. Koenig felt he
had seen everything when his legionnaires queued up for
sweet, milky tea! In March, April, and part of May, they became adept at the hit-and-run tactics of Jock Columns. Suddenly, in May, the rumor ran that Rommel might attack; the
weekly excursions to Koenig's Beach ceased; the sappers
shaved off their beards and did gas-mask drill in case the
Germans used poison gas.

    Rommel needed Bir-Hakeim. But Free France needed
it more, to restore its prestige and place in the war. How
would the Legion and the colonials stand up to lightning attacks by Panzer and mobile columns? Koenig had one
trump: his men were all volunteers. Officers such as Simon,
wearing a patch over the eye he lost in Syria, Messmer,
Captain André Lalande, Brunet de Sairigné; men who were
battle-hardened by Narvik, Keren, Damascus; Germans like
Sergeant Eckstein, who knew better than to fall into the
hands of the Afrika Korps.

    On May 26, Rommel swung to the south of Bir-
Hakeim and hurled his German and Italian divisions, supported by amor, at the rear of the Eighth Army; he planned
to drill through the center of the line and ensnare the whole
force before moving on to Tobruk. He left Bir-Hakeim to
the Italians, thinking it would crumple.

    At 8:15 on May 27 the legionnaires saw a column of

eighty tanks coming in from the southeast toward the sector held by the second Legion battalion. Identified as the Italian Ariete Division, the tanks glided across the pink sand glowing in the low sun. Within half an hour some thirty had blown up in the minefield or had been picked off by the 75-mm guns. Even in the tricky desert light Sergeant Eckstein counted seven direct hits on tanks with his gun.

Somehow six of the second wave of tanks groped through the minefield and plunged into the box, crushing a Legion command post and sending Captain Morel to burn his company standard. Bronzed legionnaires, wearing nothing but shorts and sandals, leaped on the tanks to thrust grenades under their visors and pick off the crews as they ran for their lives. Batches of men scurried across the minefields to attack the thirty tanks that lay crippled; they blew up and looted the supply trucks, bringing back Italian hams and cheeses, tins of jam, pounds of chocolate. The Second Battalion reeked of eau de Cologne, some of it on the breaths of the more dissipated veterans. A good day: thirty-five tanks, ninety-one prisoners, several score dead—all for one slightly scratched legionnaire.

Rommel and his troops had now encircled the French box. They trapped Colonel Amilakvari and a detachment commanded by Captain de Lamaze several miles north of the position and it took Messmer and his company to pull them free. Amilakvari went out the next night and destroyed five German tanks with plastic bombs.

Amilak, the new colonel, lived for the Legion, and legionnaires for him. They might have lost their Danish prince, but in Amilak they had a full-blooded, if impoverished, Georgian prince who had stridden through Bjervik, Narvik, Asmara, and Massawa as proudly as he had led them on the Bastille Day parade in 1938 along the Champs Élysées, the day they first wore their white kepis in Paris. He was, however, the antithesis of Aage: dark in looks and mood; conscious of his noble ancestry and his rank; abstemious and devout; aloof to the point of haughtiness. "On your knees in front of your colonel," he had ordered Lamaze. The brave Lamaze retorted, "No French officer kneels to anyone." He wore fatalism and superstition like the cross around his neck. "Put on your helmet, Amilak,"

Koenig would tell him during heavy bombing and shelling. "Bah! With or without, death will find you," he retorted, jamming his kepi on his head. Yet he considered his white, bullet-riddled Narvik cape a talisman and donned it in combat. Few people knew that his elder brother, who had inspired him to enter the Legion, had joined the Tricolor Legion and fought with the Germans on the Russian front— to be killed, ironically, by a bullet from one of his Russian countrymen. But more French than the French, Amilak symbolized the Legion resistance at Bir-Hakeim.

On June 2 the Italians and Germans took up attacking positions north and south of Koenig's box. Through a sandstorm a light vehicle flying a white flag approached. Two Italian officers demanded to see Koenig. Rommel summoned the fortress to surrender to avoid bloodshed. "I'm very sorry, gentlemen. Go and tell your general that we're not here to surrender," Koenig replied. An hour later two infantry divisions, supported by tanks, attacked every point at Bir-Hakeim. Shells kicked up sand geysers and Stukas flung sticks of bombs into the center of the box; but the legionnaires and colonial troops stuck to their holes, picking off the assault troops with bullets and shells and forcing them to retire. For the second time Rommel, by sending a note in his own hand, requested Koenig to give in.

Koenig replied by opening up with his guns on Rommel's advance guard. "Everyone fights where he stands— until final victory," he told his troops. The Luftwaffe dive-bombed and pattern-bombed, though the RAF made them pay dearly for those raids; heavy guns shelled the position night and day to keep the garrison awake. And for the third time Rommel suggested surrender. At 4:30 A.M. a car threaded across the minefield. Two German officers approached the German legionnaire on sentry duty. "We wish to speak to your general," they said in English.

"*Was wunschen Sie? Ich kann nicht Englisch sprechen*," said the legionnaire. The officer explained in German; the sentry pointed his bayonet at both, telling them in legionnaire German to push off. "We're not waking the general at this hour," he said. A Legion officer arrived and gave the Germans five minutes to regain their own lines. As they crossed the minefield their truck blew up; out of the smoke and fumes a German appeared to start walking. "*Schweinhund*, you've woken us all up," somebody shouted.

"*Ja*, Fritz, tell your general to have a night off."

"Send it airmail next time."

On June 6 the crack German 90th Division, supported by tanks, attacked the Second Battalion front. From his command post Captain Arnault watched the fantastic mirage effects on the tanks and men; the vehicles wobbled in the shimmering air and the infantry, running behind, seemed ten feet tall. Caught by air-burst shells from the French 75s, they toppled like giants. Speaking of his troops, Rommel wrote, "Yet, for all their dash, this attack, too, was broken up by the fire of all arms. Only in the north were a few penetrations made. This was a remarkable achievement on the part of the French defenders, who were now completely cut off from everybody. . . . When my storming parties went in the next morning, the French opened fire again

French 75

with undiminished violence. The enemy troops hung on
grimly in their trenches and remained completely invisible."

With the Gazala Line smashed, Bir-Hakeim had now
become a vital position for both sides. Rommel needed it to
allow him to thrust on Tobruk; the Eighth Army needed it to
give them time to regroup after Knightsbridge and halt the
German advance on Egypt. Koenig's brigade had come to
symbolize Free French resistance, a fact that Rommel himself admitted."If the men of Bir-Hakeim had fulfilled their
mission badly or imperfectly it would have seemed that the
knell of the French army had sounded for the second time,"
he commented.

The 3,300 men on that arid bump of pebbly ground
were hedged in by German and Italian armored and infantry
divisions. Junkers and Stukas alternated with bombing raids,
though many of these were broken up by the RAF. More serious than the attacks was the lack of water. And the stifling
heat. From May 27 the men had three pints of water a day in
shade temperatures of 120°—had there been any shade.
Several legionnaires discovered that radiator water with a
little toothpaste and whiskey made an almost drinkable
cocktail. Beards had reappeared. No one wore a shirt; the
heat and sweat cracked them in a couple of hours. About a
hundred wounded now lay in dugouts in the camp center.
What extra water the RAF dropped went to them. Just as serious, their guns now had only a few score rounds of ammunition left.

The Afrika Korps had begun to sap through the minefields to open a passage for their armor; on June 9 and 10,
Rommel's troops had surrounded Messmer's position and
crushed one of the sections. General Neil Ritchie reluctantly
gave Koenig permission to break out at midnight.

Koenig might have gone out on tiptoe, but this meant
forsaking his wounded and betraying his own feelings as a
legionnaire officer. He decided to cut a path through the
minefields to the southwest and link up with a British unit
that would cover their withdrawal. But the breakout went
awry. At midnight Koenig realized that a passage of no
more than fifty yards had been cleared for his 3,000 men
and vehicles. And the moment the first men of the Second
Battalion put a foot outside Bir-Hakeim the desert erupted

German 88 mm.

around them. Clusters of red, green, orange, and white
flares burst over the men; tracer bullets converged on them
from both flanks. The legionnaires tussled, hand-to-hand,
with the Germans and Italians. In the glow of the fires
started by the German artillery, anti-tank and 88-mm guns
were picking off the half-tracks and bren carriers. It seemed
to Koenig, standing at the breakout point, that hardly any of
his vehicles escaped either the guns or his own mines. One
by one they flamed, as shells hit them or mines exploded
under them. In the midst of this chaos, Amilakvari and
Lamaze had rallied their men with the traditional cry: *"A
moi la Légion."* The men barged through somehow. Not
Lamaze, who died with a rifle in one hand and a grenade in
the other.

Among the last to leave were Koenig and Amilakvari.
And an Englishwoman who had lived through the whole
siege of Bir-Hakeim. Romantic novels about the Legion de-
pict women who have disguised themselves as legionnaires
to share the rough life and who in the end receive medals of
honor in the Quartier Vienot at Bel-Abbès. Legionnaires
scoff at such tales. But Susan Travers had proved that fact
could catch up with fiction. She had joined the French ambulance service at the outbreak of the war, served in Finland, and found herself in England when the Legion arrived

from Narvik and Brittany. She sailed with them in the *Westerland*, attached as driver to Colonel Lotte, a divisional medical officer. Gradually she and the Legion adopted each other. Legionnaires remembered her at Der'a in Syria. After that campaign she had been attached to General Koenig as his driver and had followed him to Bir-Hakeim. When Koenig thought things were getting too tough for women, he sent her back to the base depot on May 26—only to find her back at Bir-Hakeim on June 1 with a new Ford Utility. For those ten days she lived like the men, on iron rations and three pints of water a day; she helped dig in her truck and slept in her slit trench beside it. Of her Koenig said, "We weren't women-haters, but we didn't want to be bothered by women. However, this one had been adopted by the division, in particular by the Legion, for she was exceptionally brave and had shown discipline such as few men have. She was used to the rough life that we led and her presence gave us no problems at all." Privately the general thought she had used a feminine dodge, with her new truck, to get back into Bir-Hakeim. But on that night he knew that, if anyone would get through that narrow gap, she would. Damn it! The woman seemed to be too British, too cool!

Just after 3:30 A.M. Koenig stuck his head out through the roof opening of the Ford. *"Foncez,"* he ordered. Flooring the gas pedal, Miss Travers bucketed over the shell holed desert floor. Tracers were whining off the trucks around them, spinning off the sand. They slithered into a shell hole, wheels skidding. They might have stuck but for another truck that was hit and slithered down the bank and collided with them, setting them going again. "Keep out of the shell holes," Koenig shouted from his perch. How could one keep out of shell holes in dead darkness at forty miles an hour! They used a system of signals; a touch on the right shoulder and Miss Travers slowed or stopped; on the left shoulder and she went like the devil. "I didn't have to nudge her twice," said Koenig. "She answered like a machine. The sky might have fallen on her head before she deviated by one centimeter from the route." A burst from a bren machine gun whistled around them; tracer bullets were flying past them. Somehow they seemed to have got through and left everything else behind. Beside Miss Travers sat Ami-

lakvari, a sporting gun in his lap and a compass in his
hand, verifying the route.

Koenig kicked Miss Travers' right shoulder. She
stopped. The general wormed into the cabin. "We can take
our bearings and. . . ." Amilakvari stopped him, a finger to
his mouth. "We've got company," he whispered. Twenty
yards from them was a German camp. They could hear the
voices. Koenig pressed his foot on Miss Travers' left
shoulder and they shot off, pursued by several bursts of

Bren L.M.G.

fire. "Thank God they haven't got tracers," Koenig
thought. They were zigzagging through the darkness and
the mist that had fallen over the desert when they spotted a
German machine-gun carrier on their track; gradually they
drew away from him, though he fired several bursts that
passed close. They swung south, then east and northeast as
the day broke. For hours they traveled without sighting either British or German units. What had happened to the
brigade? Koenig thought it had been trapped in its own
minefield and taken *en bloc* by the Germans. "We can't return on our own," he said to Amilakvari. "Let's go back to
Bir-Hakeim." Amilakvari replied that they would both fall
into German hands. They continued, and at 10:30 contacted the first British units.

All that day, and for three days afterward, the men of
the Free French Brigade filtered into the Eighth Army
lines. The breakout had been costly: seventy-two known

dead and 763 missing, either captured or killed or
wounded, including thirty-three officers. But in that night
of chaos the miracle was that two-thirds of the men had
come through. The thick mist had saved many of them,
though it scattered the units. When Captain Arnault called
the roll on the 11th he had one or two men from every company in the two Legion battalions.

At dawn, on June 11, Rommel walked through Bir-
Hakeim, the sandhill that had cost him his blitzkrieg on
Egypt. Several Legion and marine detachments that had
fallen back on the box were still firing at the Germans, and
some succeeded in vanishing to join the Eighth Army.
Looking at the maze of trenches and galleries, Rommel
wondered how the brigade had clung so long to this waste-
land.

No one could call Bir-Hakeim a victory. But those
fourteen days when the Legion and the colonial battalions
halted the Afrika Korps had put France back into the war.
Everyone paid tribute to the Free French; the British decorated several of the officers and men, Koenig receiving the
DSO from General Alexander. For her part in the siege and
the breakout, Miss Travers was given the Croix de Guerre
and, ten years afterward, the Military Medal. She stayed
with the Legion, the only woman ever to hold a rank in that
elite corps. She served in Indochina for two years after the
war and rose to the rank of adjutant, or warrant officer; she
married an adjutant-chief in the Legion in Indochina.

The Legion was again in action at El Alamein with the
tough job of seizing El Himeimat, a triangular peak that
dominated the sector from the south. Amilakvari had misgivings about the operation. "Not all bullets kill," he had
often said to the men; now, however, he had the presentiment that one bullet had his name on it. He visited Abbé
Mallec, a Yugoslav priest with the brigade who was lying in
a hospital in Alexandria. "I had a horrible dream," he said.
"I was badly wounded and someone was giving me the last
rites and it wasn't you."

On the morning of October 24, after the great barrage,
he led the demi-brigade across the seven miles of open
ground to the sharp peak. Apart from his Narvik cape, he
was the immaculate legionnaire prince. "When one risks ap-

pearing before God, one must be properly dressed," he said.
As they crossed the minefield at the foot of El Himeimat,
machine guns pinned the First Battalion; for hours they lay
in the sand until the Second Battalion had attempted to
leapfrog onto the hill. Captain Messmer and his company
climbed the steep slope, but the Germans threw in a
squadron of tanks against which they could do nothing.
They had no way of hoisting their guns up the slope. Until
nine o'clock they held on, but finally Amilakvari was
forced to order the retreat. He was marching back beside
the regimental doctor when a salvo of shells bracketed both
of them. The doctor was unhurt, but a fragment had pierced
the colonel's kepi. He never heard Father Jean Hirlemann
administer the last rites on the tank that transported him to
the rear. Dmitri Amilakvari, refugee Russian prince at
eleven, had never known anything else but the Legion. As
Monclar said,"Amilakvari *is* the Legion; his whole life is
wrapped up in it." As they buried him in front of El
Himeimat they remembered one of his favorite sayings:
"The only way for us foreigners to repay our debt to France
is to die for her."

Most of the demi-brigade was buried in Tunisia; the
end of that vicious campaign found it with no more than
1,000 men. But with the American landings and the finish
of Vichy rule in Morocco, the 13the received an infusion of
African veterans. In Algeria and Morocco the Legion
strength had dropped to its lowest point for half a century,
though it still provided the allies with two regiments.
Newly equipped, the demi-brigade joined the Allied forces
in Italy in April 1944. At Radicofani the advance was
halted by a miniature Monte Cassino—a sheer cliff capped
by a Renaissance castle. Three Panther tanks guarded the
approaches to the pinnacle, while the castle was still filled
with Germans. They had, nevertheless, left the cliff face un-
defended, since they thought it too precipitous to climb.
Lieutenant Jullian asked for five volunteers and set off with
ropes and pitons to claw his way up; in front Lieutenant
Poirel and a company of legionnaires took on the tanks and
kept the Germans in the castle occupied. The astonished
garrison found itself assaulted from the rear by Jullian and
his five legionnaires, who rained grenades into each room

and compelled the three officers and ninety men to surrender.

After fighting for four years through three continents, the 13th landed at Cavalaire in the South of France on August 16, 1944. They helped to take Toulon, then moved up the Rhone Valley to Lyons. Their thinning ranks suddenly filled out with a battalion of Ukrainians who had been pressganged into the German army but had escaped. The Legion liberated Belfort and fought fiercely for two of the Rhine bridges. Reunited with the Marching Regiment, formed in North Africa, it turned to attack the Colmar Pocket. In that bitter January of 1945 men froze to death among the pines and potassium mines around Thann and Mulhouse in Alsace, their rifles still in their hands. One of their tanks entered and liberated Colmar—with four dead legionnaires on its rear platform. The Marching Regiment went on to the Danube and beyond, but the 13th had fought its last battle of the war. Only seven hundred men could still march; and only a handful were officers and men who had sworn allegiance to Free France in June 1940.

FOURTEEN

Be not happy to lie
With a congaï.
Black are her designs,
Yellow her breasts,
Black their nipples.
Do not fondle the cursed things,
For if she yields them to you,
You are lost. . . .

The card, embossed with the Rising Sun and the insignia of the Japanese army of Canton, requested the honored presence of French officers of the Lang Son garrison at a banquet in the Imperial army's divisional headquarters at eight o'clock that evening, March 9, 1945. A strange invitation, the more so since relations between the Japanese and French forces in Indochina had remained cool since the invasion of 1940. Japan had broken the treaty it had made then with the Vichy Government by increasing its forces; Kempetai secret agents had stirred the Siamese and Vietnamese to rebellion against the white colonists. The Kempetai knew, too, that American arms were reaching the Fifth Foreign Legion Regiment, garrisoned all over northern Indochina, with its base in the Hanoi Delta. Why were the Japanese suddenly so friendly, especially with the Americans on Iwo Jima and virtually encircling their country? General Émile Lemonnier, French commander of the Lang Son area, pondered this question when the invitation ar-

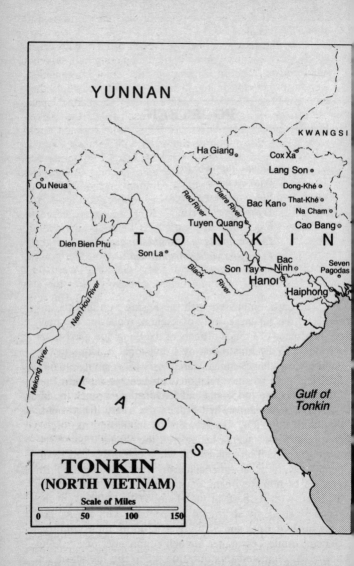

YUNNAN

KWANGSI

Ha Giang

Cox Xa

Lang Son

Dong-Khé

Ou Neua

Red River

Claire River

Bac Kan

That-Khé

Na Cham

Tuyen Quang

Cao Bang

T O N K I N

Dien Bien Phu

Son La

Black River

Son Tay

Bac Ninh

Seven Pagodas

Hanoi

Nam Hou River

Haiphong

Mekong River

L A O S

Gulf of Tonkin

TONKIN
(NORTH VIETNAM)

Scale of Miles

| 0 | 50 | 100 | 150 |

rived. Nonetheless, he gave some of his staff permission to attend the banquet.

The Japanese received the French officers with oriental courtesy, escorting them to the banqueting hall, where a band played Western jazz music and senior commanders were waiting to toast them in sake. At eight o'clock, as they prepared to sit down, the music suddenly stopped; a Japanese officer uttered an order; the French found themselves looking into revolver muzzles. Those who resisted arrest were shot or thrust through ruthlessly with Samurai swords.

The Japanese had also taken General Lemonnier and the French resident, Camille Auphelle, prisoner. A Japanese general pushed a surrender document in front of them. "You will sign," he said. "Never," cried Lemonnier and threw the paper on the ground. Both men were taken in trucks to the Kilua grottoes near the Chinese border and ordered to dig two graves. Then with their hands tightly bound, both men were ordered to kneel before the graves; an officer and a sergeant with heavy Samurai swords upraised, stepped from the Japanese company. "For the last time, will you sign?" Lemonnier shook his head. The officer's sword glinted; the French general's head fell into his grave. A moment later Auphelle suffered the same treatment.

Throughout Tonkin the Night of the Samurai had begun. In Lang Son a Japanese regiment had surprised the Brière de l'Isle fort, guarded by Lieutenant Jean-Pierre Duronsoy and just over a hundred legionnaires. Barricading one building, Duronsoy and the men fought the rest of that night and the next day until their ammunition ran out. Even when the Japanese had breached the doors the legionnaires fought them off with their bayonets. Marching the prisoners into the courtyard, the Japanese lined them against a wall. "Shoot the officers but spare the men," Duronsoy shouted. The Japanese sneered. Duronsoy started to chant the *Marseillaise;* the words were taken up by Sergeant Pilič, the Czech, corporals Tsarikopoulou and Emerich, a Greek and a German, legionnaires Shkolny, Holland, Gaesert, Ionescu, and a handful of others. At the second couplet bursts from machine guns cut their feet; the Japanese fell on the wounded men with bayonets and swords, gun butts, knives, and even picks. That grisly slaughter lasted more than an hour.

At Ha Giang, the post on the Claire River, the same scenario was enacted. At Hanoi, Captain Georges Fenautrigues was assassinated as he tried to join his regiment. Sergeant majors Roman and Demont defended the citadel. Badly wounded, Roman crawled from man to man giving orders. They opened the jails; the legionnaires spilled out, grabbed rifles and ammunition, and sold their lives at the cost of more than fifty Japanese. "Those prisoners were the pride of the Legion," said an adjutant, one of the few survivors.

The headquarters of the Fifth Foreign Legion Regiment lay at Tong, northwest of Hanoi. To spare the civilian population, General Marcel Alessandri moved the men out of the town and began to regroup the other Legion units west of Vietri. Unless he moved those 2,000 men, the Japanese army of 40,000 would catch and massacre them. But where to go? The Japanese controlled the Hanoi and Haiphong deltas; they would block the southern route, too. Alessandri decided to march west, then north into China, where Chaing Kai-shek's nationalists would give them aid. But more than five hundred miles through the worst jungles in Tonkin and Laos with men who had lived "soft" for more than five years! Wasn't it asking the three battalions to commit harakiri?

Alessandri was a remarkable soldier. World War I, Morocco, then Indochina, his second home. He spoke the languages of Annam and Laos and no Buddhist monk lived more ascetically. At fifty he would still march all day, having eaten only a ball of rice and a morsel of fruit. The jungle, he knew, had no allies; it would hinder the Japanese as well. He fined down the column by disbanding the native Tonkin troops. Since they had no vehicles, the Legion would march; it had no colonel or battalion commanders either. The battalions were led by three captains, but all bred in the legion tradition: Roger Gaucher, barrel-chested and hard-drinking, had the first; Guy de Cockborne, a gruff *"baroudeur"* had the second; Raoul Lenoir, a dedicated soldier, had the third. Alessandri's instructions were formal: a fighting retreat to China without letting the Japanese engage them too severely.

Their men had an average of fourteen years' Legion service and an average age of forty. Leaving their base and Indochina came as a wrench to most of them—and their *congaï,* those Vietnamese girls who served as wives and mistresses, hostesses and handmaidens. These *congaï* seemed to run the Legion; a legionnaire who got into trouble in town or barracks and had his pay docked and a month in the cells had to reckon with the fragile beauty who ran his home. A man with a *congaï* could not afford to tangle with his officers. Sergeant Leibner, for instance. For the first three of his fifteen years' service this Sudeten German had been in and out of prison. His *congaï,* Moona, had tamed him, made him work for promotion—which meant more pay—and converted him into an exemplary legionnaire. The *congaï* lined up with the battalions, but Alessandri was firm. "Only native guides," he said.

The day after the massacres several thousand Japanese attacked the regiment as it made to cross the Black River. Lenoir's battalion lost seventy-five men, killed and wounded, but beat back the assault until the column had swum its horses, and many of its men, across the river. Eighty miles west, Son La was signaling that Japanese had surrounded its small force of sixty legionnaires under Lieutenant Chenel. De Cockborne, who had struck north, now had to turn and march to their relief.

On March 25 the two forces clashed in the thick undergrowth, steaming with rain and mist. No question of tactics, even of firing and reloading. You bayoneted, clubbed, kicked, and gouged your way out of trouble. But at nightfall it was the Japanese who withdrew, leaving more than 150 dead.

Three days later it was the Meos Pass, where the Japanese had ringed the bridges with two regiments supported by mortars and mountain guns. Gaucher's battalion was split on the hill and valley, with de Cockborne between. For two days they staved off fanatical Japanese attacks. Gaucher charged with a company to silence a battery of guns, then covered the other two battalions as they filed across the bridges. Another forty men had gone; another forty-odd wounded, among them a Russian sergeant, Gustave Schuvetz, who would live to carry Captain Danjou's wooden hand on Camerone Day, 1971. He and Sergeant Leibner had to wade and swim the river to rejoin the battalion.

That night Leibner was standing guard at the edge of the bivouac when something moved in the scrub; he raised his rifle to cover it. A voice whispered, "It is me." Moona, his *congaï*, dripping wet. For nearly 150 miles she had trailed the battalion. She had been a stranger in her village. What would she do if she did not follow and look after him? Leibner brought her what food he had, and a blanket, and she slept at his feet. "You're a leery one, Sarge," his men said the next day. "Taking your camp comforts with you." However, they knew Leibner for a quiet soldier who would never have flouted Alessandri's and Gaucher's order. Nevertheless, Moona now marched behind them. She shared their rations, though more often brought them rice and small bits of meat she had begged from villagers; at night she crept into the camp to cook Leibner's food, to patch his tattered clothes and bandage his feet. She proved clever with her hands. From her they learned how to split female bamboo to make a bed, how to use the hollow branches to boil their rice and drinking water. Somehow she also distracted their thoughts from the long road ahead and the Japanese behind and on either flank.

Dien Bien Phu almost spelled the end of their march; the Japanese had caught up and flung in 3,000 men to capture the airstrip and surround the Legion. The airstrip guard joined the Third Battalion to hold off the thrust until Gaucher and de Cockborne broke through the west pass. Covered by the Second Battalion, Gaucher pushed through to safety, but de Cockborne found his men under heavy pressure. Riding his white mare, Estafette, armed with only a riding switch, the bespectacled captain spurred forward through shot and shell and the bewildered Japanese ranks. The regiment pressed on, over wild hills and tangled valleys, to the Nam Hou River. By now only the strong had survived. More than three hundred legionnaires had died in the fighting; in the valleys and jungles of the Nam Hou several hundred more dropped out, sick and spent. Those left walked on bare feet or strips of clothing; they existed on a spoonful of meat and a handful of rice a day. Half the men were suffering from beriberi and could march no more than a few miles a day. Sergeant Leibner was one of those affected; his hands and feet had lost their feeling and he fumbled on, supported by two of his section. Each night Moona bathed his sores and he limped on until he could continue no longer. "Leave me a bayonet," he told the men. "You can make it, Sarge. Look, there's the Yunnan hills over there." But the Japanese had not yet finished with them; before Ou Neua they tumbled on Gaucher's rear guard. Somehow, Sergeant Leibner found the courage to stagger forward at the head of his section, only to drop with a bullet in his chest. The Japanese bayoneted him where he lay, but three men drove them back and recovered the body. He was dead. They could see that. The old man who had set his heart on living and dying in this cursed country had had his wish. When they had beaten off the Japanese, Leibner's *congaï* appeared; she gazed at the body, though she did not cry; she prised the rifle he still grasped from his hand and walked like a mechanical doll into the jungle. No one ever heard of her again.

On May 2 the last of Alessandri's men crossed into Yunnan. They had marched and fought for fifty-three days against a Japanese army of 10,000; they had covered seven hundred miles of the toughest mountain and jungle in the world. More than 1,000 legionnaires still had to march, barefooted, three hundred miles through the desolate Yunnan Mountains to Tsao-pa. Not until June 15 could they rest and treat their wounded and sick. On February 8, 1946, they marched back as a fighting unit to Tonkin.

Without the Legion, France could never have reoccupied Indochina. The 1940 débâcle and nearly five years of German rule had weakened the country and soured its citizens to any type of military service. In the Liberation Day and July 14 parades Parisians saved their loudest cheers for the white kepis, on their way back to Indochina. Did those crowds lining the Champs Élysées realize they were shouting for hated Nazi SS officers and men? For with great subtlety—and not without a certain irony—the French were recruiting in prisoner-of-war camps within their own military zone of Germany. British and American military authorities might protest; so might socialist and communist deputies in the French National Assembly and the East German communist party. Legion depots at Offenburg and Landau continued to fill with thousands of crack soldiers.

The Legion had always attracted large numbers of Germans; the former German soldiers and SS men had more inducement than most to join. A soft bribe helped, too. Volunteers were sieved out from other prisoners, formed their own camp, and lived well and on good terms with French officers. They and their families got extra clothing and food rations. As for French, British, American, and German protests—why, they had volunteered. And such was the myth of the Legion that the protests dried up. What French army unit could have enlisted former Hitler Youth and SS men to fight a colonial war? What right-thinking politician, anywhere, would have tolerated it? It took the myth to blind and bewilder them. Battalions of Germans passed rapidly through Bel-Abbès and Saida. Between January 1946 and November, no fewer than five regiments and two parachute battalions landed in Indochina—mostly Germans.

General Leclerc's expeditionary force had already reconquered most of the towns and forts in Indochina. But now a new leader was preaching independence—and communism. Ho Chi Minh had proclaimed himself President of Vietnam (the old provinces of Tonkin, Annam, and Cochin-China), and though he had concluded a treaty permitting the return of French troops, he was secretly arming and training guerrillas. In 1947 the uneasy truce was ruptured when the Vietminh began to attack French posts. Legion units went back to their old role of pacification; only this time the oil-stain theory of Gallieni and Lyautey made little mark. Better equipped and trained by their own and Chinese officers, the Vietminh had forgotten nothing of the cruelty of their forebears, even adding a few novel touches. Near Saigon they crucified seventeen legionnaires from the Third Regiment. Slitting the skin on their backs with a razor, they nailed them to crosses; the men slid down the crucifixes, stripping the skin off and dying a slow, agonizing death. Others were impaled on bamboo chairs, the spikes of which entered their bodies a few inches more each day; or they were covered with honey and left for giant red ants. So that they could use even the last cartridge, legionnaires learned to place a bayonet between their fifth and sixth ribs and give a thump; that way they avoided torture.

It was nothing like the old Tonkin. Even *choum* and rice wine tasted bitter, perhaps because the High Command hinted that the Vietminh were poisoning it. The *congaï*, beautiful, submissive, devoted, were losing their charm, especially after the whisper went that the Vietminh had purposely infected the most lovely with venereal disease for the benefit of French troops. Legionnaires preferred the suspect *congaï* to the military brothel, and merely hid the disease they caught.

The French High Command seemed to share none of the misgivings of legionnaires about controlling Vietnam from isolated posts with such few troops. From Cao Bang to Lang Son they still held the towns and forts on Colonial Route 4, which ran parallel to the Chinese border. By this time several new names had appeared on both sides of this frontier: Mao Tse-tung in China and General Vo Nguyen Giap in the French territory. Giap knew that, once he had cut the RC 4, he could flood Vietnam with Chinese equipment and his troops, which were training under the Chinese. In the summer of 1948 he had drilled a new Vietminh force and was seeking the chance to rehearse it. He chose a small fort on Colonial Route 3, also leading from Cao Bang to Hanoi.

Sunday, July 25, 1948. A day like every other at Phu Tong Hoa. What can anybody do in a mud and bamboo fort overlooking a Viet village? They man the blockhouses at each corner, signal "All Quiet" to Bac Kan a few miles south. Sergeant Pierre Guillemaud, the quartermaster, and his Belgian friend, Corporal Pierre Polain, have tried fishing in the stream. Not much luck. Second Lieutenant Bevalot is settling in, having arrived only forty-eight hours before. A couple of German legionnaires, one from the Afrika Korps and the other from Koenig's brigade, are discussing Bir-Hakeim. The others are reading or playing cards for the pay they can't spend. That evening the cook does them proud by spiking their *soupe* with a bit more meat. They know it's Sunday. Captain Henri Cardinal, who commands the Second Company of the Third Legion Regiment, tells the men about the exploits of Captain Antoine Mattei, the hero who chased and all but caught Ho Chi Minh in the Tonkin jungles. A day like any of the two hundred they have passed isolated in Phu Tong Hoa. Except that, in the mist and downpour, no one has spotted any of Giap's 4,000 crack troops infiltrating the scrub-covered hills and placing artillery only 850 yards away.

Just before 7:30 P.M. Guillemaud and Polain are lighting another couple of MICs, the crude local cigarettes. This Polain, a craggy-faced giant, is a born brawler. Trained by British commandos, he has come through Narvik, Bir-Hakeim, and France with the Legion. Several wounds, but always lucky ones. An up-and-down service sheet, though he invariably lands on his feet. They say they can hear his booming voice and deep belly laugh at Bac Kan, and an officer has written in his war diary, "Legionnaire Polain's laugh prevented me from determining the real strength of the enemy fire." No one has beaten his time for drinking and holding twenty pints of beer.

The light is going when the two NCOs hear a couple of explosions inside the fort. The 75-mm shells have destroyed the main gate and are landing in the compound. "Get plenty of lemons [grenades] ready," Polain shouts and runs to his post on the bamboo wall. Shells are bursting on every building: the barrack rooms, the captain's office, the radio hut, the cookhouse. More than thirty hit their targets before the legionnaires quiet the artillery with their mortars and surviving 37-mm gun. But one shell has hit both Captain Cardinal and Lieutenant Fernand Charlotton, who now lie dying in the command post. Bevalot, a week with the Legion, now takes command. Two blockhouses have gone; huge gaps appear in the walls. The Vietminh are plastering them with mortar and machine-gun fire from the horseshoe hills. Bevalot can only fall back on the one intact blockhouse and point his mortars at the widening breaches.

The barrage ceases; in dead darkness they hear five trumpet notes. Within minutes a screaming horde of Vietminh surge through the holes and up into the third block-

house. *"Tien-Len, Anh Hai! Doc Lap! Di, di, Maulen."*
(On, on, elder brother! On, on at the double.) They yelled,
too, "Uncle Ho will live for a thousand years." The walls
bulge under their weight. Bevalot's mortars, almost verti-
cal, are lobbing bomb after bomb on the breaches. From the
radio post, where he has crawled, Captain Cardinal is crying, weakly, *"En avant,* legionnaires. At hand-to-hand
they're not worth a light."

Corporal Polain runs to the stores. "Come on, Guillemaud, more lemons."

"How's it going?"

"Not badsome. Only 4,000 to 5,000 of them with big
bangers . . . the captain's dying and my boots are full of
rain. . . . Apart from that, we're doing fine . . . if only I had
a fag. . . ." Guillemaud hands him a packet of MICs. "I
hope I see these out," Polain booms and lights one. He
grabs a bag of grenades and runs back to the main doors,
which he is defending with Corporal Huguen. Guillemaud
catches the hoarse bellow and the strident laugh as he pep-
pers the Vietminh with grenades. But, behind his own ar-
mory, he picks up the chomp of feet in the mud. "Bischoff,
do you hear. Behind the gun room."

"They've bust through, Sarge."

Guillemaud creeps up to Blockhouse Three. Hundreds
of Vietminh have filtered between the double row of bamboo stakes and are waiting to break into the compound.
From the blockhouse a Vietminh officer shouts, "Surrender,
you are prisoners." Impudent fool! Guillemaud shuts him
up with a grenade before he and Bischoff rain their
grenades into the narrow gallery. *"Maulen, maulen."* The
Vietminh stampede out, leaving fifty dead and wounded.

The downpour stops; the moon glimmers above the
hills. Corporal Polain, a sodden cigarette in his mouth,
curses as he fights off the Vietminh by the door. Huguen
falls, but the big Belgian stands over his body, clubbing at
half a dozen little men with his unloaded rifle, plying a
knife in the other hand. A Vietminh drops behind him. The
bayonet thrust takes him in the heart and the Viets clamber
over his body. At his side Legionnaire Chauve, a spaniel-
eyed little gypsy, takes a burst of machine-gun fire in the
chest. At the stores they bandage him, but have no mor-

phine. "Sarge . . . finish me off, for pity's sake." Guillemaud shakes his head. "We'll get you to the infirmary." A few minutes and Chauve is dead.

Bevalot has succeeded in mounting a counterattack on Blockhouse Three. At the breach sergeants Andry and Fissler and three legionnaires go in with their bayonets and the Vietminh recoil. Step by step they clear the blockhouse, the breaches, and the few Vietminh sticking inside the compound. At 3 A.M. the post again belongs to the Legion. Inside, forty Vietminh lie dead; they count twenty-one of their own enlisted men and NCOs dead and thirty-three wounded. Lieutenant Charlotton has died and Captain Cardinal will die that day. How many of the Vietminh dead have been carried away they do not know.

The legionnaires bury their own and the enemy dead, repair the damage, and stand on alert. The relief column from Bac Kan has been ambushed and forced back, but another force has left Cao Bang, commanded by their colonel, Jean Simon. But with five bridges blown and the road cut every few hundred yards and ambushes at every turn of the sixty miles, Simon takes two days to reach Phu Tong Hoa. As he nears the post Guillemaud has one last task—to find six new blue cummerbunds and six pairs of red epaulets. When Simon walks into the compound Sergeant Andry and five legionnaires present arms as though it were a ceremonial occasion.

Simon and other officers, such as Mattei, who were in the area found some disquieting evidence around Phu Tong Hoa: the latest American rifles, supplied to Chaing Kaishek's troops in China; recoilless guns, which even the French army did not possess, used in a concerted attack by disciplined soldiers rehearsed for the operation. That July night Phu Tong Hoa became the stage for the first act of the Vietnam tragedy. The day the legionnaires were mopping up, the French had changed their government for the umpteenth time. The new premier, Paul Reynaud, deemed it imprudent to mention Indochina. In any case, who cared about a mud and bamboo post in the middle of Tonkin? Who envisaged the attack as marking the beginning of the calvary of France—and the Legion—in Indochina?

* * *

The second act of the Indochina tragedy began in 1949, with murderous attacks on the RC 4. Those sixty miles from Cao Bang to Lang Son, with their jungle and scrub, their crags and gorges, their five hundred bends, made ideal terrain for Vietminh attacks. The Legion was losing more men on supply columns than in the posts themselves. "Ah! You're not married," they would say to young officers in Hanoi. "Good. You're for the RC 4, where bachelors can die without too much family fuss." Officers sometimes drew lots, then spent a commiserative evening drinking with the losers.

At the beginning of 1949 a convoy of two hundred trucks was ambushed. Colonel Simon formed his one hundred legionnaires into a solid phalanx, beat off the Vietminh with grenades, and salvaged 120 vehicles. Only one of hundreds of ambushes, but it changed the life of twenty-two-year-old Sergeant László Tasnády, who, like many of his countrymen, had fled the communist purges in Hungary in 1946 to join the Legion. Cut off from his section, Tasnády sought cover in the bushes; he watched the Vietminh, inflamed with *choum,* slaughter wounded legionnaires with bayonets, knives, and rifle butts; their women, even more bloodthirsty, castrated and decapitated wounded and dead.

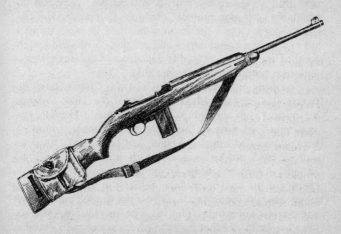

M1 Carbine

In those moments the reserved, soft-spoken Hungarian student decided that Indochina meant kill or be killed. He would survive dozens of ambushes to become one of the best guerrilla fighters the Legion ever had in its ranks. With any form of weapon he had an uncanny instinct; with an M1 carbine he could down kite-hawks on the wing, one after another, and was the finest marksman with this weapon that any modern Legion officer can remember. He once stalked ten Vietminh, crawled after them into a jungle grotto to kill five with grenades and take the others prisoner.

The RC 4 transformed Tasnády as it did everyone and everything—except the thinking of the French High Command, obsessed with clinging to this chain of posts against Vietminh twenty times their strength. Legionnaires and their officers lived with the foreboding of death. France, they felt, had abandoned them, leaving their forgotten army to wage a war that no Frenchman knew or cared about. Nonetheless, some people carried on bravely. Those in Cao Bang, for instance. The Chinese frontier lay a few miles away; the Vietminh occupied the hills around, calling on their *tannoy* day and night for the surrender of the fortress. Inside, the insouciant legionnaires were enjoying themselves. Why not? They had rebuilt the ruin left by the Japanese and the Vietminh into a modern town of 20,000 people. They had an abundance of liquor, brothels, cinemas, European and Vietnamese night clubs—the Legion thumbed its nose at Giap and his puritan communists and reveled in its own rough brand of imperialist, capitalist decadence. Cao Bang was a Legion recruiting brochure come alive.

Inspiring much of this *dolce vita* was Comte Hervé de Broca, alias Sergeant Major Burgens of the Third Foreign Regiment. De Broca, minister under Edouard Herriot, undersecretary of state in the Vichy Government, friend of Pierre Laval and Marshal Pétain, had been condemned to death in 1945, but had escaped. With more than £1 million cached in Switzerland, he might have sought refuge anywhere; for his own reasons he enlisted in the Legion and volunteered for Indochina. At fifty-eight he took part in several skirmishes around That-Khé before landing at Cao Bang to put his genius for administration at the Legion's disposal. To improve the amenities of the hill fortress, he commandeered foie gras, caviar, champagne, women, jeeps, the latest in men's and women's fashions from Hanoi and beyond. It never failed to impress the Legion that de Broca's Junkers flew crates of champagne or vintage claret directly into the dropping zone while cannons or bales of barbed wire invariably landed among the Vietminh. He dealt in everything, including secret information. In 1949 he stood up, champagne glass in hand, to address fellow NCOs in the mess. "*Messieurs*, up to now, the Third Foreign Legion has been commanded by a great gentleman whom I salute in passing—*le colonel Simon.* Tomorrow, a god of the Legion will drop from the sky—*le colonel Charton.*"

De Broca had made his last public utterance at Cao Bang. Colonel Pierre Charton thought he could deploy his talents more effectively at Lang Son, where Colonel Constans was searching for a major-domo. So for months Sergeant Major Burgens ran the colonel's house like a palace. Legionnaires, hand-picked for height and Nordic good looks, accompanied Constans everywhere, singing German *Lieder;* they waited on tables during the sumptuous banquets Constans, or de Broca, laid on for visiting American army and navy chiefs. De Broca (sometimes mistaken by visitors for his colonel) excelled himself by providing a chamber orchestra and a full-blooded Annamite princess for two American ship captains who made the tour of Lang Son.

Between Cao Bang and Lang Son, the RC 4 was anything but gay for the men. In posts like Nam Nang, Dong-Khé, That-Khé, and Na Cham, legionnaires and officers sensed that Giap would pick them off, as had happened at Phu Tong Hoa. To while away the time until the Viets attacked, some of them devised macabre sports. "Buffalo" became a favorite. Its rules did not tax the intellect. Two men got drunk, each swallowing a bottle of spirits; with hands bound behind their backs, they charged each other like bulls until one broke his head. "Cuckoo" called for a little more skill. Again, the bottle of spirits. Each legionnaire was then given a revolver and nine shots and they were left in a darkened room together. One man cried "cuckoo" and the other shot; the second man had his turn until all eighteen shots had been fired or one man had been wounded or killed. Commandant de Lambert posted an order forbidding this gruesome game the day a corporal was picked up with a bullet through his brain. Some legionnaires did not wait to be killed. A Spanish private lay down on a live grenade the day that General Monclar made a tour of Dong-Khé. "A stiff that's done himself in . . . that's unlucky. . . . If old Monclar sees that . . ." So the body was covered and switched from room to room in front of Monclar as he inspected the post; nor did he guess that it followed him and his staff car to Lang Son, where they buried it.

In May 1950, Giap hurled a strong force against Dong-Khé, overwhelming it within a few hours. Several days later a Legion parachute battalion recovered the fort, and 260 legionnaires from the Third Regiment installed themselves as a garrison. Giap spent months rehearsing an army of nearly 20,000 men to seize the vital fort once and for all. On September 15 these sixteen Vietminh battalions had encircled Dong-Khé. At dawn on the sixteenth they attacked.

First they picked off the five outposts surrounding the fort on the rocky slopes. At ten o'clock the legionnaires inside the post rubbed their eyes; the hills seethed with troops who dropped in their rehearsed positions like robots; their artillery was battering the citadel and the old fortified quar-

105 mm. Gun

ter in the lower town. Throughout the day the legionnaires stood off the attack under heavy shelling from guns and mortars. A bomb burst on their 105-mm gun, wrecking it and killing the crew. Rare survivors from the outposts fought back into the citadel to battle once more for their lives. By nine o'clock in the evening the Vietminh had breached the northwest wall and were fighting hand-to-hand with the cookhouse fatigue squad.

At ten o'clock a Vietminh hero, La Van Cau, pushed a bamboo trunk stuffed with dynamite through a loophole and blew down a section of the wall. Falling back behind their 57-mm gun, the legionnaires held off the waves of Giap's forces until dawn. Both sides seemed exhausted by twenty-four hours of combat, but somehow the 6th Company found the reserves to charge and drive the Viets out of the citadel.

The next afternoon Giap attacked again. The same pattern. Massive artillery bombardment, then waves of marionette infantry. After eleven hours of fighting the legionnaires again massed behind the 57-mm, its barrel now horizontal. Only their command post remained.

The Vietminh massed for the final charge. The twenty men had three hundred cartridges, which they shared. The solid wall of little men bore down. Into it the legionnaires charged wildly, desperately. Only five broke through to reach That-Khé to recount the horror of Dong-Khé. In that battle eight-five had died and 140 were captured, badly wounded. . . . Giap had sacrificed eight hundred men. But he had finally cut the RC 4.

In Hanoi the fall of Dong-Khé provoked a panic decision to evacuate Cao Bang. General Alessandri urged an airlift or a column along the RC 3, where Giap had fewer troops. Who listened these days to Alessandri? No, they would win back Dong-Khé and cover Charton's march along the RC 4. On September 16 a column started from Lang Son, a patchwork force of North Africans led by Colonel Lepage, a gunner with little jungle experience and no knowledge of his mission. They decided to stiffen this Bayard Group with the First Foreign Parachute Battalion, which dropped on That-Khé and linked with Lepage on September 19.

The 1st BEP was commanded by Major Pierre Segrétain, but the man who had converted the unit into the crack battalion of the Legion was Captain Pierre Jeanpierre. This dynamic and resolute soldier had virtually returned from the dead to the Legion. After the Syrian campaign Jeanpierre had chosen repatriation; but what he saw of Vichy France did not please him. In occupied France he had gone underground with the French Resistance. Under direct control from London, he had commanded a resistance area near Paris, smuggling arms into the city to train men for its defense when the Allies landed. Trapped by the Gestapo in Orléans, where he went to warn one of his network, he was tortured and deported to Mauthausen, the notorious extermination camp from which few Frenchmen came back. Jeanpierre did—with a scarred lung and a scarred mind, which relived those horrors for two years. Yet he bore no grudge against Germans; most of his battalion were former Wehrmacht soldiers he had helped to recruit into the Legion. Every step of his own promotion from private soldier had been gained on the battlefield. In his battalion he demanded only the toughest and best.

For ten days the Bayard Group played cat and mouse with Giap around That-Khé. On September 30 a coded message arrived from Colonel Constans at Lang Son: "Take Dong-Khé on October 2," it said. What! Four battalions against thirty!

The paratroopers led, of course. At their head, with the cream of the battalion, twenty-five-year-old Roger Faulques, model of the Legion paratroop officer: plucky, resourceful, and intelligent. Several miles from Dong-Khé they collided with a Vietminh patrol, to kill three but watch two others escape to warn Giap. "Go hell-for-leather," Jeanpierre ordered Faulques by radio. "It's the only chance to take Dong-Khé—if it's empty." The valley seemed deserted, but from the ruined fort and a pagoda bursts of mortar and machine-gun fire pinned Faulques and his squad. Jeanpierre, who was following with a company, ducked under the fire to where Faulques lay. It was just after six. "There aren't many of them," Jeanpierre said. "If Lepage threw in everything, we could take it." The captain and the lieutenant scrambled through the fire to within a few hundred yards of the battered citadel, seeking dead ground from which to attack. "We've a last chance to take it," Jean-pierre told Lepage by radio. Lepage ordered them to pull back. The Vietminh held the crests, he said. Maybe that quick thrust would have saved the column; maybe what happened was inevitable.

The next day Lepage split his group into two to attempt a pincer movement on Dong-Khé; the paratroopers and a Moroccan unit would hold the hills east of the fortress while he and the rest of the column came in from the west. But that day—October 2—both columns ran into trouble. Segrétain's battalion blundered into a regiment of Vietminh hidden in the jungle crests, fought them off, but had to backtrack. Across the valley Lepage and his column reached Dong-Khé airstrip only to be beaten back. The Vietminh had now surmised the French plan and French fighters overhead were signaling that a vast army was seeping over the hills and jungle tracks around Dong-Khé. Only then did Lang Son inform Lepage of his real mission. A message dropped by aircraft told him to meet Colonel Charton and his column from Cao Bang and escort them. With Giap alerted and an army sitting astride the RC 4! Could they now proceed with the evacuation? "It will be a crime to continue," cabled Alessandri to his chiefs in Hanoi.

Lepage was walking into a hornet's nest. And Charton would be late at their rendezvous, fixed north of Dong-Khé on October 3. At Cao Bang, Charton fumed about the evacuation. He could have held for two years with two good battalions. He destroyed everything that might help the Vietminh and at midday on October 3 set out with his column. Had he traveled light he might have linked with Lepage a day or two earlier. But Charton had "flitted." With him he had guns, fifteen trucks loaded with stores, and five hundred natives he had promised not to desert. The colonel reckoned that he might have to punch a hole through Giap's army and a heavy column was better than a light one. How could he guess that, by the time he quit Cao Bang, Lepage and the escort group had become enmeshed in the crags and jungle around Dong-Khé and the post could not be retaken?

Only when he got to the rendezvous on October 4 did he
learn that Lepage was fighting for existence. Lang Son sent
an SOS, ordering Charton to take the old, disused Quang-
Liet Trail over the crests to aid Lepage. Charton destroyed
his lorries, stores, his guns, and issued the men and the partisans two days' rations. Now they were cutting their way in
single file along the trail long ago reclaimed by the jungle;
legionnaires carried children and pregnant Vietnamese
women; others had their wounded on stretchers. By some
freak, they stumbled on the Quang-Liet Trail and after two
days of chopping through the jungle came within sight and
sound of Lepage and his force, still trying to make the junc-
tion. But between them lay an army of Vietminh.

First they attacked the Third Legion Battalion with artillery and fanatical charges to dislodge it from vital crests;
the legionnaires massacred the Vietminh infantry and hung
on. On another crest, however, the Moroccans fell back in
panic. "We've got to keep the crests and open the passage,"
Charton told Major Michel Forget, commanding the Third.
Forget, who had limped all the way from Cao Bang, suffering from an old wound, gathered the men and flung them at
the peaks taken by the Vietminh. If they failed, Charton's
column would be trapped and annihilated. Forget himself
hobbled into the assault with his bayonet and cleared the escarpment; this time, though, the Vietminh were determined
to deny them the passage. One counterattack was flung
back; another succeeded. Again, Forget charged. Ten times
he led the legionnaires against swarms of Giap's men until,
finally, the Vietminh ceded and disappeared into the jungle.
Forget had bullet wounds in the head, the thigh, the chest
and stomach, and several bayonet wounds. "Tell my battalion I'm proud of it," he said as he died. Despite his losses,
Charton still felt that he could break through and retreat
with Lepage to That-Khé and safety. If Lepage had any men
left. . . .

From the Na-Keo ridge east of the RC 4, through the
jungles and valleys around Dong-Khé, Giap's army was literally engulfing the Lepage Column, desperately seeking to
join forces with Charton. For five days and nights the paratroopers and Moroccans were stalked and ambushed and attacked before they saw Charton appear over the crests. On

Na-Keo, Segrétain's battalion threw back a furious Vietminh assault, inflicting more than three hundred casualties,
while Lepage was fumbling west, trying to locate the
Quang-Liet Trail. He, too, had come under attack and was
forced into the Cox-Xa gorges, penned on every side by Vietminh with mortars and artillery. Segrétain and his paratroopers had no water and few rounds of ammunition left.
Rather than risk annihilation on the crags, they began a
nightmare march, with more than one hundred wounded, to
team up with Lepage. They had to scale jagged rocks, hack
at the green gloom of the jungle. And everywhere, Vietminh. Above Cox-Xa a steep precipice halted them;
Faulques inched down a narrow ledge, trailed by his men
humping the wounded. But Lepage had again changed his
mind. "Stay on top," he radioed. For a whole day the paratroopers clung to the precipice before receiving a coun-
terorder to descend.

By now the Vietminh had caught them. As the legionnaires stumbled after each other down the twisting ledge in
the downpour, Giap's men surged out of the hills and the
valley below. A man would feel for a comrade's hand to
grasp; instead, a small yellow hand. Then a bullet or a bayonet. Exhausted legionnaires teetered on the precipice, then
dropped to their death. Another one hundred men gone. But
at last they found Lepage in the trap of Cox-Xa. That day—
October 6—they caught sight of Charton arriving to the
northwest on the ridge. But what lay between them? Jeanpierre personally carried out a night reconnaissance and
found an army of Vietminh on the hills. With Segrétain he
appealed to Lepage to wait for daylight and attack, using
every fighter and bomber in that part of Indochina. Lepage
overruled them, insisting that they attempt the breakthrough
then.

Segrétain, Jeanpierre, and Faulques knew it was a suicide mission. For the only time in his career Jeanpierre felt
like disobeying orders. They had no more than 450 legionnaires left and twenty times that number of Vietminh held
the vital peaks between them and Charton. The men had
hardly slept for two days and many had not eaten. Now the
final sacrifice. The word went around. In the downpour the
men mustered silently, picked up rifles and grenades, and

followed their officers. As they climbed the limestone crags everything erupted around them. The hills were stiff with Vietminh—in front with machine guns, to the left with rifles and grenades, to their right with artillery. Even behind, someone was firing. Vietminh? Or nervous Moroccans? The decimated first company attacked the ridge only to recoil; the third company hurled in behind them and seized the position for an hour; the second company sought to press this advantage and was scythed in half. It was blind, brawling combat in the flashes of rifle fire or mortar and shell bursts. Only the will of the battalion shook the Vietminh—these grim men lunging savagely with bayonet, rifle butt, and knife. Lieutenant Faulques had fallen, bullets in both shoulders, his right leg smashed and his left lying open. Propped against a tree, he still called the moves of his company until they were swamped by the Vietminh. Jeanpierre was still battling. As was Segrétain, who had reported for this column crippled with sciatica. At dawn the vital crest separating them from Charton was theirs; the Moroccans surged through the small gap littered with the bodies of legionnaires and Vietminh. The First Foreign Parachute Battalion hardly existed. Less than one hundred men survived that night and most of them were wounded.

Charton had heard the battle in the gorges and the crests. At dawn on October 7 he suddenly saw a horde of frantic Moroccans break on the remnants of his own column, shooting their rifles at anybody in sight. His own native troops, infected with this panic, ran after the Moroccans. This was what still existed of the Bayard Group. Charton assembled his officers. "Make for That-Khé," he told them. "It's every man for himself." He plunged into the jungle with lieutenants Bross and Clerget, his orderly, Walter Reiss, and Sergeant Chief Schoenberger. Within an hour they had walked into a Vietminh ambush. A submachine gun pointed at Charton; Schoenberger heaved himself in front of the colonel to be cut in two by a burst from it. Still, Charton fell, his nose broken, his hip opened by bullets, his body covered with grenade splinters. Bross and Clerget were wielding their rifle butts as though seeking death. Charton shot one Vietminh who charged at him; another ran up to bayonet the fallen colonel but a commissar stopped him.

In the prison camp that night Charton and Faulques met each other for several seconds. Not long enough to learn how the massacre of Cox-Xa had ended for both columns. In any case Faulques was so badly wounded that Vietminh surgeons gave him no chance of surviving. Within weeks he had been released as one of the "living dead." Somehow, Faulques pulled through; he spent a year in a Paris hospital, then his sheer guts took him back on two wobbly legs to fight again in Indochina and Algeria with his paratroopers.

What had happened to the rags of the paratroop battalion? The remaining men Segrétain split into five detachments, giving each officer a map and a compass. His own section was ambushed and Segrétain ordered his men to leave him where he lay, mortally wounded, and push on. Some paratroopers arrived at That-Khé to be confronted by Giap's men, who had taken over the post after its evacuation. Jeanpierre took no chances and made for Lang Son, keeping to the jungle. For seven days and nights he and his section cut and squirmed through miles of jungle, stumbling along by compass and by some freak avoiding Giap's patrols, which were hunting down the remnants of the column. They drank rainwater, but had no food; they marched knee-deep in streams to escape detection, for to be seen, to be heard, was to die. Only the iron determination of Jeanpierre kept himself and the men going. When they eventually tottered out of the jungle before the fortress of Lang Son, Jeanpierre collapsed and was carried into the citadel.

They would make a stand at Lang Son, Legion officers told themselves. Give the Vietminh that and they would then grab Hanoi and the whole country. Lang Son. The name breathed the bull-headed heroism of General de Negrier, the enlightened colonialism of Gallieni; it was a European city with 100,000 inhabitants, wide boulevards, modern administration blocks and dwellings; fine schools, hospitals, shops full of Paris finery. There they would surely turn and fight to win back their posts on the RC 4.

But Hanoi had already instructed Colonel Constans to clear out. Sixty-five years before, Colonel Herbinger had been court-martialed for his precipitate retreat. This was a repeat performance; the same panic, the same legacy of arms, ammunition, and stores to the enemy; the same reluctance by the other side to believe that the French had quit such a stronghold without a fight.

In the general scrum only one man seemed unruffled—the portly, dignified Hervé de Broca. He left little of value. He scratched his great head as he watched the troops leave and got on with his job of packing Colonel Constans' belongings and making a few business deals on the side with the natives who were staying. To the tired and hungry legionnaires from Cao Bang and That-Khé he offered food and liquor—free. De Broca was one of the last to leave Lang Son, though he never left Indochina. At Hanoi he fell ill; they operated, but he died on the table. "Whatever his past, he was a fine legionnaire," said one of his officers. "To join at his age, march and fight and do as much for the Legion demanded a lot of guts."

The evacuation of the RC 4 had cost the French more than 4,000 men. In Lang Son the Vietminh found thirteen heavy guns, 125 mortars, 450 vehicles, three armored cars, 940 machine guns. Five of Giap's regiments would turn these weapons against the French in the last great battle of Indochina. Few military pundits would disagree that the French lost their hold on the country on September 17, when Dong-Khé fell and dragged the whole of the RC 4 and an army inexorably behind it.

With the legionnaires of the Third Regiment who retreated on Hanoi went a young Jewish recruit, Eliahu Itskovitz. Even in the bizarre half-world of the Legion few stories ring as strange as this man's. As a boy of thirteen he was taken from his home town of Chisinau in Rumania and thrown into a concentration camp run by the Iron Guard his Nazi countrymen had formed. The Itskovitz family fell into the hands of the most brutal of the Rumanian Nazis, a guard named Stanescu, who hailed from a neighboring village. This man led Eliahu's parents to the gas chamber; the boy stood, powerless, watching the brute strangle two of his three brothers with his bare hands. His third brother had died by the time the Russians liberated the camp. Alone,

Eliahu survived, a sixteen-year-old skeleton who owed his will to live to one thing: his hatred for the jailer Stanescu.

But Stanescu had fled before the Russian invasion. Nonetheless, when he had recovered his strength, Eliahu went to the guard's home and knocked on the door. Stanescu's son appeared; Eliahu drew a knife and stabbed him in the heart. Walking straight to the police station, the boy confessed to the murder, though pleading that he had every right to revenge himself on the man who had destroyed his whole family. The Rumanian court took the boy's age and his ordeal into consideration, but still sentenced him to five years in a reform school. "I wish to emigrate to Israel," Eliahu told the school governor when he had completed his sentence. The Rumanians raised no objection; Eliahu landed in Israel and immediately joined the paratroopers. As he had envisaged, many of his barracks mates had suffered similar bereavements in Nazi concentration camps. "And one guard named Stanescu? Have you ever heard of him?" he would ask incessantly.

No one had. Until one day a young German Jew reacted to the name. "Stanescu? He escaped across the West German border before the Russians came. . . . No, nobody heard of him after that." Eliahu kept interrogating people. Stanescu had been interned, someone said. Yes, didn't he make his way into the French Zone? Stanescu? "I think that one joined the Foreign Legion, like many of them, to hide out in Indochina." Eliahu had found the clue. He approached his battalion commander. "I want to transfer to the navy," he said. Since the navy needed men, his request was granted. A few months later, when his frigate lay at Genoa picking up supplies, Eliahu walked off the gangway, took the train to Bordighera, crossed the frontier, and made for the Legion depot at Marseilles. At Bel-Abbès he did his three months' training and volunteered for Indochina.

In the barracks at Haiphong he probed discreetly for news of his good friend Stanescu. No. Nobody of that name in the Legion. In the Third there was a Rumanian corporal. Big, blue-jowled. Not somebody you'd share your *pinard* with. Anyway, who wanted the Third, which had just taken some hard knocks at Cao Bang and the RC 4? Eliahu had no difficulty in filling a gap in the Third Regiment, which was moving into the area of the Seven Pagodas in the Haiphong Delta.

And there was Corporal Stanescu; he had finally caught up with the family executioner. Nothing about Stanescu had changed—except his name. But the Rumanian would never have recognized the bronzed, broad-shouldered Eliahu as the bewildered sixteen-year-old waif he had seen in a concentration camp over five years before. Not even when Eliahu maneuvered himself into Stanescu's section did the NCO suspect his real identity. Still, Eliahu wanted to savor his moment of vengeance; this bully and brute must know who his judge and executioner was and have time to remember the father and mother and two brothers he had slain. His opportunity came when he was chosen to patrol with Stanescu in the scrub jungle between Bac-Ninh and the Seven Pagodas on RC 18. The two men found themselves alone; Stanescu was leading Eliahu by a few yards. Suddenly the Jew called out:

"Stanescu!"

The Rumanian whirled at the sound of his real name. Giving him no time to think, Eliahu said in Rumanian, "You really are Stanescu, aren't you?"

"Yes," the NCO stammered. "But . . ."

"Stanescu, I'm one of the Jews of Chisinau."

The corporal tried to say something, but Eliahu was already emptying the clip of his Sten gun into his chest. Picking up the body, he bore it back to the road. A legionnaire looked at it. "The Lemon Peels have had him—the cows!" He glanced at Eliahu. "He was a Rumanian like you, huh?"

"Yes, a Rumanian like me," Eliahu muttered.

Eliahu served his five years and survived the Indochina War. He still had one duty to perform. Presenting himself to the Israeli military attaché in Paris, he confessed that he had deserted the Israeli navy. Then he told the whole story to the astonished official who thought that this young Jew needed rest in a mental home. "Ask the Legion," said Eliahu. "They know part of my story."

Eliahu returned to Tel Aviv in handcuffs to face a

naval tribunal. Three judges gave their verdict. "In view of the circumstances, an Israeli state tribunal cannot bring itself to impose a heavy sentence." Eliahu served a year in prison and finished his term with the navy.

FIFTEEN

Repose in the grandeur of your sacrifice,
Repose, untouched by life's regrets;
Repose in that deep and liberating peace
That I evoke in my sad thoughts.

From where he stood Colonel Roger Gaucher could look northwest at Gabrielle; across the Nam Youm River lay Anne-Marie; around the road, river, and airstrip were clustered Huguette, Françoise, Claudine, Eliane, and Dominique; through the haze of ocherous dust overhanging the valley Gaucher could pick up with his glasses the remote Isabelle, five miles south. Who had chosen such nostalgic and endearing names for the strongpoints around the central base? Who had chosen the base itself—Dien Bien Phu? Gaucher knew it well. In 1945, nine years before, he and de Cockborne had all but left their skins near its tangled airstrip during the long retreat. At that time he had never imagined that the high brass in Hanoi would pick this crossroads, in hostile Thai country between north Laos and Tonkin, to stage a showdown with the Vietminh. He knew the arguments. The politicians contended that they must have a strong base to defend Laos and Tonkin now that Giap had seized the delta and was threatening Laos. Dien Bien Phu, his own chiefs had decided, would serve as a defense base and a springboard for French counteroffensives. They had air mastery, so they could land or drop supplies while Giap would have to stretch his communication lines two hundred miles to threaten Dien Bien Phu.

A natural bastion, according to the armchair soldiers in Hanoi: the higher crests ringing the huge bowl protected it from mass assault; its ridges, astride the road and river, gave them strongpoints from which they could defend the central base and ward off attacks from the twenty miles of surrounding hills.

Gaucher had watched the base grow from November 1953, when Legion paratroopers had seized the overgrown airstrip. He had brought two battalions of the famed 13th Demi-Brigade to build strongpoints such as Beatrice, on which he placed the Third Battalion and his command post. The Legion had bulldozed and lengthened the strip and constructed a series of blockhouses around it. In February the war minister, René Pleven, toured the camp and nearly fell through a dugout roof, shored with nothing but wood and earth. *"Mon colonel,"* he observed to Gaucher, "won't we unfortunately have to reckon with the Vietminh artillery. They tell me they have some." Gaucher replied, *"Monsieur le Ministre*, we shall fight here as we did at Verdun." But he and others had their doubts.

Still Dien Bien Phu swelled to the bursting point with 16,000 troops—all the air force could supply with landings and parachute drops. Of these, legionnaires formed the hard core, 5,000 in all from the 13th, the Second and Third foreign regiments, and the re-formed First Parachute Battalion. The Legion held the key points. Colonel André Lalande, a veteran of Narvik and Bir-Hakeim, commanded Isabelle, which sat astride the Nam Youm and defended the secondary airstrip. Another two battalions straddled the main airstrip at Huguette. An Algerian infantry regiment controlled Gabrielle, the most northerly barb of the hedgehog, while four French paratroop battalions, two Thai battalions, and one Moroccan battalion were disposed over the interior strongpoints in the eight-mile valley. They had a battery of 155 guns and a regiment of 105s. To command Dien Bien Phu they had chosen a cavalry officer, Colonel Christian de Castries, an exponent of mobile warfare stuck in a static base.

By March it had become evident to officers such as Gaucher that Giap had accepted the challenge; his crack divisions were moving into "grandstand" positions on the

3,000-foot hills around them. When he attacked, Beatrice and the Legion would catch it first since they sat closest to the jungle. A solid man, de Castries said of Gaucher. Now nearing fifty, he had achieved his life's ambition two years before: command of a Legion regiment. Like his demi-brigade, everything about Gaucher suggested strength and will: his square, handsome face, heavy build, his ease in command, and his gruff, patronly way with the legionnaires, whom he adored. No, Gaucher and Beatrice would not give.

Gaucher expressed his misgivings, however, to Colonel Pierre Langlais, the second in command and a hard-bitten Breton. "If we really catch it who's going to fill the hole left by your two reserve battalions?" Langlais shrugged. Where could he put reserves, or supply them or feed them? On March 13, as he made his daily tour of Beatrice forward positions, Gaucher reckoned that he might soon need those reserves. They'd said the Vietminh couldn't get guns onto those hills, yet for a month they'd been lobbing

B-26

75-mm shells and heavy mortar bombs onto the runway. They'd said Giap would charge out of the hills and break his army on their machine guns and artillery. But the day before yesterday he'd sapped to within a couple of hundred yards of the barbed wire. And yesterday they'd smashed a Dak on the runway with a 105-mm shell. A 105! God help them

with their bits of corrugated iron and wooden beams if the
Viets had many of those. The legionnaires greeted him as
he climbed out of his jeep. They liked the reassurance of his
tough appearance, his brusque humor, his unerring eye for
the badly sighted machine gun.

"Got enough Tiger's Blood?"

"Oui, mon colonel." Tiger's Blood was Vinogel, the
concentrated, canned red wine they dropped to save aircraft
space. A pint diluted with water made three pints of wine,
but it always had a rusty taste and many drank it neat—to
spare their palates. Old Sammarco, over on Eliane, had
downed two cans without reading the label and was nearly
busted from sergeant for neglect of duty. Vinogel had a
kick like a Spanish mule.

"Not too much today," Gaucher told the men.

"It's for tonight then?"

Gaucher shrugged. Major Pégot, the battalion commander, said, "The men are jittery."

"No time to be jittery. It's for tonight, sure."

As Gaucher drove back to his dugout on Beatrice,
shells and mortar bombs were raining from the hills on the
airstrip; two Dakotas lay like stricken birds, while a Curtis
Commando flamed black and orange in the saffron dust.
Where did the shells—and those 105s especially—come
from? Their Hellcats and B-26s had strafed the Vietminh
gun positions for a month with bombs, cannon, and napalm.
They must have a thousand, or move them after each barrage. In packets of a dozen the 105 shells burst on the central area, scattering men and trucks like ants. Gaucher
briefed his officers that they could expect a Viet onslaught
the moment the guns stopped. The legionnaires had already
guessed. In his machine-gun section Sergeant Kubiak noticed that the officers seemed nervous.

"The lieutenant wants to see you, Sarge."

Kubiak made his way to the command post. The lieutenant appeared uneasy. "We're expecting it tonight," he
said. "It'll be a hot one, so make sure to check the machine
guns so that they can fire all night." Walking back, Kubiak
thought, "There are some edgy ones here, but there must be
some mad ones on the other side. . . . If those Vietminh
have the notion of coming to push us off a hill like Beatrice,

well dug in and held by a Legion battalion, then it won't be
a quiet walk for them." That afternoon he went to split a pint
of Vinogel with another NCO. At 4:55 he was returning.
Was it the Vinogel? No, Beatrice looked as though it were
exploding in its own dust. Around him legionnaires were
pitching face-down, dead or wounded. He galloped for his
own section. Thank God! His men and machine guns had
escaped. Shells erupted around them like giant hailstones.
Dugout by dugout, trench by trench, everything was crumbling, burying men and weapons.

"Keep your head down."

"And they told us they'd no guns, Sarge."

"They're only 105s. Compliments of the U.S.A. via
Chunky Sheikh and Mousy Tongue."

At six o'clock a parachute flare silhouetted the enemy
massing before Beatrice; their guns continued to pummel
every yard of the hill. From his dugout Gaucher rang de
Castries. "It seems I have the honor. The Vietminh are
twenty yards from our barbed wire."

"Will it hold?"

"It'll hold. But we'll need all the guns." Twenty minutes later he called again. "Two Vietminh regiments have
attacked. I must have artillery support."

Miraculously, Sergeant Kubiak and his section had survived the bombardment. In the magnesium glow of the
flares they watched the Vietminh wading heedlessly through
their own shellfire and the machine-gun fire in their faces;
dozens hurled themselves on the barbed wire to blow gaps
in it with plastic charges and let the mass plow through.

In his underground shelter Gaucher could stand it no
longer: listening to bleak reports from forward posts, shouting orders, demanding gunfire and reserves that never came.
Emerging, he strode through the shellfire to the nearest
units, muttering about the dead, organizing the evacuation
of the wounded. "Major Pégot and his officers are dead,"
somebody said. Gaucher grunted. Looking at the splintered
surface of Beatrice and the shreds of his battalion, then at
the Vietminh hordes, he doubted if he could hold. "*Mon
colonel*, don't you think it's better . . ." said the lieutenant
who accompanied him. Gaucher nodded. To get himself
killed wouldn't help. In his command post, a series of cubi-

cles roofed with wood and sandbags, Gaucher heard the
radio reports as each forward post fell to Viets who were
climbing like robots over their own piled-up dead. Next
door, Abbé Trinquard counted the shells dropping round
them—fifteen to eighteen every minute. "I always said
those shelters were too flimsy," Gaucher growled.

His dugout shuddered. A 105 had landed on top, but
the roof had resisted. Gaucher had no time to reflect on
their good fortune. Three seconds later the whole command
post seemed to volatilize; a shell had plunged through the
ventilation shaft and exploded inside. The lights went out.
Lieutenant de Veyes grabbed a flashlight and scrambled
over the twisted beams and debris. Major Michael Vadot
was still alive, but two lieutenants lay dead and Major Mar-
tinelli was badly wounded. Gaucher? The shell had torn off
his arms and opened his chest, his eyes were wide open, his
mouth full of dirt; he was breathing desperately. "Wipe my
face," he gasped. "And give me something to drink."

They rushed him by jeep to Surgeon Major Paul
Grauwin's underground hospital. Grauwin described the
scene. "Two grave-faced legionnaires put down a stretcher
in front of me on which Colonel Gaucher lay. His legs and
arms were all literally smashed and his thorax lay open; he
was dying. 'Father, here, quick . . .' Father Heinrich just
had time to perform the last rites, and Colonel Gaucher
breathed his last. . . ."

Gaucher. Not brilliant, not flamboyant, not very articu-
late. But a born leader and one of the great men of the Legion.

Colonel Langlais took over what was left of Beatrice's
defense force. On the northeast face the fragmented sections battled on by instinct, unaware that the colonel and
most of his staff had been wiped out. For four hours
Sergeant Kubiak's machine guns kept drilling gaps in the
Vietminh ranks. "Where are they coming from?"

"Never mind. They're breeding them on the spot.
Keep firing."

How can they accept such losses? It seemed as the
night wore on that the advance slackened. A runner approached Kubiak. "The colonel and his staff are dead," he
stated simply. Kubiak raised his head. What did that mean?

Another wave of little men, sprigs of camouflage on their helmets, bore down on them. They sprayed the barbed wire with bullets. But now the circle was tightening; the dregs of the battalion retreated to the center of the position, hoping their line of march to the base still lay open.

At 2 A.M. they were still contesting the scarred, lunar-like surface. Kubiak was to write, "I am practically alone on the hilltop in the middle of the battle which continues. I look around me and am scared to see all that is left of our fine battalion. Our road of retreat is thick with bodies, with wounded men who moan and even scream at death. And the din from shells and machine guns is still at its height. The battalion radio operator is literally cut in two by a shell. He has just asked for them to fire on our position, for now everything is finished. Right to the end, he has done what he could. Not for his country, for he's not French, but for HIS Legion."

On Beatrice they lifted their wounded, placing them on stretchers or hoisting them on their shoulders, and groped back in the darkness to the underground hospital. Kubiak and his comrades were stunned, incredulous, unwilling to concede that the Lemon Peels had swamped and annihilated a Legion battalion. The evidence confronted them in Surgeon Major Paul Grauwin's dugout—the gruesome sight of amputated arms and legs heaped together.

"The High Command is confident that it can re-dress the position . . ." the Paris newscaster blandly told the millions who were learning where and what Dien Bien Phu was.

But Beatrice and a Legion battalion had gone. Six officers killed, one wounded, nearly four hundred men killed, missing, or seriously wounded. Giap had already replaced his 1,500 casualties when the remains of the battalion and two reserve companies tried to claw back the next day. The Vietminh hung on. Giap called for a truce until midday to collect his wounded. Shocked and ragged legionnaires stared at the tiny, immaculate officers ("I could have shaved on their trouser creases," said Kubiak.) who strolled in calmly to collect their men.

C-47 "Dakota"

At midday the artillery inferno started again, this time on Gabrielle. Vietminh infantry, knee-deep in their own dead, swamped a battalion of Algerian Rifles who fought as stubbornly as the legionnaires. The next day, March 15, Colonel Langlais and half the Legion paratroop battalion pushed Giap's men off in a dawn assault. But what remained to defend on that shell-torn surface where the only cover was piles of Vietminh and Algerian dead? Giap had won the strategic heights to the north and northeast at the sacrifice of 3,000 men. With his artillery and mortars he could crucify the 16,000 men in that long valley, dismember its limbs, then engulf it with his robot infantry. The long, slow agony of Dien Bien Phu had begun.

"At Dien Bien Phu, the situation is well under control," said the Paris radio.

Even the lowest coolie in the entrenched camp realized that the battle could go only one way. Colonel Charles Piroth, the one-armed artillery commander, blamed himself for Beatrice and Gabrielle because he had not muzzled the Vietminh guns. "It's finished," he wept to Langlais. "We're going to be massacred and it's my fault." He entered his dugout, primed a grenade, and lay on top of it. On March 17 the Thai battalion holding Anne-Marie deserted en masse, leaving this important bastion, their arms, and their equipment to Giap. More than 40,000 Vietminh, the cream of Giap's army, ringed the valley; while their gunners shelled the runway and the nerve center of the camp, thousands of sappers were cutting trenches to bring the infantry within rifle range of Huguette, Claudine, Dominique, Eliane, and Isabelle. With the airstrip under constant bombardment, any thought of evacuation disappeared. Even the wounded soon knew they had no escape route.

Two helicopters darted in to lift two wounded men. Vietminh shells killed the five men carrying their stretchers. Dakotas had to run a gauntlet of shells, mortar bombs, and ack-ack fire as they labored into the air with their cargoes of wounded. Kubiak saw one Dakota take off. "The desperate wounded—those who can't board the plane and don't wish to stay in this hell—grip the wings. Clusters of men cling to the plane, which now cannot stop and bears its cargo aloft. One by one our poor comrades are thrown to the ground to be killed by the fall. . . . It's a horrible sight, watching men fight to save what's left of their lives."

The planes had to land on an unlit runway at night, dropping in pairs. The first acted as a decoy for the Vietminh gunners, while men stuffed the wounded into the second. Some 240 wounded were evacuated before the Vietminh countered by shelling the strip all night. Some wounded refused to quit. Kubiak forced a young legionnaire into the first-aid center; he was hiding a fist-sized wound in his thigh so that he could stay with his comrades. Another legionnaire walked out of the surgery tent with serious chest wounds; they found him; riddled with bullets, at his post the next day.

On March 28 a Dakota threaded through the flak on one good engine to bounce along the runway. Vietminh gunners finished it off. Its crew and flight nurse were trapped. That was how Geneviève de Galard joined Major Grauwin to work around the clock in the underground hospital and infirmary, now a charnel house whose pungent odor of death and sickness drove all but the medical staff away. Somehow, Grauwin, Lieutenant Gindrey, and Geneviève ignored the stench if not the horror of the fifty-seven days and nights that they handled the human wreckage of Dien Bien Phu. The dead were so numerous that from March 22 they bulldozed mass graves.

Inexorably the Vietminh wormed nearer the key positions. "We were to discover that the pick and shovel were as powerful as the tank and the plane," said Colonel Langlais, one of the best soldiers this doomed battle produced. As Giap gradually strangled the camp, the French had to contest the vital areas. On March 30, Giap battered the four bastions commanding the airstrip and the dropping zone, then threw in infantry. Until April 6 this holocaust lasted, with the legionnaires and colonial paratroopers clinging desperately to the strongpoints.

Five companies of Legion paratroopers and the demi-brigade were cut to ribbons before they ceded Eliane, the key to the whole defense. If that fell it would mean the end of Dien Bien Phu, for Giap could then turn his artillery over open sights on de Castries' command post. At dawn on April 10 the remarkable Colonel Marcel Bigeard counterattacked with his own and Legion paratroopers in what Langlais called the finest feat of arms at Dien Bien Phu. Against eight to one odds, Bigeard's men bulldozed through a whole Vietminh regiment; they fought hand-to-hand and impaled themselves on bayonets rather than take a backward step. One by one they ferreted the blockhouses clean. "I'll never forget the sight," said Langlais. "Two paras with submachine guns bracketed the legionnaire with the flamethrower. Heavy tanks on his back, he advanced with extraordinary calm. I saw him point the lance and the flaming jet enveloped the blockhouse, which began to stream with fire. . . . A few survivors fled." For twenty days the paratroopers held that hill in face of suicidal attempts by Giap to recapture it. Huguette, too, had proved costly to defend. In ten days about 2,000 men were killed or badly wounded.

But for every man lost, the French had two or three volunteers stepping forward to take his place. Lieutenant Colonel Maurice Lemeunier, with a safe Hanoi billet, heard that his friend Gaucher had died. He went to General

Cogny, in charge of the Dien Bien Phu operation in Hanoi. "*Mon Général*, I'm the oldest legionnaire in Tonkin. Gaucher's place should come to me."

"But Lemeunier, if I said yes, how do we get you there?"

"I jump."

"Why, you don't know one end of a parachute from the other."

Nevertheless, Lemeunier jumped—and at night with only a flare to indicate the dropping zone. And Staff Captain Jean Pouget left his safe seat in General Navarre's headquarters to take his first jump. And hundreds of others, including Sergeant Chief János Valkó, a legendary Hungarian NCO, made their first parachute jump in the dark. De Castries, now a general, Langlais, Lemeunier, and Major Vadot were playing bridge in the "Subway" (nickname for the headquarters tunnel system) when a thump shook the roof. "That one didn't go off," said Vadot, who had been in Gaucher's dugout. They heard footsteps crunch; a giant legionnaire appeared, still entangled in the chute he was wearing for the first time. Unabashed by all the gold braid, he accepted and drank half a pint of Vinogel from the general. Those first-time paratroopers revised military thinking about airborne operations. More than seven hundred dropped and had no more broken bones than the 2,300 regular paratroopers who jumped alongside them. One had a harrowing experience; after crash-landing in the dark, he groped for his bearings; his fingers encountered one icy face, then another. He had landed in the morgue. It took half a pint of brandy to bring him around.

By the middle of April, out of the 16,000 men who had begun the battle only 3,500 were fit to fight. And 2,500 of these were legionnaires. The others? Killed, wounded, and missing. Among the North Africans and Thais some thousands had answered the incessant *tannoy* appeals. "Why die a slave of the colonialists? Uncle Ho offers you life and freedom."

On April 18 the Vietminh attacked the strip and the two Legion paratroop battalions were thrown in to win it back. As they charged forward, the legionnaires sang:

Anne-Marie, wo geht die Reise hin?
Anne-Marie, wo geht die Reise hin?
Si geht in's Städtlein
Wo die Soldaten sind.
Ei, ei, ei,
Junge, Junge, Junge, Anne-Marie. *

It took two days to dislodge the Vietminh from the strip.

On April 19 it was choking dust; the next day, torrential rain, with men plodding through a foot of mud and water. But the monsoon saved the camp. A Vietminh shell detonated the tanks of aviation fuel, which floated, a blazing black pall, down the Nam Youm; the downpour quenched the blaze. But now water flooded the trenches in which bodies floated; it filtered through into the surgery and hospital, spreading infection and heightening the death stench; the wounded in their camp beds sank deeper into the mud.

Sergeant Kubiak celebrated his twenty-fifth birthday on April 22 by getting drunk on Vinogel. He started to lead a party to counterattack from a post on Huguette. "But just as we were going to make the final effort, up comes Sergeant F: 'No good going to 4. It's just been overrun.' There were good friends of mine in 4! Sergeant F went on: 'No prisoners. It was a real slaughterhouse.' What a birthday!"

April 30. Camerone Day. The legionnaires celebrated with fruit juice made from dried lemon and orange powder. A Dakota had dropped them two crates of Vinogel, but a gusting wind had swept them into Vietminh territory, where they lay tantalizingly within sight. A section trained its machine guns on those crates and, at night, crept out to grenade a blockhouse and drag back the precious wine. The next day Colonel Lemeunier, in his best kepi, read the whole camp the Camerone story over the *tannoy*. They had

----

*Anne-Marie, where's she bound?
  Anne-Marie, where's she bound?
  She's off into the town
  Where there are soldiers around
  Ho, ho, ho,
  Young, Young, Young, Anne-Marie.

some new "recruits." Geneviève, in paratroop uniform,
wearing her new Croix de Guerre and Legion of Honor, became an honorary legionnaire, together with de Castries,
Langlais, and Bigeard. A sad festival. So many legionnaires
had enacted their personal Camerone there. The senior officers shared the feast: tinned beef and rice, a morsel of tinned
cheese, and half a pint of Vinogel to wash it down. Each
man got a bonus of two American cigarettes. As they ate, a
singsong voice boomed at them through sheeting rain:
"Why continue the fight? Why do what the legionnaires did
at Camerone—get yourselves massacred?" it said. "So they
knew the story," the legionnaires muttered, proud that
Camerone signified something even for Giap's fanatics. The
Boudin, sung by more than 1,000 men, drowned the insolent
voice.

A Camerone Day no legionnaire in Dien Bien Phu
would ever forget. Those who survived. For that night Giap
lunged again at the central positions—the same barrage, the
same suicidal waves of men. On Eliane and Huguette the
battle swayed one way, then the other. "It was all hell let
loose and the legionnaires going berserk," said Sergeant Kubiak. "And it didn't end with the dawn. Time after time the
positions changed hands. We were dead-beat. On our feet
by some miracle. Obeying like robots." Relieved by the
paratroopers that morning, Kubiak was sitting on the south
face of Eliane listening to the Vietminh burrowing closer.
One man, dressed in brilliant white, climbed from a trench
and walked toward them. A legionnaire ran out, thrust a
bayonet in his back, and marched him into the blockhouse.
"You bloody idiot—get that Lemon peel out of here.
Maulen! He's carrying enough dynamite to send up the
hill." They pushed Giap's death volunteer outside where a
sapper defused him.

*"Our forces in Dien Bien Phu have repulsed another
enemy attack with heavy losses," said the radio commenta-
tor.*

Now only Eliane stood between Giap and final victory.
Kubiak and forty legionnaires handed over their sector to
colonial paratroopers who had just dropped. "Watch it, the
Peels are tunneling for your blockhouse," he told the paratroop sergeant. "You've been too long in Dien Bien Phu,

mate," replied the incredulous sergeant. Half an hour later Kubiak was eating monkey and rice at another strongpoint when they heard the blockhouse under attack. "What are they copping round the earhole?" he thought. Did it matter? He and his men sprawled in the mud and slept through it. For three days, until April 6, the paratroopers weathered everything—land mines, shells, grenades, and something new, the screaming Stalin Organs, rocket batteries flown in from Russia. Eliane had to go. And with it the final hope of salvaging Dien Bien Phu and the 2,000 men who could still carry a rifle.

Even the weather seemed to have vowed the destruction of the camp. Tropical thunderstorms grounded the strike aircraft. One supply Dakota was literally wrenched to pieces in a sudden hailstorm; another had its windshield shattered and its pilot and co-pilot killed; engines iced up or waterlogged, and planes plummeted to earth. In the camp the legionnaires were dragging their feet through treacly mud; some lay down to sleep in it and did not open their eyes. In the Second Legion Paratroop Battalion, Major Lisenfeld saw two robust legionnaires topple over and die for no apparent reason. A doctor guessed that nervous and physical stress had drained their hormone system dry. Scores of men who had lived through more than fifty days of infernal combat died of this endocrine failure.

"The question is how much longer our troops in Dien Bien Phu can hold out," said the Paris radio. The time for euphemism, the muted communiqué, had passed.

For fifty-seven days Major Grauwin and his staff had worked, eaten, and slept in the dugout that did duty as surgery and hospital. No one kept count of the operations; they ignored the clock, measuring time by the crump of shells dropping around them and the carnage that followed each bombardment. They ignored the sickly tang of blood and chloroform mingled with the fetid air in the underground wards and operating room. The wounded huddled together, their canvas cots sliding on mud and monsoon rain, which seeped everywhere. They did not mind the maggots—"The doc said they cleaned the wounds."—but the flies! Geneviève slept among the wounded. And between the beds flitted a dozen Ouled Nails, the North African

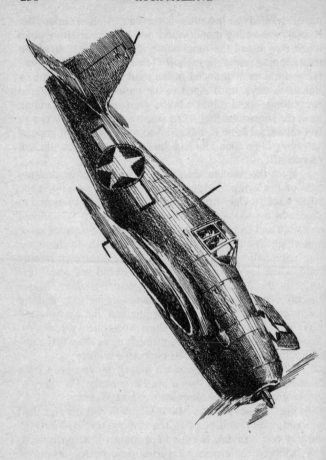

Hellcat

prostitutes from the camp brothel. Trapped, too, these fragile creatures had volunteered to act as nurses; many a legionnaire remembered their grave smiles and infinite
gentleness as they bandaged wounds or sat throughout the
night holding a hand. On the death march toward the Vietminh prison camps, no one saw or heard of them. They disappeared—like so many.

Everything else had been lost—except honor. "You must hold out," General Henri Navarre bawled into the radio at Hanoi. "We shall hold out," Castries answered from his command post, now under direct fire. Every man who could stand was mustered to defend the decreasing circle, now only Claudine and the last vestiges of Eliane. In the hospital Grauwin addressed the wounded. "I've just seen colonels Langlais and Bigeard. It seems that, with the rest of your battalion, some of you could form a small unit. Are there any volunteers to return to combat?" He had to fight them off: men on crutches, a one-legged legionnaire hopping between two wounded paratroopers, one-armed and one-eyed men who protested that they could handle a rifle as well as the next. Grauwin lost his temper. "No, not all of you," he shouted.

"Our pals are expecting us. If they're going to croak, we croak with them."

On May 6 only a fragment of the central area still flew the French flag, and Colonel André Lalande's battalion of the Third Legion Regiment at Isabelle. No more than three guns could respond to the four hundred Vietminh cannon that thundered the death knell of Dien Bien Phu. Behind the barrage, death volunteers had hurled the remaining legionnaires off Eliane and across the Nam Youm into Claudine.

At Isabelle the six hundred legionnaires, Algerians, and Moroccans had held on tenaciously to their hill for nearly two months, though Isabelle was now nothing more than an inverted colander, with water draining from its crumbling trenches and blockhouses. When the deluge let up on May 6, Colonel Lalande could observe the final stage of the battle three miles north around de Castries' command post. Through the immense smudge of fire and smoke he could pick out the flashes from the massed Vietminh batteries. Above, French planes wheeled, powerless to do more than observe. Hellcats shaved the low hills to strafe the enemy troops and gun positions. Lalande did not realize that he would make the last spasm; he knew that Hanoi had suggested to de Castries that he should try to break out south with what remained of his army.

De Castries had rejected the plan; he told General Cogny over the radio telephone. "Any breakout is bound to fail. Another night battle would mean the massacre of thousands of wounded in the shelters. We must cease firing."

At Claudine on May 7, however, they assembled a group of haggard, red-eyed men to march to Isabelle. Among them, Sergeant Kubiak. "As they line up there's a commotion. Seeing us grouped for departure, the wounded in the small first-aid posts paid no heed to the medical staff. They lifted themselves out of their stretchers and limped over to accompany us. Legionnaire S——succeeds in joining me. He has several bullets in him and walks literally jack-knifed. He's suffering terribly, but asks me to get him a weapon. He promises not to eat on the road but he'll be in trim to carry the reserve ammo. I don't know how to reason with him, but I understand his viewpoint so well." Kubiak fortified himself with rum from his water bottle. As they made ready to march, he heard his battalion commander curse. Turning, he spotted an enormous white flag floating over de Castries' command post. In front of them the Vietminh were crossing the river to take them prisoner. "It was then that the shooting started. I said the wounded had guts. It was they who were defending themselves. Captain B——, who's a highly strung character, opened up as well. Finally, everybody joined in the shindig."

Several bursts of machine-gun fire and the resistance stopped. Kubiak fell, with a bullet in his right leg, and would have died under an enemy bayonet had not one of his comrades shot the Vietminh. He would die a few years later from his wound and the privations of those two months.

At Isabelle, Lalande picked out the white flag. That afternoon Cogny asked over the radio link, "What are you going to do—fight or try to break out?"

"I shall try to break out."

At 6:30 that evening the guns turned on Isabelle; the powder magazine shot into the sodden sky with a tremendous roar; the legionnaires watched thousands of Giap's men massing to overrun the hill. Lalande summoned his officers. *"En avant,"* he ordered. The six hundred legionnaires knew it meant to ford the river and punch a gap through miles of enemy troops in the dark. The battalion barged over the river. On the far bank the Vietminh waited in thousands. About one hundred legionnaires managed to pierce the Vietminh wall. A handful stumbled into Laos weeks later. The jungle appeared to have swallowed up the others. Lalande's few men were the only ones to escape from the doomed camp.

On May 7 the world learned the Dien Bien Phu had fallen; that the Vietminh had inflicted on France the greatest defeat in colonial history; that France had lost the battle for Indochina. The new Mendès-France Government had to make peace with Ho Chi Minh. The country seethed; its politicians, its press, its military chiefs held interminable post-mortems on Dien Bien Phu. Only men like the brave Colonel Langlais posed the vital, the embarrassing question: How many French soldiers fought for that doomed valley and French colonial policy? Not more than a handful. Who then could they blame? The Legion? The Algerians, Moroccans, Vietminh, Thais? The men who had died during those fifty-seven days of hell? Or the defeated army, marching toward prison cages and a humiliating penance before their conquerors?

From the scarred earth of their impregnable fortress, the column shambled. Behind them lay 4,000 dead, including 1,500 legionnaires; on the Death March went 7,000 prisoners of whom 4,000 were legionnaires. *"Maulen, maulen,"* urged the Vietminh guards, prodding officers and men with rifles. They slogged through jungle trails in ten-mile stages; each night they had a ball of cold rice on a palm leaf. Hundreds dropped out, to be shot or left to die in the jungle. With their own wounded on makeshift litters, legionnaires struggled through bamboo groves and swamps. Many wounded died before they could receive medical attention. In the rice fields of Nadon they saw the rest of the thousands of prisoners from Dien Bien Phu. It was there that the final humiliation came. General de Castries, colonels Langlais, Bigeard, and Lalande had to parade back and forth with their men while Soviet camera crews recorded their distress.

On the Death March the senior officers began to comprehend how Giap had defeated them. On the same trails hundreds of thousands of coolies jogged along with loads of matériel for the Vietminh army. With bamboo pole or litter they could carry eighty-pound loads for thirty miles in a day. So Giap had hauled those guns over the mountains with muscle power! He had used the lowly bicycle to transport the ammunition. Two coolies and one bicycle could carry ten shells for a 105 gun. More than 30,000 coolies had thrust 150 miles of road through thick jungle in two months to bring the guns to Dien Bien Phu and dig them in. Giap had camouflaged the batteries, then further disguised them by firing blank charges to decoy the aircraft. Dien Bien Phu or some other battleground, the Vietminh would have triumphed in the end.

On May 8 the extent of the catastrophe reached Bel-Abbès. All ranks paraded in the great square before the war memorial. The spare, wiry figure of Colonel Paul Gardy stood stiff as the buglers blew *aux morts*. In a choked voice, his eyes full of tears, he read the order of the day. "We are gathered to commemorate the heroic sacrifice of those who fell during that epic struggle. We are going to present arms to the banners of those units that disappeared in the battle." To each unit the men paid their moving tribute. To the two battalions of the demi-brigade; to the battalions of the Second and Third Legion regiments; to the two Foreign paratroop battalions; to the mortar companies of the Third and Fifth Regiments; to the Legion volunteers who dropped on Dien Bien Phu during the final days.

In the summer an armistice between the French and Ho Chi Minh was signed at Geneva. After seventy-one years the Legion was quitting Tonkin for good. From 1945 to 1954 it had lost more than 11,000 dead and some 30,000 wounded. Of the 6,328 legionnaires captured during that period no more than 2,567 returned alive. Indochina and the Legion had left their marks on each other. Son Tay, Tuyen Quang, Lang Son—some of their most glorious pages had been written there. And now retreat. From their ships legionnaires watched the harrowing sight of thousands of Vietnamese men and women trying to join them. Hundreds drowned in the bay of Haiphong, trying to swim to the ships. That burned deeply into the minds of men like Adjutant Roger Degueldre. In most, the cicatrix of defeat still showed. But they were going back to their spiritual home—a home, however, that had changed in the years during which they had waged the futile Vietnam War.

SIXTEEN

With green tie and white kepi
Where away, gay legionnaire?
I'm off to make a little whoopee
Under a fine night and a moon of silver,
Out of sight and sound of MP,
Far from guards and barrack-square,
Drinking hard and getting happy.
I'm on my way, gay legionnaire,
In green tie and white kepi.

Legionnaire Jean Marsal had no doubt once been John Marshall, but this he never admitted and the Legion never verified. Many wondered, though no one asked, why an intelligent Englishman who spoke fluent French and Arabic was sweating and swallowing sand in Moroccan and Algerian outposts for a few francs a week. When his commanding officer at Bel-Abbès learned that Marsal meant to quit the Legion after ten years, he did pose a few questions: What did he intend to do as a civilian? Marsal shrugged. For his own reasons he did not want to return to England. He might head south, for Kenya or Rhodesia.

"You wouldn't like to stay here?"

"To do what, *mon colonel?*"

"What you did before you joined the Legion."

"I did quite a few things."

"I mean, intelligence work."

"How did you know I was in intelligence?"

The colonel shrugged. Marsal wondered if this was

their reason for sticking him in Timimoun and Le Kreider for months on end; they didn't trust a former British army intelligence officer who had worked in Egypt and Libya. He listened to the proposition: the Legion had information that bands of rebels were forming in the Aurès and Constantine mountains; they were establishing arms dumps in other parts of Algeria to start a revolt that would threaten French rule. They must pinpoint the source and the arms. They needed somebody they could trust, who spoke colloquial Arabic and could put two and two together.

"And if I said yes?"

"We wondered if Laghouat would suit you. Oh, it's on the road to nowhere, but it's midway between Tunisia and Morocco and we feel that the arms traffic touches that point."

"And my cover?"

"We thought a petrol station. They need another and we'll build it as your gratuity and give you a pension into the bargain."

Jean Marsal installed himself at Laghouat. His English passport and routine visits to the British Consulate in Algiers waived suspicions. Lorries, which plied north to Algiers and across country between Tunisia and Morocco, pulled in for petrol; the Kabyle drivers chatted with Marsal over a glass of tea or sherbet. Occasionally one of his old Legion officers in civies would stop to fill his tank or have some minor fault repaired and Marsal would pass on what he had heard. In the summer of 1954, a few months after the petrol station opened, he whispered to one of the officers, "I've drawn some plans—you'll find them at the usual place." This was a stone cairn several miles north of Laghouat.

Marsal had discovered that fellah rebels were buying Italian army-surplus rifles from Libya and smuggling them into Algeria across the Tunisian frontier near Tebessa. Lorries belonging to one of the country's biggest transport companies distributed them to rebel bands, who cached them. Marsal had pinpointed several of these hideouts, which Legion intelligence men visited to seize several hundred rifles, wrapped and covered with grease. The Englishman had also drawn meticulous plans of the arms dump in

Tunisia. Two Legion officers made a secret trip to an oasis in the Fezzan Desert of Libya following Marsal's information and unearthed a cache containing hundreds of unused Italian Mannlicher-Carcano rifles, left over from the North African campaign.

Later, Marsal informed them that the Fezzan Desert also hid short- and medium-wave transmitters, run by Egyptian operators, who were broadcasting propaganda and code signs to rebels in the Aurès. By intercepting and decoding radio messages, the French began to realize the size and strength of the coming rebellion in Algeria. Marsal, the British agent, was one of the first to alert the Legion that it had yet another liberation war on its hands.

In October 1954 a Legion captain drew in at the whitewashed petrol station. The Arab boy filled his tank. "Where's the boss?" he asked. "Maybe in Algiers," the boy replied. Marsal, however, failed to appear at every meeting place. Two weeks later they knew why. A dredger in Algiers port brought up the body of a blond, blue-eyed man. He had been stabbed a dozen times and his throat cut before being dumped in the bay. "He was one of your legionnaires, wasn't he?" the French police asked the Legion intelligence service at Bel-Abbès. "Yes, he was a fine soldier," the captain replied. "But he left us six months ago. . . ."

On November 1, 1954, the Algerian War began, though so quietly that the French could not believe that they had a full-scale rebellion on their hands. The Fells, as they now called the rebels, staged several raids in the Aurès: they isolated a mixed Arab-French community; they attacked a police station, killed an officer and several soldiers, and took several prisoners; finally they ambushed the M'Chounech-Arris bus and assassinated a young French schoolteacher, Guy Monnerot. A French reserve officer was killed while trying to save Monnerot and his wife, who was gravely wounded.

Who were the French fighting? General Paul Cherrière, the commander in chief, assumed that the truculent Aurès tribes had merely grown restive; his army would soon reduce the dissidence and leave the police to cope. But gradually French and Legion intelligence officers began to put names to the new movement: FLN (National Liberation

Federation) and its military offshoot ALN (National Liberation Army). Its leaders, men like Ferhat Abbas, Krim Belkacem, and Ben Bella, aimed at nothing less than expelling the French; indeed, they had already divided the three metropolitan departments into *wilayas* (military districts) and hundreds of *katibas* (companies). What was beginning with four hundred to six hundred rebels would suddenly flare into a full-scale war, involving 400,000 French troops, splitting France and Frenchmen into two hostile camps, and almost destroying the Foreign Legion.

At the outset the Legion existed only as a training regiment at Bel-Abbès; its fighting units still remained in Vietnam. When they did land at Algiers, Oran or Bône, legionnaires wondered why the concern over a few deaths and two or three hundred armed fanatics. This time, however, they were not dealing with Abd el-Kader or Abdel Krim, who at least stood and fought. The FLN worked stealthily, destroying and looting whole villages, murdering pro-French Arabs. Village chiefs and administrators were tortured, mutilated, then butchered in front of their own wives and families. When Legion patrols arrived, the terrified villagers had seen and heard nothing. Each FLN defiance brought them hundreds of new recruits, many of them infected by fear. To trace the FLN leaders and stamp out the terrorism, the French launched a vast census operation to issue every man, woman, and child in Algeria identity cards.

In 1957 another phase of pacification. The Moroccan and Tunisian frontiers were sealed by electrified wire barriers. The Morice Line, stretching from Bône to Tebessa, had nearly two hundred miles of wire, minefields, searchlights, and blockhouses; this line, and the Legion patrols, stemmed the FLN infiltration. France poured in troops to garrison towns and villages throughout Algeria and protect inhabitants from atrocities. By the middle of the year more than 400,000 soldiers had invested the country. Most were conscripts, bored with eternal guard duty, searches, identity parades, and waiting for their two years to end. The main job of tracking and destroying the rebels in the Aurès and Kabyle mountains fell to units of the 20,000 legionnaires and the regular paratroop regiments.

But what were they—soldiers or policemen? A band of
Fells would open fire on a Legion section, which would
hunt, kill, or capture them. Before they could interrogate the
prisoners, in stepped the French gendarmes to take them for
civil trial. After six months they might catch the same men
again, rifles in hand and arguing insolently that they could
not be FLN since the police had acquitted them. For the Legion the Algerian War was turning into a schizophrenic
nightmare that seemed to have no end. Legion officers, especially the younger battalion and company commanders,
began to mutter that Algeria was Indochina all over again.
Paris was dithering between governments that searched
vainly for political solutions. Another Dien Bien Phu? Another betrayal of the army and, in particular, the Legion?
Perhaps they had forgotten that the Legion was as much a
part of Algeria as the granite from which its war memorial
had been hewn. No handful of rebels would tread the conse-
crated ground of Bel-Abbès or snuff out more than 120
years of tradition and sacrifice.

One man and one unit had no illusions about the Algerian War. For Colonel Pierre Jeanpierre and the First Foreign
Parachute Regiment the FLN had to be liquidated, the war
won. Jeanpierre had watched the paratroop battalion bleed
to death twice in Indochina. He had led it on the Suez adventure—one more political fiasco. Now it was a regiment
after his own heart and the spearhead of the drive against
Algerian terrorists. In the 1st REP he had constructed a for-
midable unit, handpicking its officers and men. He had his
old comrade Captain Roger Faulques and younger officers
like Captain Antoine Ysquierdo, and lieutenants like
Philippe Durand-Ruel and Roger Degueldre. As NCOs he
had men like Adjutant László Tasnády, with his flair for
stalking and killing. In their green berets and mottled battle
dress, Jeanpierre's paratroopers soon became the *corps
d'élite* of the Legion. The legionnaires considered themselves a race apart. The old, rock-solid, slow-stepping Legion was built to bulldoze through anything—given enough
pinard; the paratroopers were leaner, more lithe, and they
flew instead of foot-slogging. Their spiritual home was Zeralda, twelve miles west of Algiers. They had taken over a
Nissen-hutted camp and converted it with their own hands

into a model barracks, with low, brilliant-white buildings set in a pine grove. Jeanpierre had them plant palms and regiments of roses.

From Zeralda the paratroopers struck at the Aurès, the Nementcha, the Ouarsenis, and the Kabyle mountains. Colonel Jeanpierre's command post was a "chopper" hovering above his men to direct the operations. Senior officers and quiet civil servants might complain about this blunt fellow with the rolling shoulders, flat gait, and rough manners of a Vosges peasant; Jeanpierre brushed them aside and got on with the war. In six months they had destroyed every important band of rebels in the mountains. Defeated in the country, the FLN moved into towns—Constantine, Philippeville—and finally into the capital, Algiers. There they sowed terror, planting bombs in cafes, cinemas, sports grounds, and office blocks. Most notorious among the FLN were Yacef Saadi, a smooth and capable *plastiqueur* who controlled the casbah, and Ali La Pointe (Amar Ali), his illiterate young lieutenant.

The new commander in chief, General Raoul Salan, called in his strong man, General Jacques Massu, the craggy-faced commander of the Tenth Paratroop Division. "I want no more trouble in Algiers," Salan said. "I leave it to you." Massu, who sided with the French *colons,* snorted, *"A vos ordres, mon général,* but you're wishing a helluva job on my paras. We're not policemen." On January 1, 1957, Massu moved his Legion, marine, and colonial paratroopers into the vast casbah slum with its dark, bewildering alleys, its hovels climbing over each other to the hill overlooking the port.

Still the bombing went on. On January 27 and February 10 five bombs killed ten people and injured forty-five. The paratroopers threw a heavy barrage of barbed wire around the casbah, isolating it. Everyone who entered or left was checked. Colonel Roger Trinquier, of the marine paratroopers, devised a "block" system whereby one family member became responsible for the others' movements twenty-four hours a day. This person had to report in turn to a floor chief and he to a block chief. That way the paratroopers could account for everyone. They even took a census of the dogs in the casbah. Flat roofs and vantage points became command posts, in touch by walkie-talkie with patrols scouring the alleys and hovels. So labyrinthine and intricate was the casbah that a man could enter a hilltop house and come out at the bottom without once using the narrow streets. Starting with nothing more than the names and addresses of the bomb victims, the paratroopers began their quest for the terrorist leaders. As each hidden arms or gelignite dump came to light, the occupants were questioned until they revealed the names of their contacts. To allegations that they wrung information from suspects by torture, Massu and his officers replied, "Let *messieurs* the FLN stop their torture and killing and we'll stop the interrogations." In less than a month the casbah had become quiet. But it still hid the two chiefs, Yacef Saadi and Ali La Pointe.

In the fourth week of September a well-dressed Arab entered the casbah checkpoint; he began to climb the twisting streets. He had impressive papers. Too impressive perhaps. The Arab glanced around for mottled uniforms, his eyes skimming over the Arab woman, holding her veil, and threading through the porters carrying meat and vegetables in the casbah. At No. 3 rue Caton he knocked at the Moorish door, then slipped inside. An hour later he reappeared. Near the checkpoint he felt a revolver in his back. It was the Arab girl he had ignored. Only when they reached the command post did he see the "girl" take off her gown and veil and realize that it was a paratrooper with a quiet face, a shock of blond hair, and blue eyes. It was László Tasnády.

The Arab, Hadj Smain, produced his authorization, signed by the minister of justice, his papers, his check book with important figures on the stubs. He protested his innocence, demanded to see his lawyer. They applied a little pressure and he broke down.

"You've seen Yacef Saadi at Caton Street," said Jeanpierre. The man nodded. "At No. 4?" He hesitated. "No—it was No. 3." Funny. The widow Bouhired lived there. She had given them information and even had a guard of his paratroopers! Nonetheless, Jeanpierre mounted the operation for dawn on September 24; the paratroopers encircled the maze of houses at Caton Street. The widow Bouhired opened the door. "What do you want. . . . I'm alone." Spotting Hadj Smain, she disappeared inside; behind her barged

Jeanpierre, Captain Ysquierdo, and Adjutant Tasnády.
Yacef's cache had been constructed behind the bathroom,
which gave onto the staircase of the slum. A legionnaire attacked one side with a pickax while Jeanpierre and his men
went through the kitchen corridor. A burst of Tommy-gun
fire halted them. "Come out and give yourself up, Yacef.
You're finished." To answer Jeanpierre, Yacef rolled a
grenade down the corridor; it exploded, showering the
colonel with splinters. Ysquierdo and Tasnády pulled him
into the tiny kitchen. While legionnaires covered them with
submachine guns, they evacuated the wounded Jeanpierre
through the narrow corridor.

"You have ten seconds, Yacef, and then we blow the
place up," an officer shouted.

"I surrender only to the civil authority, which is my
right—or to General Massu," the rebel replied.

While they waited for an administrator he burned his
documents and even a hoard of money. Finally, Colonel
Yves Godard, military security chief, persuaded him to
come out. He cursed the legionnaires, threatening to bring
down the wrath of the minister of justice on them. Jeanpierre took a month to recover from the shrapnel wounds he
had received. It did not hearten him or his regiment to see
Yacef Saadi, the terrorist, hobnobbing with administrators
and baring his soul to the world press. "We should have
tossed him that explosive," they muttered.

Two weeks later Ali La Pointe betrayed himself by
spending two consecutive nights in the same casbah
house—No. 5 rue des Abdermanes. He and a dozen terrorists were hiding in a bricked-up cellar when the paratroopers moved in just after dark on October 8. This time,
however, the civil authorities had come to take charge of
the young terrorist and perhaps to quell the enthusiasm of
the paratroopers. "You must use only enough explosive to
demolish the wall," they instructed. Of course! What legionnaire sapper could not handle a job like that. They
placed the charges and pushed the administrators back.
"You have thirty seconds, Ali—we're lighting the fuse," an
officer cried. "Merde," Ali shouted back. It was his verbal
testament. An enormous detonation shook the casbah, waking thousands of natives and the whole regiment of soldiers.

Several houses crumbled around Ali's hideout. "It must have been pretty flimsy, that clay wall," muttered the legionnaires. It took several days to unearth the frail body of Ali La Pointe; they recognized him by the French tattoo on his chest: *Marche ou Creve* (March or Die), the Legion motto. Seventeen people died with him. After that spectacular blast Algiers returned to normal; Jeanpierre and his officers could discard their "civie" disguise and don their uniforms; the paratroopers breathed more freely away from the filth of the casbah.

In many ways Adjutant László Tasnády was the antithesis of the old legionnaire NCO. He had a smooth, boyish face, a quiet manner, and drank mostly water, though he liked his big Ford convertible with two girls in its front seat. But, for the equivalent of a sergeant major, he seemed diffident, self-effacing. Some NCOs—those who had not seen him in action—thought that in Rollet's Legion he might have made a batman for the youngest subaltern.

In the last months of 1957 helicopters transported Captain Ysquierdo's company to the hills thirty miles south of Algiers to deal with a band of Fells. Within an hour they had killed and wounded a dozen rebels and taken thirty prisoners. During interrogation of the prisoners, Tasnády's section scoured the ravines and scrubby hills to flush out any rebels hiding there. When he had finished, the Hungarian NCO de-

French Machine Pistol

ployed his men in the bushes and sat with his radio operator under a fig tree.

Across the valley an intelligence officer had weeded out seven prisoners, detailing an escort to lead them to his vehicle. On the way six of the Arabs broke loose and scrambled into the bushes, out of sight and range. Unhappily they ran across Tasnády's line of fire. Without budging from his squatting position, he calmly rested his M1 carbine on the radio set. The radio operator watched his finger take the first pressure, then the second; six shots, all spaced two seconds apart; and six Arabs lying contorted on the opposite hillside two hundred yards away. Retrieving the bodies, the legionnaires found a bullet in the head or near the heart of each. Yet Tasnády had hardly seemed to take aim! Under fire he seemed to become calmer, to freeze even. "The Man with the Carbine" they called him; but automatic weapons, revolver, grenade, bayonet—they all came as easily to him.

The French had reinforced the Morice Line with the Guelma Line. These barricades halted most of the rebels, though in the Guelma area an FLN command unit was directing more than 1,000 armed men against towns and villages. Jeanpierre and his paratroopers dropped into this sector at the end of April 1958. He had a new tactic, and on Camerone Day an outlaw band equipped with machine guns gave him the chance to try it out. Between the frontier and Duvivier, Jeanpierre located the rebels and dropped one company that was pinned to the ground by machine-gun fire. Helicopters set down another company. Under covering fire the men advanced in line abreast. On a signal everyone stopped and hurled a grenade. Another hundred yards, another salvo of grenades, until they had quartered the ground. That morning they killed 192 rebels, took five prisoners and enough modern equipment to arm two companies. With Jeanpierre's method the men could clean out valleys and hills with no more than a few casualties. He had other rules for this "rotten war." Act only on precise information, then heave everything at the enemy; use fighter support rather than wait for artillery; attack in the morning and finish them off before dark; strip down the men to machine pistols and grenades to speed things up; and if in doubt, attack.

Jeanpierre had become a legend in Algeria. His regiment could parade more medals than any other. In two years it had accounted for 2,000 rebels in the most difficult of all wars, though 123 legionnaires had died and 350 had been wounded. Jeanpierre's success had destined him for high command in the French army—but did he want it? Legionnaires could hate France, yet paradoxically fight for it because they loved the Legion. There was something of this in Jeanpierre; the more he saw of French politics and political generals, the more he became a legionnaire rather than a Frenchman. He had no great liking, either, for the well-fixed *colons,* who would sacrifice nothing to keep Algeria French but sat back to let the army do its dirty work. He had been promised a more important command. Well, he would think about it in the rose gardens of Zeralda when he and the regiment had taken a breather.

But on May 29 two rebel bands were sighted on the hills around Guelma. Two companies were dropped by helicopter into the tangled scrub on Mermera Hill and immediately attacked by the Fells. The legionnaires tried grenades, called for strafing and artillery fire. But nothing would budge the rebels from their caves on a sharp rib of the hill. Not long after mid-day the legionnaires saw Jeanpierre's Alouette appear and swoop over the entrenched rebels. They could clearly discern his bulky figure, earphones jammed over his green beret, even the map on his knee. Over the radio they heard his voice. "There's only one approach. I'll see how many there are," he radioed. And the light "chopper" circled and racketed over the treetops despite the bursts of automatic fire from the rebels who were attempting to hit it. "He'll get himself killed one day," the men whispered, but nobody really believed it. Again the Alouette darted like a firefly over the caves. A fusillade of machine-gun fire came from the undergrowth; the helicopter coughed several times, its blades whirled silently; then it plunged, standing on its nose, into the skein of bushes. A section of legionnaires charged across the defile toward the machine while another stood off the advancing rebels. The helicopter had broken its back on a rock; Jeanpierre and the pilot lay unconscious. They lifted Jeanpierre and carried him to a truck. Within a couple of hours he was dead—killed stupidly by a thousand-to-one bullet that had fractured the petrol feed of the helicopter. His enraged legionnaires did not stop until the last rebel had died or surrendered on that baleful hill.

Jeanpierre, twenty-five years a legionnaire, survivor of Syria, Mauthausen, Indochina, Suez, killed by some thug! So his regiment thought when they paraded before his coffin at Guelma. More than 30,000 people turned out for his funeral at El Alia. Salan and the generals paid their tribute, then his officers, one after the other. The stocky figure of Lieutenant Roger Degueldre, whom Jeanpierre had commissioned from adjutant chief, placed his hand on the coffin. "Rather die, *mon colonel,* then leave Algeria in the hands of the FLN." That oath, and the effect of Jeanpierre's death on his men, would do much to transform the history of the Algerian War. At Zeralda his legionnaires constructed a chapel, which they dedicated to St. John and St. Peter in memory of Jeanpierre.

Since 1954 six French governments had wrestled vainly with the Algerian crisis. The day they buried Jeanpierre the government of Pierre Pflimlin toppled, following demonstrations in Algiers on May 13 and army discontent over the handling of the Algerian War. At one moment it seemed that the army might seize power in Algeria and even dictate to Paris. Salan and Massu, instead, appealed to Charles de Gaulle, who was in self-imposed reclusion at Colombey. Not blind to his opportunities, de Gaulle welcomed the army crisis and even, if necessary, a military coup. But Frenchmen, tired of paying in conscription and taxes the massive cost of a bloody and futile pacification, were calling, too, for a strong man. On June 1, de Gaulle became prime minister. Three days later he was in Algeria, placating the generals, kneeling at Jeanpierre's tomb, leaving the impression that Algeria would remain forever French and that the army had his backing to snuff out the FLN rebellion.

A brilliant air force general, Maurice Challe, took over from Salan in December 1958 and began another phase of pacification. Hundreds of thousands of villagers were uprooted from their homes and crowded into camps to make their protection easier. This population "re-arrangement" did French prestige no good and recruited several more bat-

talions to the FLN. But Challe's methods worked and he
ruthlessly pursued armed rebels when they did manage to
infiltrate the frontier barrages.

The 1st REP still spearheaded the hunt for Fells. The
paratroopers had tracked a hard-core rebel band into the
Ouarsenis Mountains, a hundred miles southwest of Algiers,
and were chasing them with units of the Third and Fifth
Foreign regiments. On May 13, 1959, Tasnády's section ran
into an ambush in the Bou Zara wadi. The adjutant worked
around and calmly picked off five Fells before the others
surrendered. Altogether, ten dead rebels. A good day. When
Tasnády returned to the camp near Orléansville the next
day, somebody broke the news. "Szüts, the adjutant in the
Third, was wounded yesterday. He's in Bel-Abbès and they
don't expect him to live. One of your pals, wasn't he?" Tasnády nodded.

*A week ago it had been János Valkó, adjutant chief in
the Fifth. Killed in the middle of the Ouarsenis at Teniet el-
Haad. Like Jeanpierre, his "chopper" had run out of air.
Valkó, who'd fought with him at Cau-Dai in Tonkin. . . .
He'd still got a scar on his brow from the day he lugged him
off that mound. . . . Valkó who'd made his first jump into
Dien Bien Phu among the no-hopers . . . who'd spent
months in Vietminh camps and come back to die like this, in
an exploding chopper . . . chasing a bunch of wogs. And
now István Szüts! They'd gone through Bel-Abbès together
as rookies in 1946. . . . He remembered they'd taken a lot of
stick, three Hungarians who could hardly say "bonjour"
between them. . . . He'd been seventeen, two years younger
than the others . . . and yet they'd all made adjutant with
more "bananas" on their chest than the new colonel, Dufour. And now Szüts, downed by some Fell near Miliana. . . .
He hoped whoever he was would come his way.*

An alert took them once again into the hills, to the
Lamartine area, where an Algerian doctor was suspected of
treating wounded rebels. A native guide led the company
into the long, deep el-Hamri wadi. Prodding forward, Tasnády was stopped by a revolver shot that came from a cave
halfway up the sheer limestone face. No use firing. The
shots would never penetrate. Too far for grenades. They
must clear the bushes. Tasnády's section clawed to the cliff-

top. The adjutant twined a rope around an olive tree and slung a bag of grenades over his shoulder. "You're not going down there, Aj—that's asking for it." Tasnády put his foot into the noose and swung down. Over the gorge a section covered the cave entrance; the Hungarian twisted himself around on the rope and hung, upside-down, by the cave mouth. Two of his grenades blasted away the undergrowth at the entrance, though the rebels were still firing.

Back on the cliff-top, Tasnády now filled a haversack with six pounds of dynamite and several grenades; again he launched into space. Above the cave mouth he primed a grenade in the sack and slung it far inside. *"Tirez,"* he yelled. He was halfway back when the grenade exploded and detonated the demolition charge. The cave erupted like a blunderbuss, discharging mattress feathers and bits and pieces of the fellahs inside. They identified the doctor and six other dead rebels.

An hour later they started down the gully, still combing the bushes. Halfway down a shot reverberated. Tasnády ran forward to lift the wounded legionnaire. Two more shots rang out. Tasnády pitched forward on his face. A dozen machine pistols sprayed the bushes from which the shots had come while two legionnaires doubled over to the adjutant. One bullet had caught him in the back, another in the nape of the neck.

Tasnády was dead—killed by an Arab graybeard with a sawed-off shotgun! The most famous Legion NCO since Adjutant Chief Mader had fallen to some frightened old Berber shepherd.

"Adjutant Tasnády is dead," the radio operator whispered to the company. Refusing to believe it, Abbé Delarue ran up the track. Too late to give Tasnády the last rites.

The men talked about him. "Remember, a few weeks back when we picked up that bit of chewed tomato skin and he led us to that hideout and killed half a dozen Fells?"

"And Suez? When he repaired that yacht engine and smuggled in enough liquor for the whole battalion?"

Recounting the triumphs of the quiet little man, whom Vietminh atrocities had converted into the most expert guerrilla in the Legion, his company forgot that yesterday and today they had killed more than seventy rebels. Had he been with them, Tasnády would have murmured in that soft voice, "Bah, another legionnaire. Does he matter?" And he would have gone back to the battle. Which is what the paratroopers did.

Tasnády, Valkó, and Szüts passed into legend. Their three coffins lay in state at Bel-Abbès while the First Regiment paraded before the great Monument aux Morts. No fewer than sixteen adjutant chiefs and adjutants, all wearing the military medal, filed on either side of Tasnády's coffin. A plaque in the Legion museum commemorates the three Hungarians who joined the Legion within weeks of each other and died in the same week. Three crosses of the Legion of Honor and three military medals glitter in the glass frame, which also records the twenty-eight other citations and the eight wounds these men received before they died.

The rift widened between Paris and Algiers; the senior officers who had campaigned for de Gaulle's return to power heard with dismay the general's broadcast on September 16, 1959, in which he outlined his alternatives for Algeria: independence, complete union with France, or self-government under French aegis. Blunt as ever, General Jacques Massu criticized de Gaulle for offering self-determination. On January 24, Massu was sacked. Crying betrayal, the Europeans barricaded themselves in university and public buildings and fought a pitched battle with the gendarmes. At the end of the Day of the Barricades, fourteen gendarmes had died and 123 were wounded; six demonstrators had been killed and twenty wounded. Paratroopers, drafted in to restore order in Algiers, seemed uncertain as to which side to take; they, too, sensed the loss of Massu, their chief. The legionnaires were the most divided; for six years they had grubbed among the djebels and thalwegs, in the deserts, in villages and towns, to round up the FLN. And now that they were licking the rebels, de Gaulle was proposing to hand Algeria over. What happened to Bel-Abbès and Saida, to Zeralda, and all they had built in this country? The Legion without Algeria was as unthinkable as France without Algeria. Their traditions, their relics, their dead lay at Bel-Abbès. And why had men like Jeanpierre and Tasnády died if the war meant nothing?

They quit Algiers to deal with Fell bands in the mountains around Constantine. But now they wondered: Is it worth it? Former Legionnaire Pierre Messmer, now war minister, hopped by helicopter from one unit to another. "Your duty is clear," he told them. "Win the war on the ground and have confidence in General de Gaulle." The paratroop officers remained skeptical; some had already lost faith. Captain Pierre Sergent's company was attacked by rebels five hundred yards from the Tunisian border. Pursuing them, he discovered an extensive camp on the other side of the frontier. Against orders, he blew it up before returning to Algeria. That same day, when a senior officer ordered him to search for Fells, Sergent refused to obey; he refused to see his men killed for no purpose. Many of his messmates, notably Roger Degueldre, felt the same way.

What was de Gaulle's game? Visiting Algeria in the spring of 1960, he urged the army to greater effort and declared that Algeria would never be ceded; in the summer he was negotiating with the FLN chiefs. On November 4, de Gaulle quashed all their doubts with a TV and radio broadcast: "Having resumed the leadership of France," he said, "I have decided in her name to follow the path that leads no longer to Algeria governed by Metropolitan France but to an Algerian Algeria . . . that means an emancipated Algeria . . . an Algeria which, if the Algerians so wish—and I believe it to be the case—will have its government, its institutions, and its laws." De Gaulle also made it clear that he envisaged an Algerian republic.

The next day the paratroopers of the 1st REP did not bother about reveille. Their officers said, "Why hunt the men who will soon take over the country?" On November 14, at the funeral of ten legionnaires in Zeralda, Colonel Dufour cried, "It is not possible that your sacrifice will be in vain. It is not possible that our French compatriots do not hear our anguished cries." Dufour was transferred to France, but his successor, Colonel Maurice Guiraud, Jeanpierre's successor, could not find the regimental standard. Dufour had taken it with him, knowing that the command could not be passed traditionally without it.

In December, Lieutenant Roger Degueldre disappeared. Though technically a deserter, no one in his regiment considered betraying him. Corporal Claude Tenne, one of his legionnaires, spotted the heavy, blue-jowled face in an Algiers cafe, but did not dare greet him in case the gendarmes pounced. Degueldre began canvassing the young paratroop officers to ascertain if they would take part in a bid to keep Algeria part of France. Disguised in an airman's uniform, he made frequent trips between Algiers and Paris to inform senior officers about the temper of the army and the Legion particularly. In Algeria, General Edmond Jouhaud was waiting for the moment to act. In Paris, cabals were convening secretly—even in the sacrosanct École Militaire—to discuss ways of reversing de Gaulle's policy or seizing power. It surprised nobody to see General Paul Gardy, former inspector general of the Legion, at these meetings. But the bulky figure of Maurice Challe! It had rankled him that de Gaulle had transferred him to a NATO command when he was winning the Algerian War. He had resigned from NATO and would make a natural leader if they had to act. The colonels and generals preferred him to Salan, who was operating from Madrid.

The more desperate right-wing political factions, allied with some army officers, had decided that only if de Gaulle disappeared would they preserve Algeria. Captain Pierre Sergent, on leave in Paris, was caught up in carrying coded messages between the capital and Algiers. Though unaware, Sergent was transmitting the order to assassinate the President. The attempt would be made between December 9 and 12 when de Gaulle toured Algeria. At Ain Témouchent, in the Oram district, the President was nearly crushed to death by the crowd. Perhaps the crowd saved him from a bullet, for an assassination bid had been planned. The story went that three partisans of French Algeria had protected him from the crush, and he had convoked and thanked them. Was there anything he could do for them?

"I'd like a Citroën DS," said the first man.

"Granted."

"I want a patisserie in Paris."

"Granted."

"I'd like to be a citizen of French Algeria," said the third.

"Sorry. You'll have to choose something else."

"A coffin, then."

"A coffin!"

"Yes. When my old father hears I've saved your life he'll do me in."

Assassination was in the air all along the President's route. Security men had a tip-off that gunmen planned to shoot de Gaulle at the entrance to Orléansville. They diverted the car and from that moment the itinerary was not published. In Algiers the FAF (French Algerian Front) had organized a strike to paralyze the city during the visit. The civilian leaders of the front expected the paratroopers from the Legion and other units to take over the city and demonstrate to de Gaulle that he could not pursue his policy. But the paratroopers were not yet ready. They had no real leader.

In the 1st REP, officers and men realized that France and the *pieds noirs* (Algerians of French stock) would collide sooner or later. NCOs like Sergeant Albert (Bobby) Dovecar and Claude Tenne and at least two companies of legionnaires had already decided to follow their officers if they revolted. The paratroopers had begun to sing something spicier than the *Boudin*—the Africans, an Algerian version of the *Marseillaise*. It had a wild lilt and fervent lyric.

> *Far-traveled are we, the Africans,*
> *Who have forsaken all for France—*
> *Our loved ones, our homes, our native soil,*
> *To fight for Frenchmen who are loyal.*
> *In our hearts we hold,*
> *A spirit bold,*
> *Which high and proud will ever bear*
> *The glorious emblem of the Tricolor.*
> *Who tries to wrest it from our grasp, be warned,*
> *To a man we shall die before we see it scorned.*

By the second week of April 1960 the Paris cabal of senior officers had decided to stage a putsch to take over Algeria. Challe would lead, backed by General André Zeller and Jouhaud, a *pied noir* idolized in Algeria. They were assured of support from the 1st REP, two Legion cavalry regiments, two colonial paratroop regiments, and a dragoon regiment. They banked, too, on the other Legion units. "When we march, the whole Legion will march with us," General Gardy told the others. They would meet in Algiers on April 20. The putsch would be carried out the next day.

On April 19 the 1st REP had returned from operations to Zeralda for a break. Commanding during Colonel Guiraud's absence on leave was a young, dynamic major, Elie Denoix de Saint-Marc. A resistance leader at eighteen, Saint-Marc had been caught and deported to Buchenwald, had then fought in Indochina and Algeria. Such was his prestige that, had he ordered the regiment to drop on Paris, it would have obeyed without question. Of course he had heard rumors of a putsch, but not until Challe threw his weight behind the movement did the Legion officer consider taking part. Even then he wanted guarantees from Challe himself. On April 21 the two men met. Challe explained his aims: to seize power, finish the war against the FLN, and set up a French Algerian state on democratic lines.

"I will have nothing to do with a fascist putsch," said Saint-Marc.

"You have my word as a democrat," said Challe, insisting that the extremists on both sides would have no part in government.

"I'm at your disposal, *mon général*," said Saint-Marc.

Challe ran over the plan to capture the nineteen key points that would give them Algiers, and the generals and civil servants they must arrest. Saint-Marc and two of his captains and their wives had been invited to dinner that evening with General Bernard Saint-Hillier, chief of their paratroop division, a man whom they would later have to arrest. To cancel now would alert the general staff. Challe postponed H-hour until 2 A.M. "Avoid bloodshed where possible," he told Saint-Marc.

That evening Captain Savary, an officer in the Tizi-Ouzou district of eastern Algeria, informed his colonel, "They've asked me to take part in a putsch tonight." General Jean Simon, commanding the zone, rang the army corps commander in Algiers, General Vézinet, with the news. But his chief, General Fernand Gambiez, who had spent his formative years in a Legion mounted company, refused to believe that the army, his army, would march against the government. The commander in chief telephoned Saint-Hillier, another legionnaire, who told him that Saint-Marc had just left his dinner table with two of his officers. Two hours later, just after midnight, security men reported vehicle movements around Zeralda. Gambiez got through to Saint-Marc.

"*Non, mon général.* Everything's absolutely quiet."

"But these vehicle movements?"

"We're holding a night exercise, *mon général.*"

"I have your word."

"My word as Saint-Marc and as a legionnaire."

At Zeralda, Saint-Marc replaced the receiver and turned to the officers he had been briefing. "That was Gambiez. They've got wind of something. We must move now." They broke up and ordered the legionnaires into the trucks. When the men learned they were carrying out a putsch, Corporal Claude Tenne saw them slapping each other on the back and rubbing their hands at the thought of seizing Algiers. "*Un putsch. Ça, alors . . .*" And after Algiers . . . Paris? And after that . . . who knew? But this was real adventure. They sang and shouted as the convoy pulled out. France's most decorated regiment was in rebellion.

In the leading jeep Captain Pierre Sergent ordered Legionnaire Sladeck to drive at top speed. He talked his way through the first roadblock; they dismantled the others while the gendarmes watched. Who wanted to tangle with legionnaires?

In his headquarters General Gambiez listened to reports and grew more dubious about Saint-Marc's reply. Gambiez, a tiny figure with a face like an archdeacon rather than a five-star general, contacted the officer from the vehicle group serving Zeralda. "Yes, a convoy of trucks left here for a mission with the 1st REP." At that moment Saint-Hillier called to say that he had talked with Saint-Marc's wife. "She admitted he had just left his home. I think the situation is serious. I'm driving to Zeralda."

"Wait for me," said Gambiez.

The two generals drove at full speed through the town. On the outskirts they saw the long convoy, its headlights stretching for miles. The first vehicles passed, but Gambiez managed to squeeze his car into a gap; both generals climbed out and placed themselves in the middle of the road. A five-ton lorry braked and came to rest two inches from the commander in chief. "Go on, squash the crazy fools," came a shout from the cabin. Luckily, Gambiez and Saint-Hillier had stopped by a petrol station; the truck detoured around them and moved on. Gambiez ran to a command car.

"You recognize me," he shouted. "The commander in chief."

Lieutenant Philippe Durand-Ruel leaned out. "You're not in the hunt. Challe and Zeller have arrived."

"I place you under arrest," Gambiez shouted.

"I'll do my time here," said the lieutenant and drove on, nudging one of the general's cars out of the way. Gambiez leaped into his car. "Pass them," he cried. But by the time he reached the General Delegation building the paratroopers were pouring through the gates. "These men are guilty of insurrection," the general yelled to the security men. They looked at him, then at the determined legionnaires, and solemnly removed the clips from their machine pistols. Carrying Gambiez and Saint-Hillier with them, the paratroopers charged into the building. Somehow the courageous little general broke free and regained his car. But before he could escape, Durand-Ruel had fired several shots into his tires and ordered his arrest.

"In my time in the Legion, junior officers didn't arrest their generals."

"The generals didn't sell out the Empire," said Durand-Ruel.

"You know my son died at Dien Bien Phu," said Gambiez.

"It's the mission and I have my orders," replied the lieutenant.

At Pélissier Barracks, Captain Sergent had succeeded in opening the gates for his legionnaires. The uncompromising General Vézinet resisted, but was marched off while the legionnaires cleared his office, smashing a portrait of de Gaulle. With the main administration building and the army headquarters in their hands, the 1st REP had virtually taken over Algiers. Two hours after leaving Zeralda they had possession of every key center; only one man had died, killed accidentally, as he resisted the paratroopers who seized his radio transmitter. Challe, Zeller, and Jouhaud congratulated themselves on a model coup d'état.

The dramatic incident of that night, perhaps the moment on which the success of the putsch hinged, came just before 4 A.M. Lieutenant Roger Degueldre appeared at the Delegation building with a handful of legionnaires and made for the room where Gambiez, Vézinet, Jean Morin, the delegate general, and Robert Buron, the French public works minister, were all under guard. Degueldre knew Challe's injunction about killing; but as a soldier he believed that a bloodless revolution was doomed from the outset. If shooting two generals and two ministers would force the vacillating, the lukewarm military chiefs to join the putsch, then it must be done.

But his way was barred by his friend Captain Bésineau. Not only his friend, but the husband of the woman Degueldre loved—Nicole, the daughter of General Paul Gardy. "I want to have a word with these *messieurs*," said Degueldre.

"I know what's in your mind," Bésineau replied. "But I have my orders. If you want to shoot them, you must first shoot me. I am ready to make the sacrifice. Go ahead."

Had it been anyone else other than Bésineau, the lieutenant would not have hesitated, not even have reflected. But how could he? There was Nicole . . . Degueldre turned away with his legionnaires.

Gambiez and the others were bundled into a plane and flown to In Salah, in the heart of the Sahara. At Tizi-Ouzou, General Jean Simon refused to join Challe. The former legionnaire could not turn against de Gaulle. "I have fired on Frenchmen three times," he said. "Not again." Disguised as an air force corporal, he slipped out of Algeria and flew back to Paris.

With fifty officers and 8,000 men, Challe had executed a brilliant coup d'état. The paratroopers, in mottled combat uniform and green berets, patrolled the streets and guarded the main civil and military buildings in the city; at Constantine and Oran, the same scenario. But a few thousand troops holding three or four towns did not signify control of Algeria. And where did the revolution go from here? Captain Pierre Sergeant and groups of militant civil leaders urged Challe to drop the paratroopers on Paris before de Gaulle could appeal to the population and convince the 400,000 troops in Algeria to resist the putsch. But Challe temporized. As some said of him, "He has every quality of leadership except one—he doesn't know how to disobey." Something stopped him. The enormity of his action? The presence of the American Seventh Fleet in the Mediterranean? The threat of a trial of strength with de Gaulle? The failure of regular French army, navy, and air force units to rally? The refusal of Foreign Legion units to march with him?

For General Gardy had not swung the Legion behind the putsch. Colonel Vaillant told officers of the 13th Demi-Brigade, "You'll have to get rid of me before the demi-brigade gets involved in sedition." At Bel-Abbès, Gardy found the Quartier Vienot and the town deserted; the men and units that had promised to help seize and hold Oran had not appeared. Colonel Brothier, commanding the First For-

Sherman Tank

eign Regiment, replied frostily to the former Legion inspector general; he told officers who wished to join the rebellion, "The Legion is foreign by definition and will not intervene in a purely French quarrel." And Brothier disappeared to his home to let tempers cool. Throughout Algeria, the same reaction. Generals and colonels who had promised backing now wriggled or waited to see how the revolution developed. Navy units declared their hostility; air force pilots flew out to France with their planes to avoid becoming embroiled.

In Paris the prime minister, Michel Debré, mobilized the army and appealed to Frenchmen to resist any move from Algeria to start a civil war. President de Gaulle, however, let the situation simmer for nearly three days. On Monday evening he denounced the putsch and the generals who had led it in a TV and radio speech. "In France's name, I order that every means, I say every means, be employed to bar the road everywhere to these men until they are forced to submit. . . . I forbid every French citizen, and especially every soldier, to carry out any of their orders." Challe realized that the majority of army officers and their soldiers were listening to Paris and not Algiers. On Tuesday he announced his decision to surrender himself. The more intransigent officers, like Sergent, discussed the possibility of liquidating Challe and continuing the revolt; instead they decided that the coup had fizzled out. They would disappear and fight with the underground movements for French Algeria.

Elie Denoix de Saint-Marc did not join officers like Sergent, Lieutenant Daniel Godot, and Degueldre; he would hand over the regiment to Colonel Guiraud at Zeralda and give himself up. On Tuesday evening the legionnaires withdrew from their posts. Many wept as they climbed into the trucks. With them went Challe, Jouhaud, and Salan, who had arrived two days before from Madrid and had decided to fight on. When Challe flew out for Paris the next day, a state prisoner, the two generals disappeared into the countryside around Algiers.

Saint-Marc and his legionnaires found their camp ringed with Sherman tanks; off the coast the aircraft carrier *Arromanches* was cruising, its decks covered with fighter

aircraft; overhead, helicopters hovered until several legionnaires fired at them with their machine pistols. Gendarmes
surrounded the barracks and called on the regiment to surrender—a unit that had won more citations in its short history than any other, that had twice bled to death in
Indochina, and that had taken most of the hard knocks in Algeria!

"We have orders to search your barracks, where we believe there are rebel officers," the chief gendarme said.

Saint-Marc glared at him. "Push off before I throw you
in the cells and let your little chums come and fetch you," he
growled. Indeed, the regiment was prepared to fight. Certain
officers suggested staging a new putsch, this time using
force; some urged Saint-Marc to send the men on leave
while the officers gave themselves up. The discussion ended
with the arrival of Colonel Guiraud, who bore a letter from
Messmer. The officers must consider themselves prisoners;
the regiment would report to Bel-Abbès to be disbanded.
This was de Gaulle's decision. Messmer had, in fact, done
much to persuade de Gaulle not to dissolve the whole of the
Legion!

The low, white-walled barracks suddenly filled with
the families of legionnaires, the townspeople, both European and Arab, for whom this regiment *was* Zeralda. They
showered the men with roses from the gardens, with cigarettes, with bottles of wine; the flowers that Jeanpierre had
planted bloomed in the hair of wives and girl friends who
had come to bid adieu. Newspapermen and photographers,
who were recording these scenes, found Tommy guns in
their backs. "Get out, you scavengers," an officer shouted.
"You'll never see legionnaires crying."

Smoke climbed above offices as the regimental
archives burned. Some enraged legionnaires smashed furni-
ture and partition walls; random Tommy-gun bursts sent the
snoopers flying. Everyone stiffened as a series of explosions
set the camp and the still air vibrating. It was the regimental
arsenal. No one else would use their ammunition, the legionnaires decided.

In silence the regiment formed up in the square; for the
last time a legionnaire ran the colors to the top of the
flagstaff; bare-headed, minus his medals, Elie Denoix de

Saint-Marc brought the men to attention and handed over his command to Colonel Guiraud. *"Vive la Légion! Vive Algérie française!"* the women and children yelled as the legionnaires crowded into their trucks. Roses, jasmine, bougainvillaea rained on them. Legionnaires wrenched from their chests the ribbons they had won—in World War II, in Indochina, in Algeria—and flung them on the ground. The officers shook each man by the hand and wept as the lorries lumbered out of the gates. A snatch of song. The Africans: *"Nous étions au fond de l'Afrique/Gardiens jaloux de nos couleurs . . ."* It was the finish of the First Foreign Parachute Regiment.

Some legionnaires did not wait for the humiliation of being disbanded or posted to other Legion units. On the outskirts of Orléansville, one truck veered left and disappeared toward the Ouarsenis Mountains. NCOs such as Sergeant Dovecar and Corporal Tenne left the convoy along the road to Bel-Abbès with many of their section; they were determined to continue the struggle with their officers. Several officers, too, had disappeared when the cars arrived to escort them to Milbert police barracks in Algiers.

In the summer of 1961, Challe and Zeller were brought to trial and sentenced to fifteen years' imprisonment. Saint-Marc, who accepted the responsibility for the defection of the 1st REP, got ten years—considered by many as a harsh punishment. Nine captains, two lieutenants and the adjutant who had killed a sergeant by accident were given suspended sentences ranging from one to two years.

More than a dozen Legion officers had gone underground in Algeria and France. One of them made his stand clear. The week the putsch failed, a leaflet circulated in army units. It said, "The state is about to abandon Algeria. And you chiefs? Will you abandon the faithful Moslems who have fought on your side? Would you like to see hundreds and millions of men, women, and children throw themselves into the sea to join the ships embarking you? Remember Tonkin!" The document bore the signature of a paratroop officer—Lieutenant Roger Degueldre.

SEVENTEEN

Farewell, farewell,
O Bel-Abbès, hallowed by blood eternal,
We will guard and honor
Our traditions, our legend, our banner.

The morning after the failure of the putsch, Sergeant Albert Dovecar walked through the rich residential district of Bouzareah to a villa set behind walled grounds, the rendezvous Roger Degueldre had given him two days before. The legionnaire barely recognized his old lieutenant. Degueldre had dyed his dark hair and eyebrows blond; his civilian suit sat awkwardly on his massive shoulders and bulky body. Dovecar saluted and reported that several score of legionnaires from the 1st REP had decided to desert. "They're taking the breakup of the regiment badly," he said.

"I'm suffering, too," said Degueldre. "The 1st REP is finished, but it will rise again." Dovecar estimated that some two hundred legionnaires had escaped from Zeralda or jumped from the lorries taking them to Bel-Abbès. Degueldre ordered him to round them up; he handed him the addresses of villas and houses in the Bab el-Oued district, where they would find friends who would also fight for French Algeria. Within a few days they would receive clothing, equipment, new identity cards, and instructions about the coming battle. Degueldre and his legionnaires were to become the iron core of the struggle against de Gaulle, whom they viewed as a traitor to France, and against the FLN, with whom the President was negotiating.

In the succeeding days Algiers witnessed a new symbol of revolt floating over its port, a black flag with the letters OAS pricked out in white; the same letters appeared on the walls, on cars and vans, on the streets and pavements. Seven weeks before the putsch the OAS (Secret Army Organization) had proclaimed its existence, though the government did not take it seriously. But now the three dissident generals and the cabal of colonels who had directed the putsch were shaping the OAS into a fighting arm to contest de Gaulle's Algerian policy. General Salan (the Mandarin, because of his inscrutable face and Vietnam background) directed the movement from a farm near the capital. General Jouhaud had taken over the Oran sector and General Gardy, the Algiers network. The mastermind was Colonel Yves Godard, a Resistance hero and former security chief in Algiers who used the Resistance and the FLN methods as a model for the new organization. At no time did the OAS have more than 3,000 militant members, of whom only 1,000 were combatants; yet its campaign of physical and psychological violence would bring Algeria to the verge of civil war, poison Franco-Algerian relations, and split both countries into two camps. The OAS aimed at keeping Algeria within the French Union; but many of its members saw themselves fighting on a border front. For some it was the menace of communism or the antichrist taking over North Africa then Europe; others were right-wing reactionaries, a few with fascist leanings. Many of the army men just refused the humiliation of yet another defeat. Among these new revolutionaries Roger Degueldre stood out as the most ruthless, the most enigmatic, the most dedicated.

But dedicated to what? To the Legion, certainly. He had served sixteen years: as a private in Algeria; as an NCO in Indochina; as an officer from 1958 in Algeria. A hard man, but as tough on himself as on the men. No one knew, for instance, that he covered up a heart attack in 1959 to return to the fight against the FLN. His whole life seemed to begin with the Legion. He had enlisted under a false name, giving his nationality as Belgian, though he would later insist on being French. Some officers whispered that he had joined the Nazis in Belgium and fought with their Rex Division against the Russians. Degueldre denied this, claiming he had fought with a communist cell in the French Resistance and joined the Liberation army in 1944. Why then did he serve in the Legion as a foreigner—even after being commissioned and assuming his real name? Like most questions about Degueldre, it remains unresolved. His motives for joining the secret army seem equally cryptic. Anti-communism? The honor of the army? The image of Vietnamese drowning in Haiphong Bay when the French quit Tonkin? His links with the *pieds noirs,* whom he admired? Perhaps a mélange of these sentiments. Perhaps, like so many legionnaires for whom Bel-Abbès represented a place of rebirth, he felt that when Algeria had gained its independence he would again become a displaced person. Degueldre had also given his word as a legionnaire. He had sworn his personal oath on the coffin of Jeanpierre. And, after the barricades in January 1960, he told his senior officers, "You say nothing will stop you from keeping Algeria a part of France. I have given my word. But understand that, as far as I am concerned, it will be honored. I shall go on to the end." Degueldre believed that two factors would assure victory for the OAS: they would succeed in assassinating President de Gaulle and thus change French policy; they could inflame the populations of cities like Algiers, Oran, and Constantine into open rebellion and force the French Government to change its ways. "We'll do what they did in Budapest—fight in the streets," he told Captain Sergent, who was leaving to organize the OAS in France. "The *pieds noirs* will follow us."

Degueldre became Delta, the strong man of the OAS Action and Operations Bureau. He split his legionnaires, who numbered more than one hundred, into commando cells. The FLN had made violence their political weapon; the OAS would do likewise. They did not lack targets. Godard, Degueldre, and others had waged the battle of Algiers and had gathered intelligence about FLN leaders, their groups, and their hideouts. Armed with submachine guns, revolvers, and plastic explosives, the Delta commandos worked from cars, bombing or shooting up FLN meeting places and homes, then disappearing. They had the population of the European quarter—and many of the police—with them. Some *pieds noirs* did not think that the commandos went far enough; they must kill those European traitors who sided with the FLN. When anyone voiced such opinions to Degueldre, he would say blandly, "Right. Perhaps you'd care to volunteer to execute a terrorist or an FLN collaborator? I will brief you, give you a loaded revolver, come with you, and point out the man. Then, if you hesitate, I will kill you with my own hand." Few accepted the challenge.

One policeman with no divided loyalties about the OAS was Roger Gavoury, the spare, bespectacled police commissioner for Algiers. OAS men, arrested and interrogated, complained that Gavoury was too zealous in his efforts to stamp out the movement. The leaders of the movement condemned him to death and handed the warrant for his execution to Degueldre. The lieutenant could trust only one man to carry out the assassination: Sergeant "Bobby" Dovecar. Though Yugoslav by birth, Dovecar had taken Austrian nationality. He had already proved his courage many times over in the djebels and the battle of Algiers, having been cited several times. Loyalty to Degueldre had impelled him to join the OAS, and the lieutenant had made him a party to the oath he had sworn over Jeanpierre's body. "Gavoury is standing in the way of French Algeria and must be killed," Degueldre told the sergeant. "But I want no shots."

Dovecar took two legionnaire members of his commandos, Corporal Claude Tenne and Legionnaire Herbert Petri. For Tenne the Legion had meant redemption, converting him from a footloose Parisian youth, in and out of trouble, to an exemplary soldier. He admired Degueldre intensely. Petri, a tough, resolute German, was following orders. Besides the three legionnaires, there were three civilians, one the son of a police commissioner. They began by watching Gavoury's office and flat, checking his routine. On the night of May 31, Dovecar posted himself in a student's flat opposite the commissioner's studio in Docteur Trolard Street. At 11:30 P.M. Gavoury returned, opened the door, and then, as if sensing danger, banged it shut in Dovecar's face. But waiting for him in the studio were Petri and Tenne. Gavoury ran for the bathroom, but the legionnaires pounced. Petri struck him with a truncheon; Tenne leaped on him, seized him by the throat, and stabbed him in the heart and chest.

The OAS publicly claimed responsibility for Gavoury's murder. Only when they listened to the radio that night did Tenne and Petri realize they had killed the police commissioner. "We did a good job." They grinned at each other. But the hunt was on. Dovecar and his legionnaires flitted from one apartment to another, finally finding refuge in the opulent villa owned by Madame Gauthier-Saliège in Bouzareah. The lady, one of the aristocrats of Algiers, hid the legionnaires among the thousands of rare books in the library that her husband had made famous throughout Europe. However, someone had tipped off the police. They almost caught Degueldre, who had come to issue new orders; he broke through the roadblocks in his car. "You'll have to fight it out," he told Dovecar. Around the luxurious villa a battle developed between Dovecar, his legionnaires, and the police. The sergeant escaped, but Tenne was picked up, seriously wounded, in the library; and six other legionnaires were arrested with him. But it would be nearly a year before the police could bring all the killers of the Commissaire Gavoury to justice.

Throughout that long, torrid summer, Algiers lived the daily drama of bomb, grenade, and machine-gun attacks by the OAS and the FLN. The OAS stepped up its psychological campaign, destroying radio and TV transmitters or interrupting programs to make its own announcements to the population. It published its own newspapers, proudly announcing yet another list of FLN and Gaullist supporters who had been killed. As these execution lists grew, so the gulf between the French and Moslem communities widened. This, according to President de Gaulle, had become the OAS aim. In his *Mémoires d'Espoir,* de Gaulle wrote: "For more than a year, the OAS expanded its bloody activities. It worked under the theoretical authority of Salan and Jouhaud, hidden respectively in Algiers and Oran, who kept a certain influence in the administration, the police, and the army. In reality, it obeyed their henchmen like Jean-Jacques Susini, possessed by totalitarian passion. It used the deserters and the fanatics, procured from the scum of military men, particularly from foreign units, and the underworld aroused as always by latent tumult." De Gaulle recorded that the OAS made 1,500 plastic-bomb attacks during several months of

1961, as well as daily raids with guns and grenades in Algiers and Oran. He accused it of killing 12,000 men, women, and children in the course of a year, of wounding several hundred policemen and assassinating some thirty police commissioners, officials, and magistrates.

Degueldre played a major role in this terrorist work. Jean-Jacques Susini, member of the OAS supreme committee, considered the lieutenant's dozen Delta commando units to be the pillar of *pied noir* resistance in Algeria. Degueldre handled his small private army with an iron fist; but such was his personal magnetism that only one man deserted and informed on the Delta units. The lieutenant's astringent personality did not, however, appeal to his chiefs, like Colonel Godard, who regarded him imprudent and too prone to mix in politics. His fellow legionnaire General Gardy defended him. "Psychologically he feels on his own," he told Godard. "Partly disavowed by his serving comrades in the legion, especially since the Gavoury business, he's not sufficiently directed and supported by our organization. He might assume more and more the mentality of a desperado, become discouraged, and disappear."

Even General Gardy, who was genuinely fond of Degueldre, found it hard to forgive his association with his daughter, Nicole, the wife of a fellow officer. Nicole and Degueldre not only shared a mutual love but they both had a passion for French Algeria. A strange love affair, the more intense, the more poignant because it was played out by two people who lived from one violent moment to the next, who were now the hunters, now the hunted, who stood at the center of a nightmare of bloodshed.

In the second week of October, one of Degueldre's commandos was arrested and, under pressure, informed the police that the lieutenant's headquarters were three apartments in the Boulevard Marcel-Duclos. What? In the center of Algiers? The police would have been more incredulous to learn that Salan had visited Degueldre just two weeks before. However, they acted on the information, surrounding the block on October 12. Degueldre walked through the cordon, but Dovecar and five of his men fell into police hands. The swoop also gave them most of the Delta arms, ammunition, and archives. Dovecar submitted quietly to arrest; he feared to fight it out and risk blowing up the stocks of plastic explosive, which would have wrecked the building and killed innocent people. The police could hardly believe that this soft-spoken, smooth-faced boy had caused them so much trouble; or that he would confess so readily to his part in the murders of Commissioner Gavoury and many others. Two weeks later they arrested Claude Piegts, one of the oldest members of the OAS. Dovecar identified him as the man who had furnished a revolver for the Gavoury murder and had helped to brief him.

Degueldre was living dangerously every moment. Later that month two policemen walked into a cafe in the El-Biar district, spotted someone they were sure was Degueldre; they opened fire, but the man fled. Degueldre and his Delta commandos appeared invulnerable. In Algiers and Oran the OAS appeared to have the upper hand. In Paris it was decided to form an anti-OAS brigade that would copy the terrorist methods to exterminate the movement. Thus the Barbouzes came into existence.

Barbouzes was the music-hall label pinned to this polyglot collection of undercover men who arrived in Algiers at the beginning of December—a nucleus of Free French and Resistance fighters, a group of former colonial paratroopers that included Vietnamese and Tunisians. They operated alone and their main objective was to arrest Salan and Jouhaud and kill or capture Degueldre. They had their minor successes, seizing and grilling more lowly OAS members. But what could a handful of amateur agents hope to achieve against the hardened professionals led by Degueldre? As soon as they arrived, Degueldre knew what and who they were. The OAS commandos and the Barbouzes had several running battles and a few duels—for some of the rival gangs knew each other. Degueldre bided his time until he had located their headquarters near the summer palace. Then he struck in the last hour of 1962.

The legionnaire lieutenant posted his best commandos around the villa Dar Likoulia. Forty-five minutes before midnight, seven rockets from his homemade bazookas blasted the front of the villa; one exploded a stock of grenades. Degueldre and several ex-legionnaires rushed the building from a flank and grenaded each room. The Barbouzes, however, hit back with machine guns and grenades; for half an hour the grounds of the villa became a battlefield. It was the Delta commandos who had to withdraw, leaving one OAS member dead and carrying a wounded man. The Barbouzes had no casualties, but they had to quit the wrecked villa for another hideout at rue Fabre in the El-Biar district.

By now the Barbouzes and their new secret headquarters were known. Godard and Degueldre circulated their names and their pseudonyms. At the end of January a crate arrived at Algiers airport addressed to Mr. Jim Lassus, No. 8 rue Fabre. The cover name of Jim Alcheik, one of the Barbouze leaders. So they had ordered a new printing press to step up dissemination of anti-OAS propaganda! The packing case came first to Degueldre. "We must see that they're not disappointed when they open it." He grinned, handing it over to one of his booby-trap experts. The legionnaire stuffed it with more than sixty pounds of plastic explosive and, for good measure, placed some grenades between the press and the wooden planks. A battery of detonators was tied to the outside with parachute silk. At 3:45 P.M. on January 29 a truck unloaded the crate at the Barbouze headquarters; one of the freight men demanded money for carriage, then told the Barbouzes, "The customs will be here at five o'clock." At that hour, no customs men arrived. The Barbouzes crowded around the crate to watch the press being removed.

At 5:05 the El-Biar district shuddered with the blast; the villa seemed to disintegrate in a mess of crumbling walls and erupting roof. Few of the Barbouzes survived. From the debris the gendarmes and firemen dug out the remains of eighteen of the undercover men. The bodies were flown to France and buried secretly in case the OAS should attempt to assassinate the few mourners.

The new Barbouze team had scarcely installed itself in the Raja Hotel when Degueldre pounced again. For forty-eight hours he attacked the hideout until the Barbouzes fled. Four agents who tried to drive a wounded comrade to a hospital were gunned down by five OAS men. Their car rammed a wall in the center of Algiers. Before the wounded passengers could escape, the inhabitants of apartment blocks ran out to surround their car and set it ablaze. In that fire per-

ished the last of these curious agents. Degueldre had won the
battle against the Barbouzes.

When the French Government began the Evian negotia-
tions with nationalist leaders, Salan called for an all-out war
to halt the peace moves. But the Evian Agreements on
March 18 granted Algeria the right to choose her own form
of government and fixed a cease-fire for the following day.
Not for the OAS. Now Moslems feared to step outside their
own quarter of Algiers. The OAS singled out groups of people thought to be collaborators of the FLN. One day it was
pharmacists, the next postmen who were butchered. To
Degueldre's credit he and his Delta commandos refused to
take part in these massacres. Barbouzes and gendarmes, yes.
But not just anyone. Toward the end of March an OAS commando attacked a patrol of half-tracks, leaving eighteen gendarmes killed and twenty-five wounded. Next it was the
army—two lorry loads of native conscripts. After these out-
bursts General Charles Ailleret, the commander in chief, decreed that the fanatics of Bab el-Oued must be taught a
lesson. Armored cars cleared the streets, spraying anything
that moved in this armed camp; fighter aircraft strafed the
rooftops that hid OAS guerrillas. Bab el-Oued was block-
aded and isolated from the rest of the city. The OAS reacted
by staging a peaceful protest march out of the quarter to beat
the blockade. At the rue d'Isly it ran into a unit of native riflemen. Who provoked the massacre? Some say the OAS
fired first on the soldiers, others that the unit panicked and
fired into the surging mob. At the end of that day, March 26,
forty-nine people lay dead and 121 wounded.

Only the diehard OAS militants now believed that they
could win. Algiers had seen enough blood. Salan believed
that they could still take to the hills and fight as a *maquis*.
But in the first serious engagement in the Ouarsenis Mountains, Colonel Roger Gardes and his *maquisards* were defeated, caught between the FLN and the French forces. The
forty prisoners taken on April 2 were persuaded to talk; time
began to run out for Degueldre and the others. Still the lieutenant refused to admit that he was beaten. He tried to coax a
former officer to join him. "We'll get rid of the generals and
colonels and form our own organization," he said.

On April 7, Captain Lacoste, the police chief, picked up a legionnaire deserter who named several of Degueldre's hideouts. One by one Lacoste eliminated them until he was left with a block of flats at 91 boulevard du Telemly. Inside, Degueldre and several other OAS leaders spotted the gendarmes surrounding the building. Degueldre refused to follow others into a secret hiding place; he had walked through security checks so many times. "I'll be all right," he said. "I have *la baraka*." At the door he showed his papers. "Joseph Esposito, Primary Schools Inspector." The policeman was waving him on when a lieutenant suddenly held up his hand. Degueldre's blond hair stank of dye.

"You say you're a schools inspector?"

Degueldre nodded. "Phone the Algiers Academy if you want to check."

"We'll confirm your identity at the Hussein-Dey police station."

And there Captain Lacoste saw through Degueldre's disguise immediately. The lieutenant did not deny his identity. "No use questioning me," he told Lacoste. "I won't tell you anything." That night they put him on the Paris plane and into a cell at La Santé Prison. With the arrest of Lieutenant Roger Degueldre, the OAS dream of keeping Algeria a part of France evaporated.

As Algerian independence drew nearer, the OAS began a final violent spasm. It ordered the destruction by bomb and flame of buildings in Algiers and Oran; universities and schools, town halls and public buildings, stocks of fuel, factories, shops blazed, illuminating the fury and despair of the movement. In May and June the French left the country in boatloads with the blessing of the OAS. Of the 1,000,000 Europeans, no more than 100,000 remained by the end of June. Salan and Jouhaud had been captured and, from their prison cells, gave their organization instructions to cease its campaign of violence. General Gardy slipped into Spain and eventually to South America; other leaders followed him into exile. The Algerian referendum took place on July 1 without incident; France formally recognized the country's independence on July 3.

The Gavoury case was heard two weeks before Degueldre's arrest or he might have stood trial with the three legionnaires and four civilians accused of murdering the police commissioner or being accessories. Laconic and neutral the legionnaires confessed to their part in the crime with no attempt to justify or excuse their action. Dovecar testified how Degueldre and Claude Piegts had briefed him; how Corporal Claude Tenne and Legionnaire Herbert Petri had volunteered. Tenne electrified the court with his bland description of the killing—the classic sentry treatment, a kick, an arm around the throat, and a stab in the heart. Asked by the advocate general how he felt about murdering in cold blood, Tenne replied, "I'm a soldier. They trained me to kill . . . I worked on dummies."

Colonel Brothier, who knew all three men as their former commanding officer in the 1st REP, appeared as a character witness. Dovecar, he said, was a model legionnaire combining intelligence and courage; he had won his NCO stripes and three citations in only three years. Tenne, the turbulent civilian youth, had developed into one of the best legionnaires, the colonel considered. He had been cited twice for bravery and had no blot on his service record. Petri, a Berliner, was the classic legionnaire type—rough and hard to command but splendid in combat. Brothier stated that the 1st REP seemed not so much a unit as a solid phalanx of officers and men. "One of the exceptional characteristics of the Legion is the dog-like devotion of the men to their officers," he said. "It is from them that they find the structure and balance that civilian life did not give them. Thus, they transfer all their attachments and affection to their officers. For they have no critical sense. In their officers they will forgive everything, even the most extravagant actions. This is what I believe has brought them here. They followed those they were used to following. . . ."

That appeal probably saved Tenne and Petri from a firing squad; the advocate general agreed that they had acted like robots in striking down the commissioner. But Dovecar and Piegts must bear the responsibility for organizing and planning the crime. They were sentenced to death. Tenne and Petri each received life imprisonment; the three remaining civilians got lighter punishments. The legionnaires heard the verdicts while standing to attention in new uniforms adorned with medals. Petri shouted, "I ask the court to grant me the favor of dying with my sergeant." His request was refused. Tenne ripped off his medals and hurled them into the courtroom; Dovecar and Petri followed his example.

Appeals for Dovecar and Piegts failed. Degueldre broke his silence to plead for Piegts, who, he avowed, had played no part in the Gavoury assassination. A strange confrontation took place in a room in Fresnes Prison, where Degueldre met his old sergeant, Dovecar, and Piegts. But the lieutenant's evidence and arguments failed to convince the state prosecutor and the judges. Another of Dovecar's officers, Captain Pierre Sergent, planned a bid to rescue him from the condemned cell at La Santé. An OAS captain explored the sewers under the prison. They intended to approach through the sewers, grab Dovecar, and make their escape while a commando unit covered them with machinegun fire. At the last minute, however, Dovecar was transferred to another cell and they had to abandon the idea. On June 7 an armed convoy escorted Dovecar and Piegts to Fort Trou D'Enfer. The sergeant wore the green beret and the leopard battle dress of the 1st REP. At 4:12 A.M., his hands bound to a post, he gazed at the firing squad raising their rifles. *"Vive la Légion,"* he shouted as the officer ordered, "Fire."

Both General Jouhaud and General Salan had been captured. Brought before a High Military Tribunal, Jouhaud was sentenced to death on April 13. But six weeks later the same tribunal brought in a verdict of life imprisonment on Salan. Under pressure from several of his cabinet ministers, General de Gaulle grudgingly spared Jouhaud's life; but he scrapped the tribunal and replaced it with a Military Court of Justice. The first man to be tried by this court was Lieutenant Roger Degueldre.

The chief of the Delta commandos had no illusions about the coming trial. "I don't wear kid gloves and carry a brief case," he said. "I shall be shot as an example to the soldiers who erred." He sat mute before the examining magistrate in prison, merely observing that the man had no jurisdiction to interrogate him. Apart from his intervention on Piegts' behalf, he said nothing, though he did not deny his responsibility for the actions of his commandos. In his spartan cell in the Santé he had few visitors: his lawyers,

J. L. Tixier-Vignancourt and Denise Macaigne; the wif
from whom he had been separated years before, but who loy
ally supported him throughout his imprisonment and tria
Roger Degueldre wanted only one thing—to see his an
Nicole's son, Philippe, born in the first weeks of June
"Surely you can smuggle him in by putting him in a valise,
he suggested to one of the lawyers. But the law permitte
neither the child nor the mother to visit him.

At the end of June the trial took place in a recreatio
room at the Chateau de Vincennes. "It's fourteen years, da
for day, since I enlisted here as a legionnaire," he told hi
lawyers. Both advocates protested vainly about the jurisdic
tion of the military court to try their client; finally, they ap
peared as ordinary citizens, without their robes, to make the
plea. Degueldre, who had instructed them to make no de
fense, listened impassively as they recited his record of ser
vice, his years in the Resistance, his service with th
Liberation army, his Croix de Guerre, his military medal, hi
ten citations for bravery. When the moment came to answe
the charges, the President, General Gardet, barked, "Degue
dre, stand up." The lieutenant sat, his arms folded. "Degue
dre, stand up." He rubbed his dark chin but did not budge. T
not one of some 170 questions did he reply nor did he eve
react. Tixier-Vignancourt made a final appeal: if Lieutenar
Degueldre deserved death, then his OAS chief, Genera
Salan, must surely have deserved it several thousand time
over. But the verdict was death. Even that left Degueldre ur
moved.

On July 2, four days before his execution, Degueldre se
down on paper seven hundred words as cryptic as his life an
actions. He wrote:

> After a certain trial which took place last
> Thursday, Degueldre Roger has been transferred to
> his cell at Fresnes.
> That's what they say; I, who know D.R., hav-
> ing been with him for thirty-seven years, affirm
> that it's false. D.R. is not here. The person impris-
> oned in Fresnes is called Jules (at least it's the
> name that I've given him).
> Jules is very different from Roger. Since ar-

riving, he does nothing but sleep, read, drink, and eat. Everybody treats him kindly. One would say he is a great personage who is recovering from an illness which brought him to death's door. He is convalescing but must be carefully watched in case he relapses. . . . Everybody who meets Jules has a sad smile, full of understanding. Jules answers with a big smile and a kind word and each time he seems to hear a sigh of relief from the people he meets. This sigh appears to say, "Ah! He's feeling better." And Jules is quite happy with the game he's playing.

Sometimes, though rarely just the same, a blue funk comes over Jules; it is quickly thrown off since this fear really belongs to R.D. and Jules wants none of it. . . .

I think I have said everything about Jules and his very calm and quiet life.

And R.D.—tell me, where is he then? What is he doing? What is he thinking?

That is a secret that I know well, but only I know it.

Psychiatrists might infer that Degueldre invented Jules to relieve his guilt complex. Legionnaires have less difficulty understanding his form of camouflage since most of them lived a dual existence too.

Only the President of the Republic could save Degueldre. . . . General de Gaulle listened with a marble face and eyes hidden behind tinted glasses as Maître Denise Macaigne made her fifteen-minute plea for mercy. It was rejected and Degueldre was transferred to Fort d'Ivry.

Before dawn on July 6 they woke him and led him, handcuffed, a cigarette between his lips, to the wall where the firing squad was waiting. One captain had refused to command the squad and another was ordered to carry out the execution with a handful of nervous conscripts. As Degueldre faced them, calmly, he noted their agitation. "I don't hold it against you," he said. "Do your duty." His remarks only increased the tension. As they raised their rifles, Degueldre began to sing the *Marseillaise*.

There will always be doubt about what happened in the next ten minutes. Beyond the prison wall, journalists heard a ragged, dislocated volley; inside, some of those witnessing the execution, which included the two lawyers, Tixier-Vignancourt and Madame Macaigne, saw several bullets hit the wall well above Degueldre's head. For a moment it was thought that the OAS had succeeded in planting some of its members in the firing squad. But Degueldre had fallen. The sergeant major walked forward and gave the *coup de grâce*. Behind him came Tixier-Vignancourt and the priest. The lawyer contended that, had he moved to the left instead of the right side, Degueldre might still be alive; he would have noticed that the lieutenant had no head wound, that the revolver bullet had hit his left shoulder. At that moment, knowing that Degueldre still had a chance to live, he could have stopped the execution, invoking the grace of God. But already the sergeant major was firing the second mercy shot. His revolver jammed and it was only after the sixth attempt and the third shot that Degueldre died. The lawyers estimated that he lived for ten minutes after the order "Fire." Tixier-Vignancourt maintained after the execution that, since Degueldre had survived the firing squad and the first *coup de grâce*, the authorities should have halted the execution. The War Ministry rebutted his arguments, however, insisting that the execution had been carried out normally.

No record of Lieutenant Roger Degueldre exists in the Legion archives; his personal ideals and the methods he employed to achieve them evoked little official sympathy. To the authorities he was a deserter, a traitor, and an assassin. But many Legion officers and men saw Degueldre as a strangely symbolic figure, personifying the trauma of the legionnaire at having to quit Algeria, the birthplace of the Legion. If they did not admire his role in the OAS, they acknowledged his courage and refusal to break faith with himself. In the crypt of the Legion museum, legionnaires and friends deposit dozens of cards, similar to those commemorating a saint's day or bearing a religious text. . . . These text cards carry the pictures of Roger Degueldre or Sergeant Albert Dovecar, and the oath they both took when Jeanpierre died.

*   *   *

After Independence Day the Foreign Legion had four months in which to efface the traces of 131 years of its presence in Algeria—four uneasy months in which it had to turn its back on victorious parades of FLN troops around their barracks at Bel-Abbès and Saida. The French Government had decided to scatter the combat units of the Legion—to Corsica, Djibouti, Madagascar. It had designated a new headquarters at Aubagne, ten miles east of Marseilles. To this Camp de la Demande legionnaires ferried the symbols of their history and traditions; stone by stone they dismantled their Monument aux Morts, to erect it on the new parade ground, facing south toward Africa, of course. They packed their relics, such as the hand of Captain Danjou, the small treasures left by the Bazaine family, the swords of princes Aage and Amilakvari, the wax effigy of Colonel Rollet, the medals of the three Hungarian adjutants, the portraits of those such as Conrad, Bernelle, and his wife, Tharsile. Finally, they brought the flags, which bear more decorations than those of any other military unit—except two: the black flags that Captain Vicomte de Borelli had seized from the Chinese during the last days of the siege of Tuyen Quang in 1885. In his will Borelli had specified that, if the Legion ever quit Algeria, those flags must never accompany it to France.

In the evening of October 24, 1962, the seven hundred remaining legionnaires paraded in the vast square of Bel-Abbès; silent, the men stood at attention as an officer paid tribute to the dead they were leaving behind them. Then he read the long poem, dedicated by Borelli to Legionnaire Thiebald Streibler, who had given his life to save the captain.

Et quand donc les Français voudront-ils bien entendre
Que la guerre se fait dent pour dent, oeil pour oeil,
Et que ces Étrangers qui sont morts, à tout prendre,
Chaque fois, en mourant, leur épargnaient un deuil?

In the square, the two black, silken banners were spread; a legionnaire lit a torch and applied the flame to them. The seven hundred men lit their torches and sang the *Boudin* as they watched the tiny blaze die in the twilight.

BIBLIOGRAPHY

French

Aage, Prince Christian. *Mes Souvenirs de la Légion Étrangère*. Paris, Payot, 1936.

Aimable, Eugène. *Légionnaire au Mexique*. Brussels, Dessart.

Ainley, Henry. *Mourir pour Rien*. Paris, Stock, 1955.

Aublet, Capitaine Edouard. *Conquête du Dahomey*. Paris, Berger-Levrault, 1897.

Azan, Général Paul. *La Légion Étrangère en Espagne*. Paris, Plon, 1907.

———. *L'Armée d'Afrique*. Paris, Plon, 1936.

Bazaine, Maréchal Achille. Unpublished letters.

Beauvoir, Roger de. *La Légion Étrangère*. Paris, Maison Didot, 1897.

Bern, Légionnaire Jean. *L'Expédition du Dahomey*. Sidi bel-Abbès, Lavenue, 1893.

Blond, Georges. *La Légion Étrangère*. Paris, Stock 1964.

Bodard, Lucien. *La Guerre d'Indochine. L'Enlisement*. Paris, Gallimard, 1965.

———. *La Guerre d'Indochine. L'Humiliation*. Paris, Gallimard, 1965.

Bonnecarrère, Paul. *Par le Sang Versé*. Paris, Fayard, 1968.

Buchard, Robert. *Organisation Armée Secrète*. Paris, Albin Michel, 1963.

Camps, Sergeant-Major. *Le Siège de Tuyen Quang*. Verdun, Imprimerie Militaire, 1902.

Carteron, Capitaine. *Souvenirs de la Campagne de Tonkin*. Paris, Baudoin, 1891.

Castellane, Comte P. de. *Souvenirs de la Vie Militaire en Afrique*. Paris, Victor Lecous, 1852.

Cendrars, Blaise. *L'Homme Foudroyé*. Paris, Editions Denoel.

———. *Histoires Vraies*. Paris, Editions Denoel.

———. *La Main Coupée*. Paris, Editions Denoel.

Changarnier, Général. *Mémoires*. Paris, Berger-Levrault, 1930.

Coipel, Capitaine. *El Moungar*. Paris, Berger-Levrault, 1908.

Courrière, Yves. *La Guerre d'Algérie: Les Fils de la Toussaint*. Paris, Fayard, 1968–71.

———. *La Guerre d'Algérie: Le Temps des Léopards*. Paris, Fayard, 1968–71.

———. *La Guerre d'Algérie: L'Heure des Colonels*. Paris, Fayard, 1968–71.

———. *La Guerre d'Algérie: Les Feux du Désespoir*. Paris, Fayard, 1968–71.

Diesbach, Lieutenant Comte Gabriel de. *Notes et Souvenirs*. In manuscript.

Dominé, Lieutenant-Colonel Edmond. *Journal du Siège de Tuyen Quang*. Paris, 1886.

Dorgelès, Roland. *Sous le Casque Blanc*. Paris, Éditions de France, 1941.

Doumic, René. *Historique du Régiment de Marche de la Légion Étrangère*. Paris, Berger-Levrault.

Duchesne, Général Charles. *L'Expédition du Madagascar*. Paris, Berger-Levrault, 1897.

Esparbès, Georges. *La Légion Étrangère*. Paris, Flammarion, 1909.

Favrel, Charles. *Ci-devant Légionnaire*. Paris, Presses de la Cité, 1962.

France, Lieutenant de. *Orléans*. In manuscript.

Gaulle, Général Charles de. *Mémoires d'Espoir*. Paris, Plon, 1948-62.

Grandin, Commandant. *De Veracruz à Mazatlan*. Paris, Tolra, 1895.

Kubiak, Sergent. "Diary of Dien Bien Phu." *Képi Blanc* (the Legion magazine). Aubagne.

Lacretelée, Général de. *Souvenirs*. Paris, Émile-Paul, 1907.

Langlois, Lieutenant Pierre. *Souvenirs de Madagascar*. Paris, Charles Lavauzelle, 1900.

Le Poer, John Patrick. *La Légion Étrangère: Journal d'un Irlandais*. Paris, Juven, 1905.

Louis-Lande, L. "Camerone," *Revue des Deux Mondes,* Vol. 134. Paris, 1896.

MacMahon, Maréchal de. *Mémoires*. Paris, Plon, 1885.

Maire, Colonel Fernand, with Jean-Pierre Dorian. *Souvenirs de la Légion Étrangère*. Paris, Albin Michel, 1939.

Manue, Georges R. *Têtes Brulées*. Paris, Société d'Edition, 1929.

———. *Vu du Rang*. In manuscript.

Martin, Jean. *Je suis un Légionnaire*. Paris, Fayard, 1938.

Massoul, Marquis de. *France: Algérie: Orient*. Versailles, 1860.

Maurois, André. *Lyautey*. Paris, Plon, 1931.

Mordal, Jacques. *Bir Hakeim*. Paris, Presses de la Cité, 1970.

Nicolet, Arthur. *Mektoub*. Éditions Antipodes, 1939.

Paillot, Claude. *Dossier Secret de l'Indochine*. Paris, Presses de la Cité, 1964.

Pechkoff, Zinovi. *La Légion Étrangère au Maroc*. Paris, Le Sage, 1927.

Pfirmann, Sergent. *L'Humble Vie Quotidienne d'un Légionnaire*. In manuscript.

Pouget, Jean. *Nous Étions à Dien Bien Phu*. Paris, Presses de la Cité, 1964.

Reybaz, Georges-Jean. *Le Premier Mystérieux*. Paris, André Barry, 1932.

Saint-Arnaud, Maréchal de. *Lettres*. Paris, 1864.

Sergent, Pierre. *Ma Peau au Bout de mes Idées*. Paris, Table Ronde, 1968.

———. *La Bataille*. Paris, Table Ronde, 1970.

Silberman, Legionnaire Jean. *Souvenirs de Campagne*. In manuscript.

Susini, Jean-Jacques. *Histoire de l'O.A.S.* Paris, Table Ronde, 1963.

Tenne, Claude. *Mais le Diable Marche avec Nous*. Paris, Table Ronde, 1968.

Vial, Médecin-Capitaine Jean. *Le Maroc Héroïque*. Paris, Hachette, 1938.

Weygand, Jacques. *Légionnaire*. Paris, Flammarion, 1951.

Ysquierdo, Antoine. *Une Guerre pour Rien*. Paris, Table Ronde, 1966.

Zédé, Général Laurent. *Souvenirs de ma Vie*. Paris, 1895.

LE LIVRE D'OR. de la Légion Étrangère. 1931 edition.

The combat diaires of the Legion from 1831 to 1962 and the issues of the Legion magazine, *Képi Blanc*.

English

Alexander, Michael. *The Reluctant Legionnaire*. New York, Dutton, 1956.

Brace, Richard, and Joan. *Ordeal in Algeria*. Princeton, New Jersey, Nostrand, 1960.

Brogan, D. W. *The French Nation from Napoleon to Pétain*. New York, Harper, 1940.

Burton, Sir Richard Francis. *A Mission to Gelele*. London, 1864.

Carlé, Erwin. *In the Foreign Legion*. London, Duckworth, 1910.

Cooper, Adolphe. *The Man Who Liked Hell*. London, Jarrolds, 1933.

———. *Born to Fight*. Edinburgh, Blackwood, 1968.

Doty, Bennett J. *The Legion of the Damned*. London, Jonathan Cape, 1928.

Duncan, Major F. *The English in Spain*. London, 1877.

Fall, Bernard. *Street Without Joy*. Harrisburg, Pennsylvania, Stackpole, 1961.

Grauwin, Major Paul. *Doctor at Dien Bien Phu*. New York, John Day, 1955.

Guedalla, Philip. *The Two Marshals: Bazaine-Pétain*. New York, Reynal and Hitchcock, 1943.

———. *The Second Empire*. London, John Murray, 1922.

Hart, Adrian Liddell. *Strange Company*. London, Weidenfeld and Nicolson, 1953.

Kanitz, Walter. *The White Képi*. Chicago, Regnery, 1956.

Kraft, Joseph. *The Struggle for Algeria*. New York, Doubleday, 1961.

Leclerc, René. *Sahara*. Garden City, New York, Hanover House, 1945.

Loehndorff, Ernst F. *Hell in the Foreign Legion*. New York, Greenberg, 1932.

Mannington, George. *A Soldier of the Legion*. London, John Murray, 1912.

O'Ballance, Edgar. *The Story of the French Foreign Legion*. London, Faber, 1961.

O'Reilly, "Tiger." *The Tiger of the Legion*. New York, Greenberg, 1930.

Perrott-White, Alfred. *French Legionnaire*. Caldwell, Idaho, Caxton, 1951.

Price, G. Ward. *In Morocco with the Legion*. London, Jarrolds, 1934.

Rockwell, Paul Ayres. *American Fighters in the Foreign Legion*. Boston, Houghton Mifflin, 1930.

Seeger, Alan. *The Letters and Diary of Alan Seeger*. New York, Scribner's, 1917.

———. *Poems*. New York, Scribner's, 1917.

Sheean, Vincent. *Personal History*. New York, Doubleday, 1934.

Salzberger, C.L. *The Test: De Gaulle and Algeria*. New York, Harcourt, Brace and World, 1962.

Swiggett, Howard. *March or Die*. New York, Putnam's, 1953.

Tiria, Ensio. *Raft of Despair*. New York, Dutton, 1955.

Ward, Edward. *Sahara Story*. New York, Norton, 1954.

INDEX

291

Join the Allies on the Road to Victory
BANTAM WAR BOOKS

The history of man in flight...
THE BANTAM AIR AND SPACE SERIES

The Bantam Air and Space Series is dedicated to the men a
women who brought about this, the era of flight—the century
which mankind not only learned to soar the skies, but h
journeyed out into the blank void of space.